OVER THE HILL IN HUNGARY

OVER THE HILL IN HUNGARY

To Padma Daryanani
With Best Wishes,

VIRGINIA WHITE

Virginia White

Kroshka Books
Commack, New York

Editorial Production:	Susan Boriotti
Office Manager:	Annette Hellinger
Graphics:	Frank Grucci and John T'Lustachowski
Information Editor:	Tatiana Shohov
Book Production:	Donna Dennis, Patrick Davin, Christine Mathosian and Tammy Sauter
Circulation:	Maryanne Schmidt
Marketing/Sales:	Cathy DeGregory

Library of Congress Cataloging-in-Publication Data
available upon request

ISBN 1-56072-631-8

Copyright © 1999 by Virginia White
Kroshka Books, a division of
Nova Science Publishers, Inc.
6080 Jericho Turnpike, Suite 207
Commack, New York 11725
Tele. 516-499-3103   Fax 516-499-3146
e-mail: Novascience@earthlink.net
e-mail: Novascil@aol.com
Web Site: http://www.nexusworld.com/nova

Printed in the United States of America

PREFACE

When I arrived in Hungary three years after its rejection of communism, it still had the atmosphere of a war-ravaged country, not the burned-out look and rubble-strewn landscape left by bombs, but the forlornness of a place that has withstood years of deprivation and neglect. During the communist regime Hungary's Moscow-trained government officials, monitored by Soviet troops quartered in strategic emplacements, turned Hungary into a production facility for the Soviet Union. Denied many of the commonplace amenities and services that differentiate civilized life from a bare existence, the population was appeased, that is to say, controlled by cheap and plentiful fat-filled food, alcohol, and cigarettes, resulting in a high percentage of overweight, depressed and demoralized people who died young, more often by their own hands than in any other country. Hungary had one of the shortest life expectancies in the modern industrial world, and after the Cold War was surpassed only by Russia. It is also among those countries with the most heart disease and cancer and a high percentage of deaths from cirrhosis.

The whole country has not advanced at the same pace, but today Budapest is a thoroughly modern city, beginning to approach its glory days of the late nineteenth and early 20th century. Tourists by the millions are thrilled with the things they can see, do and buy here. The market place is glutted with commodities of every kind, the telephones work, people on the streets are as well-dressed as in London, Paris or New York, and a new restaurant seems to open every week. Budapest has historically had a rich musical life and it is a rare day or evening when there is not a music program worth attending. Opera, ballet, musical theatre, and classical, rock, jazz, even rap concerts abound. Sports contests are held in several large arenas; theatre is showing signs that it may rise to its pre-World War II level. The National Theatre is being rebuilt on Elizabeth Square and expects to be operating by the year 2000. Some English language theatre is even beginning to appear. Many of the long neglected architectural landmarks of the city have been restored and work continues on others; statues of communist leaders have been removed to a "Statue Park" outside of the city, and those of Hungarian heroes have been cleaned up and restored to their pristine esthetic elegance.

The change in the past six years has been so complete that if I were not a compulsive note-taker, it would be easy to forget how it was when I arrived. I came to Hungary with the United States Peace Corps to teach English in a Hungarian "*gimnázium*," a secondary or high school, for two years. Young people in post-communist Hungary, especially teen-age students, were avid to learn everything about the United States. Hollywood movies and television, which flooded the country as soon as all restrictions were lifted, became their main reference sources, and they mimicked the speech, music, dress and behaviors depicted in those usually unrealistic, exaggerated, and often unflattering representations of American society.

The newly-arrived, native-born-American English language teacher was an instantly anointed authority, qualified or not, on all things American, a living reference source to whom the students turned for confirmation, interpretation or explanation of anything about the United states that they read or saw in films or on television about which they wanted more information.

Given such power to influence young, impressionable minds, it is tempting to promulgate one's own value system, and it was sometimes difficult to resist sermonizing. For better or worse, I was not always able to resist. They knew how I felt about cigarettes, and alcohol and drug abuse. They also knew what I considered the strongest features of democracy: freedom of speech, a free press, and freedom of religion. It takes years before teachers can know if their instruction and philosophy, conveyed consciously or unconsciously in the classroom, had any effect upon the lives of their students, and, indeed, most never know. What I know for certain is that two years in a classroom with young Hungarians made a dramatic change in my own life in many ways for which I feel most fortunate.

After Carol Bellamy was appointed director of the U.S. Peace Corps, in early 1994, her first visit abroad was to Hungary where a new American ambassador and his wife had just arrived, Donald Blinken and his Hungarian-born wife, Vera. Bellamy and the Blinkens were friends of long-standing, and on her first evening in Budapest, she was the guest of honor at the Blinkens' first dinner party in their new home, the Ambassador's residence on Zugligeti Street, not far from the memorial monument to Raoul Wallenberg. I was happy to be invited as a representative of Peace Corps teachers in Hungary. Carol, an early Peace Corps Volunteer, who served in Central America, spoke briefly, and one of the things she said was that although the Peace Corps was established to assist people in needy countries, its dirty little secret was that volunteers probably gained more from the experience than the people they were sent to help. I have thought of that many times, and what I thought was, "How true."

Hungary is very small in area, a mere 36,000 square-mile spot almost in the exact center of Europe. What is not immediately apparent, however, is that it is a hub from which countries totaling approximately half-a-million square miles fan out like the spokes of a wheel. It shares borders with Romania, Yugoslavia, Croatia, Slovenia, Austria, Slovakia and Ukraine. From Budapest, by overland transportation, it takes as little as one hour and not more than four to reach the border of any of those seven countries. The first two years here, I was totally absorbed with teaching, learning enough Hungarian language to function in the community, and cultivating relationships with my colleagues and other Hungarians. When my Peace Corps service ended, I decided to remain a while since there was so much I had not seen and done in Hungary. Also, the ease of travel – that does not imply comfort – within Europe was so alluring that I not only explored Hungary but extended my travels to other European countries. Brief accounts of some of those adventures have been included in this book, as well as a few Hungarian highlights, under the heading "NOTES FROM THE JOURNAL."

A number of people in a number of ways helped to make this book possible. Some, day after day, patiently helped me cope with the arcane Hungarian language, and briefed me on the customs and courtesies governing sensitive situations. Others talked with me freely and lengthily, giving me first-hand information about life in Hungary as it is now, and as it was from World War I up to the present time. Several invited me to their homes and introduced me to their parents, grandparents, children, other relatives and friends.

And some good friends, Hungarian, American, English, Russian gave me encouragement and moral support that enabled me to continue in times of discouragement. To say "Thank you" does not appropriately convey my gratitude and there were so many I cannot name everyone, but I would like to acknowledge my indebtedness to the following people who, *in addition to those to whom this book is dedicated*, were especially helpful:

For reading parts of the manuscript and making valuable suggestions and comments: Donald Higgins, J. W. (Jody) Goodman, Roger Karz, Sally Oleon, Anikó Korenchy; for practical assistance, useful information, and/or inestimable moral support: András Baranyai, Joanna Barnes, Peggy Chisholm, Jack Conway, Péter Dékany, Imre Fülöp, József Garai, Debra Gillers, Joseph Gonzalez, Jeff Labovitz, József Kapás, Irén Takács Kapásné, James Leavey, Ralph Magnus, Ildikó Pusztai, Felicitas Ruccius-Koss, Charles Setlow, Ludmilla Shelenkova, Anikó Szabó, James Viera, Eliot Werner, my son Charles White, and Pauline Wickham.

I would also like to express my appreciation to the library of the Central European University in Budapest for their excellent research collection, ideal environment for study and research, and an outstandingly pleasant and helpful staff, headed by Dr. Mária Szlatky.

And very special thanks to Alexander Sabelnikov.

VW
May 1998

ARRIVAL

During my lifetime, I have made two significant automobile purchases, both sight unseen. The first was a 20-year old car owned by a friend who left it parked in a field in Hyde Park, New York, where she had been working in a summer theatre, because she could not afford to pay New York City's exorbitant insurance. I was leaving the city and needed a car so she sold it to me sight unseen for $75. After driving it for 10 years, I sold it for $50. When I could finally afford to buy one, I called up the Volkswagon dealer in the city nearest to where I lived and asked to have a "Beetle" delivered, naming the color I preferred. It arrived with the bill and papers ready to be signed; I paid for it by check. After driving that car for nearly 10 years, I sold it for half of what I had paid. My late brother-in-law, a tire-kicking, road-testing, Consumer Research-reading car owner said of my automobile-buying experience, "There's just no beating blind, fool luck." He was right. And not just for automobiles. It was that same blind, fool luck that brought me to Hungary.

When the Peace Corps announced that it was starting a program in Eastern Europe and the former Soviet Republics, it seemed like a perfect opportunity to make use of the Russian language I had been studying for several years, so I applied to go to Russia. The Peace Corps does not take applications for specific locations but does allow applicants to indicate a preference. However, they were not yet sending volunteers to Russia, so they gave me a choice, by telephone, of Poland or Hungary. When I hesitated briefly, trying to envision those two countries on my mental map of Europe, the caller said, very gently, "We're leaning toward Hungary." That did it. I accepted immediately.

Friends who heard that I had joined the Peace Corps appeared to be delighted, and congratulated me. But not everybody. Some looked puzzled, even a little embarrassed and asked, with slight hesitation, "Don't they have an age limit?"(They do not.)

Certainly it had crossed my mind that at an age when most people are thinking about retirement or are already retired, my Peace Corps colleagues were likely to be considerably younger than I. But I anticipated no difficulty in keeping up with them. I was still enjoying hiking, camping, climbing. And dancing. When I applied to the Peace Corps, I was still taking dance classes at the Martha Graham School. And having worked in the theatre for several years, some of the time in regional companies with actors of all ages from very young children to quite mature character actors, I was used to and felt comfortable with people in all age groups. Then, too, I counted on the European tolerance, even respect, for age, often cited in marked contrast to America's youth worship.

When my New York physician, who knew me well, completed the rigorous examination required by the Peace Corps and filled in their detailed form, he remarked, "You are in remarkably good physical condition," omitting to add "for your age," but he and I both knew what he meant. My medical certification was promptly granted and forwarded to me. It contained a fine-print notation that I read but gave little thought to, as it was not likely to concern me, that in case anything "medically significant" occurred between the time of the certification and the date of departure from the United States, volunteers were obligated to inform the Peace Corps Medical Office.

A few weeks before my departure date, set for early June 1992, I went to California to visit friends whom I would not see for two years. They also were enthusiastic walkers and we had been on many hikes together through the Blue Ridge and Cumberland Mountains in Tennessee, Kentucky and Virginia. After they went to California to live, we had walked together in the Muir Woods and I was hoping for another hike in the same area. But during the flight, my right knee began to hurt and walking on a level was painful; climbing hills or even stairs was nearly impossible. The New York orthopedic specialist, with impeccable credentials, whom I consulted as soon as I got back to New York, looked at my knee, then at my birthdate, and came up with the diagnosis of "Arthritis." For some reason it did not sound right to me: perhaps it was that old standby "Sixth Sense," or perhaps I recalled that in the final weeks of my dance classes, any movement involving my right knee had become painful, and I started wearing a knee pad in class, assuming that would take care of it. So I questioned him, asking if he was absolutely sure, and he looked me in the eye, and repeated,

"Absolutely." Then he prescribed medicine that took effect immediately – it gave me a rash all over my body.

Unwavering persistence, and a threat to camp out in the doctor's office was necessary before he was convinced to order a diagnostic MRI. He was much more surprised than I when the picture revealed a torn cartilage in my right knee. (If doctors would only look at our bodies as well as our birthdates!) Expecting him to be chagrinned at his early mis-diagnosis, and eager to make up for it, I said the surgery had to be done immediately in order for me to meet my departure date to go to Hungary with the Peace Corps. Impossible, he said. The operating room, or even a hospital bed for me, had to be reserved long in advance and he knew they would not be available for some time. So I sat down in his office and said I would remain there until they found facilities to perform the surgery the next day, and they did.

The surgery was very skillfully completed, at 7 p.m. the following day, which I spent in the hospital without food or drink, waiting until the surgeon fulfilled his long-standing scheduled operations. He was visibly proud of himself for having come through in the emergency and I was delighted. He was honest enough to tell me that he had repaired the torn cartilage and found no trace of arthritis. As for my traveling to Europe in exactly twenty days, he said, "You will be able to kick field goals in 10 days!" An interesting prediction considering that I had never kicked a field goal prior to the surgery, but then he had not asked about that.

Those twenty days went by in a blur: learning to use crutches and giving them up for a cane after three days; preparing my apartment for occupancy by the subleasing tenants; assembling the many items that might not be available on the Hungarian market, especially cosmetics and toilet articles, still almost as scarce as they had been during 40 years under the communists; and seeing friends who invited me to gatherings or visited me to say good-bye. It is not surprising that informing the Peace Corps Medical Office about my "medically significant" incident never crossed my mind.

Only when I was on the way to Philadelphia, our designated "staging area," where we would gather for final instructions, signing of papers, and (we were informed) a final medical check-up, did I remember. Since I was fully recovered, although I could not yet lift heavy objects or walk up stairs comfortably, I assumed that a simple explanation to the doctor, who could see that I was fine, would take care of the matter. As it turned out, no explanation was necessary. There was no doctor, no final check-up. We rushed through the departure requirements, signing papers, receiving final immunizations, meeting the other 49 volunteers (we were 50 in all), in one day instead of the three we expected. It felt a bit as if we had joined the army and were leaving for basic training. My moment of truth came when we were instructed to bring our baggage down from our rooms and put it on the bus that would take us to John F. Kennedy Airport. Two suitcases stuffed – overstuffed, that is – with everything to see me through the next two years, and I was expected to bring them to the lobby, carry them out to the curb and hoist them onto the waiting bus! (Was somebody humming "You're in the Army Now"?) After I persuaded, and overtipped, a hotel porter to bring my bags into the lobby, I stood beside them wondering what to do next. Merely lifting them was out of the question. To ask for assistance would call attention to my weakness, and consequently to my age, the last thing I wanted to do. A tall, strong, young man in the group earned my undying gratitude by snatching up my bags and stowing them in the bus without a word. Grateful as I was, it was distressing too, as any hope of appearing strong, agile, youthful, crumbled at my feet. What I projected at that moment, at least in my own mind, was a little old lady who walked with a limp and could not lift and carry. My impulse was to loudly explain that my handicap was only temporary, that I had recently had surgery for a knee injury suffered in a dance class for God's sake. I wasn't a cripple! But, of course, I couldn't explain anything, since I had not reported the incident to the Peace Corps.

Seats on the plane were pre-assigned, all in the Non-Smoking section, and mine was an inside one in a six-seat row with very little leg room. After a while, my right leg began to hurt, and there being no place to stretch it out, I took a walk through the aisles. On the way, I spotted a vacant aisle seat on the left side of the plane, perfect for stretching my right leg into the aisle. It was in the Smoking Section but that seemed unimportant under the circumstances, so I sat down. (My seat mate later told me that some of the passengers in that section had already run out of cigarettes.) "I've just had a torn cartilage in my right knee repaired," I said to the man in the next seat, as I stretched my right leg into the aisle. "Oh, I had that once," he replied. "What you need is Ibuprofin: it's the only thing that helps." He dug into his brief case, brought out a bottle of Ibuprofin and insisted that I take one immediately. "It's the only thing for that pain," he repeated, and added, "You must get some as soon as you get home." "That may not be much help," I said, "I won't be home for two years," and explained that I was on the way to Hungary with the Peace Corps. He instantly opened his briefcase again and insisted upon giving me the whole bottle. In reply to my weak demurral, he said he was on the way home and could get more. I have no idea what that man's name is or where "home" was, but I have called down blessings on his head many times, wherever he is!

After the long flight, we hoped for at least a one-night stopover in Budapest when we could have a brief look at the famous city and a comfortable night in a bed. But it was not to be. We were taken by bus from Ferihegy, the Budapest airport, directly to Szekszárd, 130 kilometers to the South, without so much as a glimpse of Budapest, not even a church spire in the distance. It reminded me of the famed story of Lenin's trip across Europe in a sealed train from Switzerland to St. Petersburg during the Russian Revolution.

We were assigned rooms for the night in the dormitory of the college where our training classes would be held (we would go to our local homes the next day), and went to dinner in the school cafeteria. The building that housed the cafeteria looked quite near but there was a narrow canal (they called it that, but it was only a very long, deep gully) between it and the dormitory and we had to walk a short distance and cross over on a footbridge. After dinner, a very good typical Hungarian meal, there was no signal that we should return to the dormitory; everyone milled around for some time in a large open area adjacent to the dining room. After a while, to my dismay, a dance band appeared and began to tune up. Not for us, I realized with relief, as I noticed that a number of people in dressy clothes had arrived for a dance evening. I wondered why we did not return to the dormitory, and asked the person next to me what we were waiting for. He looked at me as if he thought I was blind or retarded and said we were waiting for the rain to stop. Rain? It had not been raining when we came to the cafeteria or even threatening to rain, but when I looked toward the windows, rain was sloshing against them as heavily as if we were under water. Then I looked down at the floor and saw that water was already seeping in under the outside door. Some of us decided it was better to brave the rain sooner than later when the water in the gully would be deeper. A man who seemed to be in charge, led us through the kitchen on the side of the building nearest the gully and said the temporary footbridge was already under water so we would have to wade across. The water was up to our knees or higher for some people, and the mud underfoot was treacherously slick. It was frightening but we all got through safely with the help of the strong, tall young man who had loaded my bags onto the bus in Philadelphia. His name was Jeff and being well over 6 feet tall he could stand in the middle of the gully, and hold up the women as we waded across. The men were all able to manage alone, I believe. Still, there were some losses. The only pair of good walking shoes I brought with me were ruined since I did not, as the smarter people did, remove my shoes and wade barefooted. It was heavenly to get into some warm, dry cotton tights and a sweat shirt. My first night in Hungary! Grateful for a narrow dormitory cot with a very thin mattress, I slept soundly.

The next day we began the ten week orientation and training course designed to give us the tools we needed to fulfill our assignment, which was to teach English to Hungarian students. It included instruction in Teaching English as a Foreign Language (TEFL), and lectures on the culture and history of Hungary. But the emphasis was on Hungarian language, and several hours a day were devoted to that. But the most effective orientation was a truly inspired plan for volunteers to live in private homes during the ten-weeks. Thus we were forced to communicate with the family, mostly or entirely in Hungarian, and in the course of our daily lives we learned more about the courtesies and customs of the country than many months of lecturing would have taught us.

Accommodations were arranged by the training staff before volunteers arrived. They screened applications submitted by local people who wanted to be hosts to Peace Corps volunteers. "Home-stay families," as they were called, were selected only after a staff member visited the home to ascertain that the space and conditions in the household were adequate. They attempted to place each volunteer in the most suitable home, based on the meager information they had in writing, since this was done before the volunteers arrived. The placements were not always successful, but considering the difficulties, especially the limited living space in most Hungarian homes where, for example, such things as a second bathroom are almost unheard of, it is surprising how well it worked. It was the policy to select families where at least one person knew some English but that was not always possible. In the home where I lived no one spoke English.

Standing at their gate to greet me when I arrived, my hosts, Anna and János, might have been posing for a picture meant to depict the good life under the socialist system. She was short, plump, rosy-cheeked, with a warm smile. White hair framed her pretty face. János, also short, was squarely built, with thinning, half-gray hair, and a ruddy complexion that bespeaks long hours in the hot sun or heavy drinking. I soon learned it was the former. He gave the impression of being packed with energy; standing still, he seem to vibrate like an idling motor, straining to be on the move. Behind them was a small garden; half of the space was filled with flowers in glorious summertime bloom: hollyhocks, marigolds, cockscombs, zinnias, petunias, daisies, the same old-world flowers I grew up with in Virginia. The other half was given over to vegetables: corn, tomatoes, cucumbers, and the inevitable paprika. A tall sunflower stood guard over it all. I put out my hand meaning to shake hands, but Anna enfolded me in her arms and gave me the traditional Hungarian greeting, a kiss on each cheek. János followed her lead and did the same. There was no doubt I had found a home.

Our training sessions were held in a three-story college building, meaning four levels. As in all of Europe, the ground floor is the first level and the first floor is up one flight of stairs. The cafeteria, auditorium, and library were on the ground floor and classes were on the upper floors. Most of my classes were on the third, the top, floor – no elevator, no escalator. It was a mercilessly hot summer, no air conditioning, of course. Relief came late at night when the temperature fell after midnight. Despite the flood that greeted us on our first evening in Hungary, it rarely rained the rest of the summer, and then, as in Camelot, only after sundown, which did nothing to relieve the burning heat of the day. I thirsted for a mid-afternoon thunderstorm like those that used to blow up suddenly in the Southern United States to relieve the sweltering summer days of my childhood, after which the trees dripped water and the air was sweet and cool until sunset. But there was no such respite from the heat in Southern Hungary in the summer of 1992. When I returned home in the late afternoon the sun was still high, and the temperature in the upper 30s Celsius, between 95 and 100 degrees Fahrenheit. My fantasies of a tall, cool drink verged on becoming a mirage like those that delude nomads crossing the desert, straining toward the next oasis, only there was no oasis.

Climbing stairs several times a day with an armful of heavy books made my knee ache constantly and I soon used up the Ibuprofin given me by my seatmate on the plane to Budapest; painkillers were sold in Hungarian pharmacies but only with a prescription. So I had to ask the Peace Corps medical office, located in Budapest about 130 kilometers away, for a prescription or some medicine. That meant I had to tell them about the surgery, and although I tried to play it down as a minor incident, it caused a bit of a stir. My explanation by that time sounded lame. The medical officer insisted that she had to talk with the surgeon in New York who performed the operation before she would give me anything. He must have allayed her concerns (perhaps he told her I could kick field goals) because she gave me some medicine for pain. She also instructed me not to carry anything heavy and not to climb stairs! And said I must lie down with an icecap on my knee every day when I returned home! An icecap! She did not know what she was saying. It was impossible to avoid climbing stairs or to refrain from carrying heavy books. Using a backpack helped some and often one of my classmates, especially Jeff who had put my bags on the bus in Philadelphia, carried my backpack when we were in the same class, but ice! Ah, that's another story.

Ice was not something that Hungarians put in drinks. They might keep soft drinks in the refrigerator and serve them cold but the idea of putting ice into the glass with the drink struck them as quite strange. There was a söröző (something akin to a British pub) near the school where we sometimes went for drinks and I always asked for ice. The invariable reply was, "It is cold." After a while, I started saying, "I know the coca-cola (or whatever) is cold, but I would still like some ice." Occasionally, not often, a good-natured waiter or waitress would humor me and bring a drink containing, at most, two pieces of ice the size and shape of large marbles, and place the drink in front of me as if it contained pearls.

There was a refrigerator in the Kovács kitchen that had a small inside freezing compartment. Once when I was there alone, I peeked into the freezer and saw that it was crammed full of food; not an inch of space remained, much less enough to insert an ice tray. But that was irrelevant as I had never seen an ice tray in the house. It was small comfort that my colleagues all found the same situation in their homes and we talked about ice the way dieters talk about food, as if we could imagine it on our tongues.

All day after I was told to put ice on my knee, I tried to compose the request to Anna. To explain in Hungarian what the doctor said. That meant I had to learn some words and phrases I had not used before; I wanted to be very tactful so I would not embarrass her. As I rehearsed the conversation to myself, an idea sprang up. If I succeeded in obtaining ice for my knee, perhaps some of it might be diverted into a glass of water!

When I got up the courage to speak to Anna, she was, as I should have known she would be, immediately responsive and sprang into action. "No problem," she assured me, as she hurried into the pantry and emerged carrying two much-used, but intact, plastic bags. They were the first plastic bags I had seen in Hungary, and I could not guess how old they were. The sight of them dashed my hope of filching a few pieces of ice to cool my water – they were not dirty but they did not look very fresh. She removed some packages of food from the freezer to make room for the bags filled with water, and said, "You will have ice in a couple of hours." True to her word, after a while she brought me some ice wrapped in a towel and placed it firmly on my knee.

The next day when I returned from school, Anna proudly waved before me something I had never seen before – an ice tray! It was very small with ten compartments the size of, yes, large marbles. So I knew how the söröző made their ice. The entire tray might yield almost enough ice for a glass of water. She also had plastic bags with ice ready for my knee; they not only eased the pain but made me feel cooler all over. Occasionally, I would transfer the pack to my forehead and that was nice. A few days later, Anna again greeted me brandishing a metal ice tray. It was rather beat up but was a standard-size tray in which real ice cubes could be made! But what did she have in mind? Ice for my knee continued to be made in plastic bags, and no ice cubes appeared.

About that time, one of my Peace Corps colleagues announced that his family had given him ice water the previous evening. This cheered us up immensely. We had discovered that despite the scarcity of telephones, our families had some means of communication.Whenever someone reported a new offering or practice, it was not long before similar things appeared in all our homes. And sure enough, the dinner table at my home was soon graced with a bowl of ice! My gushing gratitude must have overwhelmed them: they never stopped the practice. Whenever I visited them afterward, at any time of year, there was always a bowl of ice on the dinner table!

By great good fortune, the Kovács family spanned four-generations, the entire twentieth century, a great rarity in Hungary. Grandpa (Nagypapa), past 90 and bedridden, was born just after the turn of the century, about the time 23-year old Béla Bartók and 22-year-old Zoltán Kodály were touring the Hungarian provinces collecting folk songs and recording them on a phonograph. His great-grandson, Gábor, born in 1979, would not have recognized a phonograph. With a Walkman so permanently attached that it seemed to grow out of his head, he listened to Rock 'N ' Roll and what he called "Pop" music, meaning anything he could dance to. He loved and lived to dance. His happy-go-lucky personality did not fit the Hungarian personality I had been led to expect.

Hungarian gloom is legendary. There were numerous statistics, facts, and related evidence showing that Hungarians were stressful, depressed, dying young, leading the world in suicide rates. They were said to be hard-drinking, hard-smoking, hard working people who ingested an amazing amount of fats and sweets. Figures published by their own country's Statistics Office in the early 90s stated that over one-third of Hungarians could not name a friend, and that 3 to 4 million, out of a population of a little more than 10 million, were alcoholics. The same report said that the chance of suicide was 55 times greater among alcoholics than among moderate or non-drinkers.

It is tempting to think that Hungarians became depressed, pessimistic and self-destructive because of modern historical events. But these behaviors are not of recent origin. Hungarians learn from childhood that many of their country's heroes have killed themselves. Count István Szechényi who built the first bridge across the Danube River shot himself in 1860; Pál Nyári, a leader in the 1848 Revolution who later turned pacifist, killed himself in 1871; Attila József, one of Hungary's most beloved poets, jumped in front of a train in 1937 at the age of 32, an act later emulated by quite a few of his admirers, some of them lesser and would-be poets. The Hungarian composer of the 1930s song "Gloomy Sunday," made popular by Billie Holiday and played all over the world, Rezsó Seress, was blamed for a spate of deaths and later killed himself. The communists banned "Gloomy Sunday" in the 1950s saying it was too pessimistic. Until quite recently it was played by the pianist in the popular *Kispipa* restaurant on Akácfa Street in Budapest, and still may be, the place where the composer himself used to play it in the 1930s. In 1941, Count Pál Teleki, then Prime Minister, shot himself. The pageant of Hungary's tragic history began a long time ago, before János Kádár, Mátyás Rákosi, World Wars I and II, Admiral Miklós Horthy, the German occupation, the Russian occupation. The Hungarian "Himnusz" is unique among national anthems in that it not only says God is not on the side of the Hungarians, but rails at God for deserting them. The words, written as a poem by Ferenc Kölcsey in 1823 and set to music by Ferenc Erkel in 1844, suggest not an anthem, but a dirge:

God, the Magyar bless with grace
On whom sorrow falls like rain
*****
The people have long paid the sum
For sins of past and all to come
*****
But all those who on knees did bend
Were cast to darkness at your hand

"If you find us pessimistic and overly sensitive, just try to imagine what it must be like to have been losers for 500 years!" so spoke Professor Gyula E. Szöny of Attila József University, Szeged, in a lecture on Hungarian history. The last victorious Hungarian ruler was King Mátyás who died in 1490.

Despite defeats in battle and humiliation at the hands of foreign invaders, despite the nation's reputation for melancholy and gloom, despite the national anthem, the people I lived with during my first three months in Hungary were among the most optimistic, cheerful, and determinedly happy people I have ever known.

II

THE KOVÁCS FAMILY

The dense forests of Hungary, populated with wild boar, deer, pheasants, hares and other game, were once a favorite hunting ground of European royalty. Much of the woodland area was stripped during the communist regime and turned into lumber for the Soviet Union. Reforestation is restoring many areas, easy to recognize by extensive stands of young trees all the same height, having been planted at the same time. One once-great wilderness is now protected by its designation as a nature preserve, the beautiful Gemenc Forest standing on the edge of the city of Szekszárd.

This has been a wine-producing area for almost two thousand years; red wine of vineyards dating from the Roman era in the second century is still available here. The business center is built on a flat plain, surrounded by hills. The Kovács's home was up on the outer rim, reached by bus from the center of the city where our classes were held. As the bus ascended to the higher levels, one could look down on a blanket of red-tiled roofs, reminiscent of a Cezanne painting of such roofs in the South of France. Here they are pyramid-shaped, four triangles rising from box-like houses, coming to a point in the center. Some are built to accommodate two or four families; in those the outer shape is larger but still rectangular; the pyramidal roofs are larger, and there are more chimneys. Every family has its own chimney, so two chimneys means two families, four means four families.

The Kovács's house was large by local standards, with a separate room and bath that had been added on for Anna's bedridden father. János had rigged up a bell with which Nagypapa could summons them at any time, day or night. He was never kept waiting; whenever the bell rang, someone went immediately to attend him.

The kitchen in the Kovács house was large and was the most used room. With a table that could be extended to seat ten or more people, it was the dining room as well as kitchen, and also the informal living room. Neighbors who dropped in entered through the kitchen door and never went farther. I often sat there and read, wrote letters, or talked to Anna while she cooked. There was a living room in the house, a pretty sunny room with upholstered furniture, coffee table, and a nice rug on the floor, but it was rarely used. On a few special occasions, I was invited into that room, usually to receive a gift. We would go in, the presentation would be made, and if food or drink was served, back we went to the kitchen-living room. Anna and János's bedroom became yet another sitting room during the day. The television was there and the sofabed where they slept was folded into a large, comfortable couch. A low table with four chairs, two on each side, was where they sometimes served pastry and coffee or wine to guests whom they considered too important to be entertained in the kitchen – not many. I never saw guests being entertained in the living room.

Since no one in the family spoke English and I knew very little Hungarian, we ate our meals with a Hungarian-English dictionary within their easy reach, and an English-Hungarian one beside my plate. Little by little, we managed to exchange a lot of information. My classes included four hours of Hungarian language each day and I often asked for János's help with my homework, which he, who had only a grammar school education, was very willing, even proud to give me. It is a tribute to his native intelligence and to the Hungarian public school education of his day that he knew the language and grammar quite well.

János surprised me one evening by announcing that, contrary to what I thought, he did speak some English which he had learned during World War II. His eyes were dancing so I knew it was a joke, and asked him to say something in English. He sat up very straight, and with precise articulation, said, "Goddamned son-of-a-bitch!" This from a man I had never heard utter a harsh word, much less a profane one, stunned me. It was just the reaction he expected and he hastily explained. When the American soldiers liberated the German labor-camp where he had been sent when the Germans occupied Hungary in 1944, it was a while before the Hungarians could be returned to their home country, so the soldiers passed the time by teaching them some English. Of course.

A system of government dedicated to leveling the social and economic status of the population inevitably benefits most those people who have the least. And the ones among them who are willing to work hard, live frugally, and obey the dictates of the country's leaders may well have an improved economic situation. Thus the communist regime in Hungary that shattered the lives of the country's aristocrats, stifled its intellectuals, and terrified its creative artists into inaction or chased them away, gave the Kovács family and others like them the opportunity to have a better life than they had ever known or even dared to hope for.

Anna and János were born in neighboring villages and grew up between the two World Wars, that period once described as a time when Hungary was a kingdom without a king, a landlocked country without a seacoast ruled by an Admiral who had no Navy. Miklós Horthy, a former Rear Admiral in the Austro-Hungarian Empire, was elected Regent of Hungary in January 1920. He was a self-styled "supreme warlord," right-wing, conservative, autocratic and anti-Semitic. He set up his residence in the royal castle in Buda and for the next 24 years headed the Hungarian government.

Six months after Horthy's election, the World War I allies, at Versailles, divided up three-fifths of Hungary's land and one-third of her ethnic population among neighboring countries known today as Slovakia, Ukraine, Romania, Croatia, Serbia, Bosnia, Slovenia, Italy and Austria. This dismemberment not only displaced Hungarian people, changing their nationalities overnight, but reduced the natural resources of the country, crippling its ability to recover from the first World War. Through that Treaty, Hungary lost 64% of its mineral energy resources; 80% of iron ore and iron production; 88% of the forests; 20% of paper production capacity and all its salt mines. Transportation routes were blocked and world markets disintegrated. Economic growth was slow in those years; lack of capital for modern machinery resulted in high labor costs and low production, and thus inability to compete in world markets. The Great Depression of the 1930s affected the economies of all countries and contributed further to Hungary's decline.

Agricultural production suffered severely for the lack of capital. Peasants were especially hard hit; they were unable to obtain loans for modern machinery. One-third of the country's productive land was then in large estates owned by 0.1% of landowners; approximately 85% of farmers owned 19.3% of the arable land in holdings of less than 6.5 hectares (16 acres) and 10% of these holdings were less than 3 hectares (4-1/2 acres). The families of Anna and Janos owned very tiny plots of land and eked out a living as part-time, seasonal employees on large nearby estates, as many smallholder peasants did in those days. Anna had six years of schooling, János had eight. They were married at the end of World War II, just about the time that plans for a communist-controlled government for Hungary were being hammered out in Moscow.

One of the earliest communist programs in Hungary was the enforced collectivization of farms that began in 1948. But the collectives performed very poorly, and in 1949, the Communist Party proudly announced that it was planning to turn Hungary into "a country of iron and steel," and decreed a 200 percent increase in the output of heavy industry in the next five years; in 1951, that number was raised to 380 percent. Hungary was becoming an industrial machine for the Soviet Union, and much of the agrarian population was shifted to the cities and to the industrial centers where factories were located. It was then that the real social, economic and cultural transformation took place in Hungary and the social structure underwent its unprecedented equalization. It was then that János and Anna moved to the city nearest their village and found factory jobs. The industry was badly managed and inefficient, the workers did not live well and were not happy; however, compared with the poor circumstances of village life, and their prospects for the future there, János and Anna found life in the city and factory work a tremendous improvement, and set about creating an agreeable and prosperous life for themselves and their family.

Events that transpired in the Soviet Union inevitably affected the political climate in Hungary: Stalin's death in 1953, followed by the fall of Beria; Malenkov's succession in 1953 and dismissal in 1955; Krushchev's denunciation of Stalin at the 20th Party Congress in February of 1956. Workers' demands for self-government at the factories was a major, perhaps primary, element in Hungary's 1956 Revolution. Many young workers and the country's intelligentsia wanted more of a voice in the management of their workplaces, in the communities, and in national politics. They were inspired by Imre Nagy, a visionary who, when he was Prime Minister from 1953 until 1955, tried to reform the communist system in Hungary. Like Gorbachev in the Soviet Union a few decades later, Nagy was a life-long dedicated Moscow-trained Communist who never renounced the party but believed it only needed reform and that he could do it. He did not fare so well as Gorbachev. When the Revolution was crushed by the Red Army, Nagy and his revolutionary government fled to the Yugoslavian Embassy, having misread Tito's sympathies. They were not given asylum there, but were turned over to the NKVD and deported to Romania. In 1958, he and several members of his government were returned to Hungary and, after a brief "show" trial, all were executed. In 1989, one of the first acts of the new democratic government in Hungary was the reburial of Nagy in Budapest with great ceremonial honors. In 1996, an impressive, esthetically pleasing statue of Nagy was erected in Kossuth Square near the Parliament building.

When I joined the family in 1992, Anna and János were both pensioners; the retirement age for women then was fifty-five and for men it was sixty. They owned their home, with space for a small vegetable garden in back and in front a larger space where they grew both flowers and vegetables. Although consumer goods had been scarce for years, they had managed to acquire an amazing number of household appliances, some of which – refrigerator, washing machine – resembled those used in the United States thirty or forty years earlier. They had been on the list to get a telephone for 17 years but the usual waiting period was 20 years, and they were happy that they had only three years to go. They both had pensions and Anna's father also received a government stipend, but János worked at various jobs whenever he could find them. The summer I was there he worked as a vacation-replacement guard at a local factory for one month. He went to work at 4 o'clock in the afternoon and worked until midnight. He got up at 5 a.m. and went to his large rented garden space 9 kilometers away where he worked until 1 or 2 o'clock. On weekends, he caught up on sleep. Anna always got up to prepare his breakfast and open the gate for him to drive out. Their place was enclosed by a fence, the gate was always locked at night. After seeing him off, she returned to the kitchen and sailed into her household chores which, in summer, included canning and freezing fruits from their trees and vegetables from their gardens.

Their only child, Kati, was born in the late 1940s at the dawn of Hungary's communistic era. She was educated entirely in the school system introduced in 1949 with the goal of creating the "new socialist man" conforming to the Soviet ideals. Kati belonged to the Pioneers at the appropriate age, and since she was bright, ambitious and the child of working-class parents, she had no trouble gaining admission to a gymnasium – the academic high school that prepares students for university. She now has a very good administrative job in a local medical institution. When I was there, she used to stop by every day to see her parents on the way to or from work. Since they could not communicate by telephone, it was how she assured herself that they were all right and checked to seek if they had errands to be run or needed any other help. Like her father, she drove a small East German Trabant, with its two-stroke, 26-horsepower engine, and its amazingly economical use of benzene. The power of the "Trabi," as they are still called, had to be limited because its fragile body, a composition of steel, pressed cardboard and plastic could not support a stronger engine. When Trabants were being turned out in communist East Germany, there was a five-year wait for one in Hungary. Anywhere from 55 percent to 80 percent of the car's price had to be paid at the time it was ordered and the remainder paid before delivery. There was no choice of color or model – only one model was produced at any one time and buyers took whatever they were given. They prayed, it was said, that they would not draw the least desirable colors, dubbed "hospital green" or "toilet light-blue". Six years ago Trabants were the most commonly seen private automobile. They are still being driven but are far less numerous and are most likely to be the last Model made before the reunification of Germany, the 601, outfitted with a four-stroke, 50 HP engine, originally used in the Volkswagon Polo. The more powerful engine turned it into what was described as a "shaky and unmanageable bomb, public enemy number one." No further improvements were made as the last Trabant was manufactured in Zwickau in 1992 and the factory was transformed into a modern Opel plant. The Trabis were reputed to emit about 1000 times the pollution of modern Japanese or Western automobiles. The East European Regional Environmental Center, city governments and the national government of Hungary, as well as European, American and Japanese auto makers are all very anxious to get rid of them. The problem is that they are still the only car some people can afford. The original cost is low – only old, used ones are available; they are inexpensive to operate, and can be parked in a small space. And like the Model T Ford in early Twentieth Century America, they have a mechanism so simple that almost anyone can learn to maintain and repair them. Also like the Model T, they have some drawbacks – the pollution emission is a major one, and they do not always make it up the steep hills, especially in the wintertime.

Kati's husband, Zoltán, a big muscular man who had been a much-admired local athlete, was a fireman. Nobody could be further than he from the Hungarian stereotype of the flashing-eyed, black-mustachioed, guitar-playing Lady Killer. He was rather shy, spoke very little and always in a soft, low voice. His attitude toward me can only be described as "gallant." Like his father-in-law, he seemed to look for ways to be helpful. Kati was devoted to him and obviously felt secure in his devotion to her. Unlike most middle-aged Hungarian men, he frequently helped with the household chores, including cooking, and was both willing and capable of assisting when necessary in the care of Kati's bedridden grandfather with such things as bathing and shaving him, which János usually did.

Kati and Zoltán had two children, a daughter born in the early 1970s and a son in 1979. The son, Gábor, was twelve years old when I first met him; since both parents worked, he stayed with his grandparents in the summer. He slept a lot, watched television, and was always hungry. He was a polite, loving boy, who adored his grandfather and cheerfully helped him in the garden, fed the chickens, walked the dog, or ran errands. He never complained about anything except a delay in mealtime, and that was always done with humor and a smile, as if his perpetual hunger amused him. The one thing he really cared about was dancing. He had danced in public with school groups and with an older group that traveled to other cities and occasionally to other countries to take part in competitions at dance festivals. His parents were disappointed in his academic achievement. He did not like school very much and made poor grades, and their efforts to motive him proved futile.

The daughter, Judit, could not have been more different from her brother. She was a dedicated student who always earned the highest marks. She graduated from gymnasium, the high school that prepares students for university. Afterwards, she attended and graduated from the Police Academy in Budapest, the academic equivalent of a teacher's college, called *"föiskola"*, where she was one of three females in her class. During three years at the Academy, she fell in love with a classmate and they were married soon after graduation. Then, in the fall of their graduation year, they both enrolled at the law school of one of Hungary's finest universities. Thus, in three generations the family progressed from impoverished peasantry to university graduate. Judit's great grandfather lived until she finished the Academy but died at the age of 93 before she finished law school. At a time when the life expectancy of Hungarian men is less than 60, he was himself a remarkable figure.

This warm and loving family accepted me into their circle of belonging and affection so naturally and easily that I never questioned the quality or extent of their benevolence, assuming at first that it included the whole human race. It was, therefore, a surprise to learn that, like most people, they dispensed their love and acceptance of other people selectively.

From the Kovács home near the end of the residential area one could see where the line of dwellings ended and the vineyard region began. That line was changing rapidly as the vineyards were being thrust farther out by new homes encroaching on the prosperous wine-producing area. Constructions sounds – cement mixers, shifting gears of trucks grinding uphill, crane operators shouting instructions to each other – created an air of progress, of things being built, of money being spent. This did not accord with the mournful pronouncements heard everywhere about the terrible state of the economy. This looked like evidence of prosperity.

One evening after sunset when it was still light and the late-day breezes had cooled the air, Anna and I went for a walk through the section where new homes had recently appeared and others were under construction. The new houses were very modern and much larger than those in the neighborhood where we lived. Those already occupied had shiny new foreign cars parked in front, an indisputable token of wealth. "Where does the money come from?" I asked. Anna's replay was a shrug, tightly-pressed lips, raised eyebrows – an expression that can mean, "I don't know," but usually means, "I know, but won't say." She pointed to several houses naming the owners and after their names, added, "Business man." When I asked what kind of business she only shook her head. She obviously had information, but perhaps it was only gossip that she did not want to repeat.

As we passed one especially large, impressive house, Anna leaned toward me, lowered her voice, and spat out the word, "Szigane!" (Gypsy). Her facial expression and tone of voice were understandable in any language. "There goes the neighborhood!" they said. And how do Gypsies acquire so much money, I wanted to know, but she just put on her stuffed-with-secrets look and said nothing. Although there were quite a few educated and successful professional Gypsies in Hungary – at that time three or four were members of Parliament – the standard assumption was that all prosperous Gypsies were involved in some kind of illegal activity. The word "Mafia" had entered the Hungarian vocabulary and become a generic term for anyone suspected of making money by questionable means. The epithet, "Mafia!" or "Mafiószo!" could be heard frequently, muttered in contemptuous undertone, when well-dressed, dark-skinned persons passed in the street, or drove by in an expensive automobile. I never heard anyone in the Kovács family use that term, but the expression on their faces as they almost hissed the word, "Szigane!" made their feelings clear.

It sometimes occurred to me that it was my duty to bring up with my hosts the subject of human rights, especially minority rights, but I thought it might be only a gesture toward fulfilling a self-imposed mission and anyway might have no effect. Now, looking back, it seems likely that I may have underestimated them.

III

CULTURE SHOCK

E nglish teachers sent to Hungary by the Peace Corps were college graduates and had been exposed to European history but very few of us knew much about the history of Hungary. And even fewer had any acquaintance with the literature of the country from which we might have gained some insight into its culture because, unfortunately, very little of Hungary's remarkably fine writing was available in English translation. That is becoming less true as publishers are now bringing out English language versions of the work of some of Hungary's great writers.

Young Hungarian writers of the nineteenth century who came to the capital from the provinces were bedazzled by Budapest and described it in awe-struck phrases inspired by the romantic imagination of youth. Gyula Krudy, considered by many to be Hungary's greatest novelist, arrived in Budapest at the age of 17 in 1896. His descriptions of Váci Street scenes published a few years later (translated by John Lukacs in "Budapest 1900") evoke a picture as vivid as a painting or photograph: "...the silvery heads of the booksellers gave tone to this district... old pensioners sat on benches in their spotless clothes... the merchandise from Paris arrived directly, scented like women before a grand soirée... the grocer with his wicker baskets and the baker smelling of his fresh kaiser rolls kissed the hands of the chambermaids, in their black bombazine... the serpentine waists of the vendeuses, the white blouses of the millinery girls... the famous shops that sold the best goods from London, suits, hats, gloves... banks paid out brand-new bills."

Contemporary novels by English and American writers depict Hungary, particularly Budapest, as a hotbed of international political intrigue, a place were spies meet and exchange information with exotic women (or are themselves exotic women), where glittering-eyed Gypsies play either sadly romantic or madly frenzied music on violins and the cimbalom. And, of course, there is Dracula. Transylvania was, until 1920, a Hungarian province, and Hungarians, both inside and outside of the province still mourn its award to Romania by the Allies after World War I, but much of the world is oblivious to the loss or to the implications of the Trianon Treaty.

An Italian Renaissance saying declared that the three pearls of Europe were "Venice on the water, Buda on the hill, and Florence on the plain." Lying in the very center of Europe, Hungary has been both a hospitable crossroads for travelers from every direction and an embattled target of marauders from the East, West, North and South. The generous fertility of its soil yields an abundance of luscious fruits, vegetables and grains, that is, when it isn't rivuleted with the blood of its people flowing in defense of their nation. The capital, Budapest, created by the fusion of Buda, Obuda and Pest at the end of 1872, once ranked with Paris and Vienna; it was arguably the most beautiful city on the Danube in the early twentieth century, its charm and refinement recognized worldwide. Hungary's legendary hospitality has been abused throughout its history by uninvited guests who demanded entrance at sword and gun point and repaid that hospitality with subjugation and oppression until they were forcibly driven out.

Given that invading armies always leave behind a generous sprinkling of their genes, any Hungarian walking the streets today may have flowing through his veins the blood of ancient Celtic-Illyrian Eraviscans, Romans, Huns, Ostrogoths, several Germanic and Iranian tribes, mixed with strains from sixteenth and seventeenth century Turkish, and twentieth century German and Russian occupiers. It would be as difficult to define what is mean by "Hungarian" as it is to define what is meant by "American."

The Hungarian-American physicist, Leo Szilárd, one of the most brilliant men of the twentieth century, whose "chain-reaction" theory led to the development of the atomic bomb in the 1940s, never forgot that he was born Hungarian. Because of his highly individual, some said eccentric, personality and the great respect his colleagues had for his intelligence and wit, stories about him and remarks attributed to him were circulated throughout the scientific community. One story told in various versions was about a seminar being led by his friend and colleague, Nobel Laureate Enrico Fermi. Fermi, who was known to muse upon not-always-serious propositions, posed a question. After a wordy discussion about the probability that life-forms superior to ours existed on other planets, he surmised that beings of such advanced intellect would surely have sent explorations into space, and would no doubt have discovered the planet Earth. "Therefore," he said, "if this is true, they should be here by now. So where are they?" According to the story, Szilárd replied instantly, "They are here. They call themselves Hungarians."

At that time there were, besides Szilárd, three other Hungarian scientists working in the United States who were recognized as among the brightest in their fields: János (John von) Neumann, developer of the computer; atomic physicist Ede (Edward) Teller; and 1963 Physics Nobel Laureate Jenő (Eugene) Wigner, who died in 1995. In 1937, the Nobel Prize in Physiology or Medicine was awarded to Albert Szent-Györgyi von Nagyrapolt of Szeged University for the discovery of Vitamin C. He died in 1964. The intellect of these men certainly seemed to be superhuman, and they had all been heard speaking a language incomprehensible to the rest of the world, so the suggestion that they came from another planet did not seem too far-fetched.

Hungary has been a country for about 1000 years. After the Germanic tribes moved on in the fifth century, the Avars, a horse-riding nomadic people from the Asian steppes came and stayed until they were routed by Charlemagne late in the 8th century. A later Carolingian emperor called upon a nomadic group, the Magyars, to subdue a Slavonic duke who had established an independent dukedom within the emperor's domain. Thus the Magyars discovered that on the other side of the Carpathians lay plains that would make an excellent homeland. They finally stabilized the war-torn area and established a country sometime around 900. Hungary was invaded by Mongol grandsons of Genghis Kahn in the thirteenth century; defeated in a two-hour battle by Sulieman the Magnificent at Mohács in 1526 and subsequently ruled by the Ottoman Empire for 160 years. Austria helped drive out the Turks in 1686 and thus achieved their country's long-held dream of annexing Hungary to the Austrian Empire. Hungary chafed under the domination of Austria; they wanted a greater role in the Empire's policy-making and administrative affairs, and in 1848 they mounted a revolution that failed. But less than twenty years later, they reached a compromise agreement with Austria whereby Hungary was given three of the Empire's ministries, and the Emperor of the Austro-Hungarian Empire became also King of Hungary. In 1867, Emperor Franz József and his Empress Elizabeth were crowned King and Queen of Hungary. At last Hungary had a measure of sovereignty, but the triumph was to last only about five decades. The Austro-Hungarian Empire was dissolved following World War I and Hungary was left at the mercy of the Allies who were not inclined to be merciful to a former ally of Germany. In 1920, Hungary was forced to accept the ignominious Trianon Treaty which divided up approximately two-thirds of her land and people among her neighbors.

World War II brought German occupation in 1944, when in a period of two months (14 May to 8 July) approximately half-a-million Jewish men, women and children were sent to Auschwitz. Those who remained were rounded up in ghettos; many were forcibly removed from comfortable homes they had owned for years and placed in crowded ghetto quarters where they lived in daily terror. Liberation by the Soviet Red Army in 1945 brought hope that was short-lived. Persecution of the Jews ended but the German occupation was soon replaced by a repressive Soviet one that oversaw the installation of a government headed by obedient Moscow-trained Hungarian communists backed up by Red Army troops on Hungarian soil.

The constitution voted in by the 1949 Parliament was based on the Stalinist Soviet constitution of 1936. Between 1949 and 1953, the year of Stalin's death, hundreds of thousands of Hungarians were investigated for suspicion of "political deviance," a large number of whom ended up in prison or in concentration camps. Many were executed on trumped-up charges; even more were permanently maimed or scarred by cruel treatment during investigations.

It is remarkable that a people so brutalized could muster the optimism and courage to mount a revolution in 1956, one that actually succeeded! For ten days the country enjoyed real independence before the budding new government was crushed by tanks of the powerful Red Army and once again Hungarian freedom vanished. But thirty-three years later in 1989, Hungary dismantled the barb-wire fence on the Austrian border, thus freeing the East Germans and presaging the fall of the Berlin Wall and of communism not only in Hungary but in Eastern Europe and eventually even in the Soviet Union.

After rejecting communism in 1989, Hungary like the rest of Eastern Europe, was suffering from over 40 years of centralized control of all resources and production, control that decreed and enforced maximum output regardless of deleterious side-effects. Experts from all over the world visited the area after 1989 and were aghast at what they found. One said, "If we had one-tenth this amount of pollution in my country, we would consider it a disaster!" The waters of the beautiful and mighty Danube, the longest river in Europe at 3000 kilometers (2000 miles), flowing through eight countries, were heavily polluted. Many architectural treasures, churches, synagogues, basilicas, theatres, opera houses, music and dancing schools were crumbling after more than 40 years of neglect. Buildings pockmarked with bullet holes from the 1956 Revolution and even from World War II were a common sight. Some of the 1400 mines that the Royal Air Force dropped into the Danube in 1944 to prevent Germany from getting oil supplies from Ukraine and Romania were still lying there. In 1990, a World War II bomb surfaced by the Chain Bridge near one of the large tourist hotels; in 1993 another bomb from that war turned up near Esztergom at the Danube Bend close to the Slovakian border, where the river turns from its Eastward course to run directly Southward. Hungary's first king was born in Esztergom and crowned there in 1000 (or perhaps 1001) when he brought Hungary into the Holy Roman Empire. The dome of its great Basilica, the largest in Hungary, is visible for miles around. A Soviet tank division north of Esztergom and a smaller camp beneath Peace Square near the Basilica were among the first Soviet troops to be withdrawn from Hungary in 1990 on the direct order of Mihail Gorbachev. The Hungarian Army's Bomb Squad safely detonated both of those bombs which rose to the surface of the Danube nearly 50 years after the end of World War II. But the soldiers who tried to defuse a Soviet-made World War II grenade found in the front yard of a house in the town of Dunaharaszti a short distance south of Budapest, in 1997, were not so fortunate. They were both killed.

In the one-hundred years between the last decade of the nineteenth century when Krudy described Váci Street and this last decade of the twentieth century when I first saw Budapest, great changes had occurred. Forty years of isolation behind the Iron Curtain had left the country technologically backward, and Soviet demands on its industrial capacity seriously restricted the production of consumer goods; many household and personal articles in everyday use in Western Europe and the United States were unavailable and some almost unknown. What struck me most forcibly at first was the almost complete lack of paper goods of all kinds – ordinary or gift wrapping, grocery bags, stationery, paper towels, napkins. Toilet paper was the rough brown sort used in England during and right after World War II. The first gift I mailed from Hungary to the United States, went in a flimsy, somewhat battered cardboard box that my resourceful "home-stay" hostess dredged up from somewhere, and wrapped in paper that had seen previous use at least once, maybe twice, similar to that which we call "butcher" paper. She even came up with some cord to tie around it, without which the Post Office would not accept it. Every mailed package had to be wrapped with cord no matter how small it was or how tightly sealed. It was the rule.

No millinery girls in white blouses presided over elegant shops on Váci Street. There were no elegant shops. No lit, decorated windows beckoned to customers. There was nothing to display, and if there had been there was no need to entice customers. The problem was to keep fights from breaking out if anything desirable was on sale. Stores were little more than distribution points for mass-produced government products. Grocers and bakers did not kiss the hands of chambermaids as they delivered their wares. There were no chambermaids, and nothing was delivered. Hungarian housewives carried heavy shopping bags, balancing themselves with a full bag in each hand. And no scented merchandise arrived from Paris, or suits from London. The bank did not pay out brand new bills. The money all looked old and very much used. Merchants refused to accept torn bills.

It seemed inconceivable to me at first that there could be any cultural misunderstandings between me and the Kovács family. Their warm welcome told me they were understanding, forgiving people, and the cultural orientation we received was quite thorough. But even the best designed orientation courses must deal broadly with prevailing national customs, manners and taboos. Those are easily and quickly learned and well-meaning foreigners are unlikely to commit such gaffes as scoffing at the gods of their hosts, insulting their ancestors, or touching the monarch. The things that trip most of us up are the little, insignificant things that seem too unimportant to include in an orientation course.

A great deal of thought and effort had gone into preparing a room for me. There was a large window to let in light, with a slatted wooden blind to provide shade and privacy; a standard Hungarian couch-by-day, bed-by-night, attractively upholstered; desk with straight chair and nearby bookshelf; comfortable armchair; clothes closet, bedside and desk lamps. Perfect. As I started to unpack, I looked around for a trash receptacle and there was none. A mere oversight, I thought, and was halfway out of the room to ask for one when I remembered that we had been instructed to accept whatever was provided in our homes and make no demands. They will think of it later, I said to myself. I can wait. And wait I did. No trash basket ever appeared and I never saw one in any room except the kitchen.

Much later, when I told a Hungarian friend about my surprise at having no trash basket, she asked, "What did you do?" I told her that I wrapped trash in newspapers or put it into a bag when I had one — paper and plastic bags were very rare items — and carried it in my backpack to school where I disposed of it. Or, occasionally, when I was passing through the kitchen late at night on my way to the bathroom, I would sneak trash into the metal can in the cabinet under the sink. Hoping she would tell me what I should have done, I looked at her questioningly, but all she said was, "You did the right thing." Eventually, I learned that waste baskets are not normally found in homes except in the kitchen. It was a relief to know that I had not made the mistake of asking for one, thereby suggesting that the arrangements they had made for me were not perfect in every detail.

One cultural hurdle that I completely mis-managed, however, and have not yet fully mastered is the established conventions for gift-giving. The practice of gift exchange among people has been going on as far back as, even further back than, recorded history. The various customs associated with this practice have evolved in every culture over such eons of time that their sources are untraceable, their rituals meaningless. Religion, superstition, legend, history, geography, economics, demography, weather and often the idiosyncracy of some powerful ancient monarch have all played a part in the evolution of the behaviors and courtesies foreigners must learn. In Japan, where I lived for more than three years, gift-giving is a precisely choreographed ceremonial obligation, a rite that has become as automatic as the instinctive bow, and as meaningless. Affluent families have cupboards where they put away gifts as they are received, sometimes without even unwrapping them. When a member of the family goes visiting or attends an occasion where a gift is obligatory, they may reach into the cabinet and take one at random. Stories, not all apocryphal, are told of people whose gifts are returned to them years or even months later in the original wrapping! For close friends and family, they select gifts with great thought and care.

Gift-giving in Hungary has not become so ritualistic as it has in Japan, but there are occasions when the omission of a gift would be a social error. Taking flowers to the hostess, even for a very informal visit, was the invariable custom when I first arrived, and it is still the usual custom, although I believe not so scrupulously observed since the cost of flowers has sky-rocketed. Now, bouquets may be smaller and consist of less exotic flowers. One perfect rose and a bit of greenery, artistically wrapped in cellophane and ribbon, is not unusual for the seemingly endless number of occasions when flowers are expected, a birthday, a name day, a promotion, a departure, an arrival, or some special holiday like International Women's Day. There seems to be a flower shop in every block in the central area of Budapest, and they are abundant in other cities or even small towns. In addition to the shops, flower stalls are everywhere, always near metro entrances, and even inside the stations. Women with baskets of flowers stand at the top of the escalators in the metro station holding out bouquets and urging the hurrying travelers to stop and buy. A surprising number of them do. Giving flowers is a gracious custom, easy to learn and comply with, difficult only for foreigners with very little money and those who are stingy. But selecting a personal, not ritual, gift is quite another matter and in those days of consumer goods scarcity it was not easy.

Hungarians love to give. It has been said that those who truly understand the joy of giving are people who have once been very poor. The Hungarian generosity may in part stem from those years when commodities of every kind were in short supply and few people had anything to give, but their open handedness suggests a more instinctive behavior, one that goes far back in their culture. They appear actually to enjoy giving more than receiving to such a degree that I have sometimes accused them of being "poor receivers". They make very little fuss over gifts, and never write "thank you" notes not even for wedding gifts or for gifts sent through the mail, to let the sender know it arrived. Never have I heard any Hungarian refer to a past gift with a comment like, "We placed the beautiful vase where we could see it every day," or "The flowers lasted for a whole week!" This behavior may stem from the same philosophy of the Russian people who consider it impolite to make a fuss over gifts and do not write thank you notes. A Russian friend inadvertently clued me in to this when telling me about an American birthday party he attended. He said the honoree received a large number of gifts, and with astonishment in his voice, added, "She unwrapped everyone of them, and exclaimed over each one, 'Oh, it's beautiful! It's wonderful! I love it! You are so generous!'" He shook his head, and added, "It was amazing!" I didn't understand him and asked, "But don't you unwrap gifts and thank the persons who brought them?" Then he explained, "Yes, we say 'Thank You', but not effusively. To praise a gift excessively would be discourteous; it would appear to place more importance on the gift than on the giver." The memory of that explanation gave me some consolation when I brought gifts to Anna and János from Budapest on my first visit to that city.

They had been so kind to me and done so much for me that I wanted to give them something special. After a great deal of thought about it, and some searching, I bought a bottle of bath oil for Anna. János was more difficult until I remembered that Anna had once told me his favorite drink was brandy. After a lot of searching, I found a bottle of good French brandy in a shop obviously set up for tourists, atrociously priced, of course. I felt good about my choices, and looked forward to the pleasure with which they would be received.

At dinner on my first day back home, I brought out the gifts, which they opened, and acknowledged with perfunctory thanks. It was obvious that they were pleased I had brought them gifts, but I could not tell whether they liked what I had brought. After dinner, János invited me into the almost-never-used living room, and I knew it must be for a special purpose. He walked to the far corner of the room and opened a cabinet I had not noticed before. It was used for storing alcoholic drinks and quite full. He pointed out to me how much brandy he had. The message was clear: he appreciated my gift, but he did not need brandy. And not for the first or the last time, I recalled Professor Szöny's advice: "If you find us pessimistic and overly-sensitive, try to remember what it must be like to have been losers for 500 years."

Although I am still not completely versed in the subtleties of gift-giving, that experience taught me one thing. Whatever the circumstances of the recipient or the occasion, the gift should never imply that you have perceived a "need." One must always take into account what I have come to think of as "that Hungarian pride." Flowers, candy, books are excellent, or for those who can afford expensive gifts, paintings, sculpture or a piece of the beautiful Hungarian porcelain. But restraint is necessary unless you want to be inundated with gifts, as they are likely to be reciprocated many times over.

There is no doubt that I committed many social blunders out of pure ignorance, probably even offended people on occasion but my Hungarian friends were so polite they always acted as if whatever I did was all right. Only from strangers did I occasionally get a clear indication that I had committed a faux pas. But as I learn more through the years, I can find myself blushing even when I am all alone in the privacy of my home and recall some of the deplorable things I did or said, especially in the first year or two.

NOTES FROM THE JOURNAL – SWIMMING IN THE DANUBE

It is always hot in Southern Hungary in August and very dry. Hungarians accept this stoically and when foreigners complain they may reply with a shrug and the comment, "It is very good for the grapes." Ice or iced drinks were almost never available my first summer there, and air conditioning was unheard of. So when Márika invited me to go to the beach with her and her two teen-age children the following Saturday, I enthusiastically accepted. Only later did I wonder what "beach" in land-locked Hungary meant and where we were going. It surely meant adjacent to water I reasoned and that made it very enticing.

It turned out that we were going swimming in the Danube River. The Mighty Danube. Wending its shallow and somewhat quirky way from the Black Forest in Germany near the Swiss border through Austria, Hungary, Yugoslavia, and Romania, past the great cities of Vienna, Bratislava and Budapest, emptying at last into the Black Sea. Its swift flow, controlled by dams and locks, makes it one of the world's fastest commercial waterways. Nevertheless, it has inspired poets, composers, and novelists and become many things to many people all over the world. But there are some things it is not. It is not, as everyone now agrees, blue, despite the lyrics of the famous Johann Strauss waltz. And it is not clean. Europe's grandest waterway is the main transmission belt for waste, running the gantlet of discharge from eight countries as it sweeps through Central and Eastern Europe.

During the communist regime, environmental considerations took second place to industrial production, and the waterways of Hungary as in all of that region were contaminated with fertilizers, toxic waste and untreated sewage. Whether capitalism increased or decreased pollution in Eastern Europe is debatable, because only after its arrival were there instruments to accurately measure it. Air quality specialists from other countries flocked to the area like tourists visiting a chamber of horrors. Pollution from heavy metal waste declined somewhat after the arrival of democracy because state-owned factories were closed down or their production lowered. But some new problems appeared: more traffic, more plastic foam, not to mention the toxic waste from abandoned Soviet military bases.

Communist Hungary like the Soviet Union had a network of holiday resorts where workers, upon the recommendation of their trade unions, could go on vacations at reduced prices, or, as a special reward, even free. They were called "Rest Houses" (roughly translated), and in both countries they were a highly valued "perk" as it was the only way many people could vacation at all. These were still in place when I arrived in Hungary. The rest houses for workers were not the same as those set aside for top-level party people. The elegant Hungarian ones on the shores of Lake Balaton were, like the Soviet ones at Sochi on the Black Sea, reserved for the communist elite. The one Márika took me to was quite obviously a workers' resort. It was very clean, very well managed, but Spartan.

The area was fenced in and guarded. Márika had to show a pass to get through two guarded gates along the road before we reached the compound and the house where we changed our clothes, for which she had a "permission slip" authorizing its use. The house we were in, and I think they were all alike, consisted of 3 bedrooms, a common kitchen, a shower room that could accommodate several people, and men's and women's toilets. Each bedroom had two double-decked, double beds –enough sleeping space for the average Hungarian family of two parents and two children, even if grandma came along. Each family was assigned one room, and the three families in each building used the common kitchen, bath and toilets. It was spotlessly clean – the kitchen looked as immaculate as an operating room in a good hospital and the bath and toilet facilities were the same. The normal length of stay was one week; families arrived on Friday afternoon, bringing their own food which they prepared in the common kitchen and left the following Friday morning. At least, that was the normal procedure. I asked how we happened to have a room for one day on a Saturday and Márika shrugged and smiled saying she guessed the people to whom it was assigned were late in arriving. My guess is that, as the secretary to a local official, she could arrange to use the facility for an occasional day.

It was a short walk from the house to the waterside and, like everyone else there, we brought a lunch and drinks with us. There were no hawkers of food, drinks, chairs, umbrellas or anything else. We spread a blanket on the grass under the trees where there was some, but not enough, shade. The sun was very bright and in spite of my apprehensions, the water looked inviting. Many people were cavorting in the water, tossing balls, laughing, happily at play. A low concrete wall separated the grassy area from the water, and there were a few steps leading down to the river edge where a narrow strip of rocky sand had been hauled in to make a "beach." My friends made no move to go into the water immediately so we sat for a while and I watched the people, noting the differences between them and beach crowds I was used to. It was my first experience of seeing Hungarians at play. It was nothing like any seaside scene I had ever witnessed. There were no loud radios, although a few young people had Walkmans on their heads; no alcoholic drinks, which was a great surprise, as Hungarians are very heavy drinkers and alcohol is normally a part of any recreational outing. But the only way to get to that place was by car, and the penalties for drunken driving are so severe that practically nobody in Hungary will risk it. The only time I saw anyone decline a glass of wine or a beer was when they had to drive later. The fact that it was a sober crowd seemed to make a difference. There was no shouting, or rough-housing, or quarreling. Another big difference was that everybody seemed to be completely unconcerned about bodily appearance. Swimming costumes were very brief – an approximately 300-pound woman in a string bikini caught my eye, but no one else seemed to notice. Men with huge potbellies hanging over their tiny bathing trunks showed no trace of self-consciousness. Most women in Hungary do not, or did not then, shave their legs or underarms, and would not know what a "bikini wax job" is, so their postage-stamp size suits revealed not only most of their body skin but quite a bit of pubic hair as well. The lack of concern with which people displayed their bodies no matter how unattractive, and viewed or rather ignored equally unattractive bodies, was surprising. But what was even more surprising was their indifference to gorgeous bodies, and there were also quite a few of those around too. But no show-offs paraded the beach to display their shapely bronzed bodies or their manly "pecs." When nearly nude girls beautiful enough to model for a Playboy Calendar strolled past, men didn't even look up. It reminded me of what I was told in Japan about their public baths: "Nudity is often seen, but seldom noticed."

In spite of my nervousness about swimming in the river, it was somewhat reassuring to see so many people obviously enjoying themselves and that, plus the heat, eventually lured me into the water. It had been a long time since I swam in a river, and when I stepped in and sank almost to my ankles in soft, slimy mud, it was a shock. It was not the same thing as swimming in ceramic-lined pools or the sandy-bottomed ocean. There were some rocks and enough debris to make me think of broken glass, but I took courage from the many other bathers around me. When I was waist-deep, it was clear that there were only two choices; I could stand on the mucky bottom, or lie down in the water and inevitably drink some of it. In the end, I alternated. We played ball, standing, and from time to time I would cool myself by lying down and taking a few strokes in the water.

The 1400 mines still lying on the bottom of the Danube where they had been dropped by the Royal Air Force in 1944 did not bother me. I had no idea they were there. The Bosnian War, approximately 60 miles south of where I was standing, did not enter my thoughts as it would later when Hungary took in more refugees from that war than any other country. My mind was then beginning to be absorbed in the fantasy of a tall glass filled with ice and coca cola or a double-dip ice cream cone. I grew up less than one-hour by car from Virginia Beach which, in my youth, was famous for its wide sandy beach and my favorite seaside memories are of strolling on the beach eating an ice cream cone in any weather, hot and sunny preferred. Ah, me, the memory plays tricks upon us and makes us long for the return of things that never were, so perhaps I was only dreaming. Hungarians are so fond of ice cream that I was sure it would be available somewhere nearby. There was a Kiosk but it was near the exit and too far to walk. So we stopped there when we drove out. We sat down at a table, fully dressed, and ate ice cream. It wasn't the same thing, but it sure tasted good.

The sun, the water, the long drive all made me feel healthily tired and sleepy when I got home. And neither I nor my friends suffered any ill effects from our dip into the dirty Danube River. Tactlessly, I commented on this to Márika, reflecting my surprise. She only laughed and said, "Persze!" (Of course!)

IV

OUR DAILY BREAD

All during that hot, dry summer, household activities went on as usual in the Kovacs's home: cooking, canning and freezing, gardening, entertaining relatives with or without children who came for vacations, and always guests for meals on Sunday. No matter what the temperature, Anna and János never slowed down.

The Kovácses grew a surprising variety and quantity of vegetables in the small garden plot near the house. And the harvest from the large rented plot nine kilometers from their home was astonishingly abundant. Many people in Hungary rent garden spaces, even those who live in cities. On days that János worked in the large garden, he left home at 5 a.m. with a lunch of bread, zsir (lard), and salt, and worked until after sundown. He returned home sunburned, sweating, tired, carrying bags and baskets of peas, corn, beans, cabbage, potatoes, tomatoes, carrots, cucumbers, onions and paprika. While he bathed, Anna put the finishing touches to supper, called *vacsora*, normally a light meal, but on those days it was the big meal of the day. She considered herself an artist in the kitchen and refused all offers of help, but she enjoyed an audience and so I often watched her cook.

Typical Hungarian dishes today are not the same as those the Magyar tribes brought over the Carpathian mountains a millennium ago, but the modern cuisine still contains traces of the ancient past. The enormous quantities that are routinely prepared, the huge size of an average serving, the meal-in-one-pot dishes hark back to the nomadic tribes who often did not know when they would next stop for meal preparation.

Although I never heard Anna or János utter a doleful word about the past, including their early childhood, the almost frenzied activity they put into garnering and preserving food for the winter suggested memories of hunger and deprivation.

"For the Winter!" she would say as she lifted a glass jar from the boiling kettle, filled it with vegetables, sealed it and set it on the shelf. All summer, she peeled, chopped, sliced, blanched, and pickled, stored jars on shelves, and bags or boxes in the freezer. She prepared for Winter as though for an oncoming cyclone. The urgency of preparing for leaner days must have been magnified greatly by the food shortages during the Second World War and the first years of the communist regime.

Beginning in the late 1960s, the Kádár government saw to it that food, cigarettes and alcohol were plentiful and cheap, purposely so, in order to keep the workers happy and thus fulfill Kádár's commitment to the Soviets that there would be no repeat of the 1956 Revolution. But memory of want is very persistent and people who have once known it find it hard even in prosperous times to have faith in continuing sufficiency.

Conversation in the Kovács' home between Anna and her sister-in-law who lived next door was almost entirely about food. I never heard them gossip about their neighbors or discuss clothes, books, cosmetics, or television. When the sister-in-law, or any neighbor for that matter, dropped in for a visit, she usually brought a sample of something she had just cooked, and always asked, "What are you cooking for dinner?" No matter what the answer was, the next question was, "How are you going to fix it?" Every woman has her own favorite way of preparing Hungarian dishes, such as stuffed cabbage, goulash, chicken paprika, and especially soups. Hungarians make delicious soups and every main meal, usually served at mid-day, always begins with soup.

The amount of food Hungarians consume at one meal continues to astonish me. Having always had what my family and friends considered a healthy appetite, it came as a surprise to discover that the Kovácses thought I ate nothing, and Anna repeatedly asked me if there was something wrong with her cooking. She never accepted my protests and assurances that her food was delicious. She, herself, was a prodigious eater and very proud of it. Taking ten roast potatoes on her plate from the serving bowl, she would announce boastingly, "I eat a lot!" Later, I wondered if that was meant as a kind of rebuke, a way of expressing disdain for "picky" eaters. It was one of her many qualities that I admired and could not help comparing with the stinginess with which some American women take tiny portions, nibble daintily, and look horrified at the suggestion of seconds. Then, they agonize over the decision to have dessert as if they were deciding to sin or not. Anna thought eating a lot was a virtue in the same class with working hard.

One day János brought home from the large garden the first fresh peas of the season, so we decided to have some for dinner. They tumbled out of the shells firm, plump, pearly green and made my mouth water. (I was allowed to shell peas.) Anna thought good cooking depended on how much the cook did to the food, the more effort and the more additives, the better the dish would be. I watched in disbelief and dismay as those darling little green peas were dumped into a pot of melted lard in which chopped onion was simmering. Seasonings were added, salt and powdered paprika. "I no longer use as much paprika as I used to," Anna said, as she ladled several large tablespoonsful into a paste of milk and flour, a roux, which she then stirred into the pot. "I now use only three or four kilos a year; it used to be six or seven." They make their own ground paprika after the fresh red pods have been hung from the porch ceiling on the sunny side of the house until they are dry enough to grind. So she knows exactly how much she uses and considers between six and nine pounds a year to be moderate usage. Paprika gives food a unique Hungarian flavor. The planting and growing of paprika (peppers) in vegetable gardens started in the seventeenth century. According to some sources, the grinding of red peppers into paprika was a Hungarian invention of fairly recent times. An 1830 cookbook called for the use of pepper, not ground paprika. Red paprika contains vitamins A and C and is said to be beneficial for the digestive system. The revised edition of the *Gundel's Hungarian Cookbook*, 1995 edition, advised cooks not to worry about the "seemingly excessive amount of paprika" in the ingredient lists, "it is necessary to obtain the proper flavor." The flour, milk and paprika paste which Anna added soon thickened the mixture into a pudding-like texture. Having steeled myself against the temptation to criticize any aspect of Hungarian culture, I was determined to say nothing, but that time I was only partly successful. In what I hoped sounded like an offhand comment, I said, "In America, we just steam fresh peas for a few minutes and add a bit of salt and butter." She stirred in another large spoonful of the thick paste, and almost snorted as she spoke, "Oh, then you eat them raw!" The final result was a pot of gray peas held together in what appeared to be a pink aspic, which she served proudly, beaming expectation of approval. János and I both raved and she promised to give me the recipe. Once, before I knew better, I made the mistake of describing this preparation of fresh peas to a Hungarian friend, a university graduate, a gymnasium teacher; she looked at me questioningly and said, "Of course. How would you cook them?"

The Kovácses rarely ate raw vegetables; tomatoes were turned into juice, or a delicious sauce used in cooking pork, chicken, fish or even beef, on those rare occasions when they ate beef. Cabbage, cauliflower, and cucumbers, even the tender little Kirbys, were steeped in brine. When I suggested that I would like a "natural," that is, unpickled, cucumber, they dismissed the idea as too silly for consideration, as if I had asked for a green apple. They considered raw cucumbers inedible. I never got up the nerve to suggest a wedge of steamed cabbage with butter and salt and pepper, which I would have liked. Cabbage was eaten pickled and that was that. Fresh paprika uncooked, in its many delectable varieties, is usually served only at *vacsora*, the evening meal, rarely or never at the big mid-day dinner. I have also known them to be eaten at breakfast. And what paprika! Before coming to Hungary, I thought paprika was a ground red spice that came in small boxes and cans and sat on the shelf for a while before being thrown away. Its shelf-life was always shorter than the time it took to empty the small container. In America we have green, red, and yellow "Bell peppers," all the same globular shape. Paprika in Hungary is something else. The shapes, sizes, colors, and varieties seem endless. There are long, slender red ones, and fat, round, large, and small ones in various shades of red – some as bright as the stripes in the American flag, others as dark as ripe plums. There are yellow ones ranging from pale ivory to lemon, some with delicate pink stripes. And there are green ones, mostly rich, dark green, some long and slender, others small and round, resembling young, green tomatoes. Bell peppers can now be seen in the market occasionally, always clearly labeled "California," at a cost of five to ten times as much as the local ones. The most important thing to learn about the fresh paprika is that although many are sweet (*édes*), some are hot (*erös*). The dark green ones are the fieriest. The most effective way to learn the difference is the hard way, that is by eating a hot one. You can learn that the word for hot is *erös*, but you cannot possibly understand the real meaning of that word until you have bitten into an *erös* paprika and your mouth is still burning several hours later. That's HOT! That is also the favorite of many Hungarians.

After dinner, János settled down in front of the television set, I washed the dishes (Anna allowed me to do that but always protested and stuck around to see that I put things away in the right place), while Anna prepared for the next day's labor which inevitably involved food preparation.

The preparations were all familiar to me, not only because they had become a ritual since I arrived there in mid-June, but because it was very much like what went on during the summers in semi-rural Virginia where I grew up and I could easily envision the next day. The kitchen is filled with steam from boiling water on the stove in which glass jars are being sterilized, and from other large pots of boiling water for blanching vegetables to be frozen. On a small gas stove set up in the garage (the car was backed out into the driveway) a huge cauldron will be simmering. Every counter and table surface is filled with broccoli, green beans, corn-on-the-cob, all ready for the blanching pot; cucumbers, cabbage, and paprika ready to be put into brine; washed tomatoes waiting to be cut up and carried to the outside cauldron where they will simmer slowly all day becoming, with time and the addition of seasonings, the spicy sauce Anna uses for flavoring soups and meats in the winter. The floor will be covered with baskets, boxes, and bags of potatoes, squash, rutabagas, carrots and apples to be put into the root cellar beneath the garage floor. János had dug out a space under the wooden floor where these things were stored. It was no deeper than his arm could reach and covered an area slightly larger than the chassis of the East German-made Trabant they owned. The hinged access door was centered so the wheels of the car stood on either side of it. In order to put fruit and vegetables into storage there, and to retrieve them later, the car had to be backed out into the driveway.

Anna will be flushed and damp from the steam and the late summer heat, as she wields heavy tongs to lift scalding jars from the sterilizing pans, and pours fruit and vegetables into them; fills jars with cabbage, cucumbers and tomato sauce and freezer bags with freshly-blanched peas, beans, broccoli, squash and corn. Sometimes her daughter and her sister-in-law help, and even I am allowed to peel fruit, but she is the Maestro, directing all activities from her podium in front of the stove. She relinquishes her command post only to check on the tomato sauce simmering on the stove in the garage, or to answer the bell that calls her to her father's bedside. At the same time, she prepares the next meal, bakes pastry (*sütemény*), and chats with anyone, relative or neighbor, who drops in. "Aren't you tired?" I asked her occasionally, and the reply was always the same, "I never get tired!" She said this with exactly the same expression and the same pride as she said, "I eat a lot!" Her zest for life was phenomenal! "What do you do in the winter?" I once asked her. "O winter is lovely," she replied. "I have none of this to do, no garden, no chickens. That is when I do my embroidery." I had seen the drawers full of embroidered linens, tablecloths, napkins, bureau scarves, doilies, which are, she told me, for her 19-year-old granddaughter's trousseau. All she had to do in the "lovely winter" was the housework, laundry (a daily chore), cook three meals a day, bathe, feed and talk to her bedridden father, and look after two dogs and a cat. The rest of the time she watched television or embroidered and sometimes did both simultaneously. She smiled as she spoke of this as if the thought of such a pleasant, easy time sustained her through the arduous summer.

If Anna or her brother and sister-in-law who lived next door ever read a book or a newspaper, I never saw it. János bought and read a daily newspaper, and listened to the news on television. He also listened to the classical music programs on the Hungarian television on Sunday afternoons. Anna was only interested in the daytime drama or "soap opera" programs. If our evening meal ran late, and on canning and freezing days this often happened, and there wasn't time to wash the dishes and clean up the kitchen before 8:40 PM on the day old re-runs of Dallas were aired (without commercials), Anna would shoo everybody into their bed-sitting room to the television set. No matter how much I urged her to go and watch the program and let me clean up the kitchen, she would not hear of it. Since I was fairly familiar with the story line, it was not too difficult to follow, so I considered it as a language lesson. She never talked about Dallas and I never knew what appealed to her so much. Some Hungarians see it as a kind of window on American life, thinking all Americans live like the characters in that show. They love Dallas and watch it as faithfully as Americans used to watch, well, Dallas.

One Sunday in August, Anna and I went with János to the big garden when he needed help with picking vegetables. They were "getting ahead of him" as we used to say in Virginia. It was a very long day! The plot was large by Hungarian standards, but modest compared to vegetable gardens in the United States. Even so, I was amazed at the amount of vegetables it yielded. We picked and picked and it seemed to me that the more we picked the more there was. We came home with boxes and bags and baskets full, as much as could be packed on top of and inside the small car, along with ourselves. I was very glad to go to bed that night, and just as glad I had to go to classes the next day and could escape the kitchen activity.

The Kovácses had cherry trees, both sour and sweet, and that year they were loaded with fruit, yielding enough for gorging on during the season, and canning for the winter when they would be made into pastries of various kinds.

It is not only fruits and vegetables that they prepare for the winter. Early in the Spring, in March, I think, they buy baby chicks and raise them to broiler or fryer size. As they reach that size, Anna kills them, cuts them into serving sizes, and puts them in the freezer. From time to time during the summer, she spends a day at this, processing approximately fifteen chickens in one day. By the end of August all the chickens are gone, and the area where they lived is prepared for other uses. As with the chickens, they buy very young shoats and raise them up to the right size for butchering. The chicken and pig pens were very close to the house, but were kept so meticulously clean that there was never a whiff of odor from them.

Everybody knows that hogs are butchered in cold weather, or at least they always were in the days before modern refrigeration and freezing facilities were available. Be that as it may, on a hot summer afternoon, I returned home to find that Anna and János had emptied their largest freezer and were industriously scouring it, preparing it, they explained, to store meat of the pig that would be butchered there at 4 A.M. the next morning. They invited me to attend but assured me that I was under no obligation to arise that early. Mainly they wanted to warn me that I might be awakened by the unavoidable sounds. It was obvious that this was an occasion of some importance and that it was an honor to be invited. In the "bad old days" under communism and collectivization, the private butchering of an animal for one's own use was a crime against the state. There is a wonderful Hungarian film called *A tanú*, (The Witness), made in 1969, a satire on the communist regime by the now-famous director Péter Bacsó. It opens with a scene of an illegal butchering, in which school children were brought into the house to sing lustily during the process in order to drown out the animal's squeals. But in the summer of 1992, it was a social occasion, primarily a male gathering but some women had to be present to assist with the processing of the meat. The next morning at 4 A.M., in addition to the screams of the dying animal, there were also sounds associated with merriment – clinking glasses, laughter, several people talking at the same time, having a good time. Although the primary function of this event was to provide a future supply of food, it was also an occasion for consuming a great deal of food and drink, as at all Hungarian gatherings – not uniquely Hungarian, of course. There may be cultures in which celebrations do not include food and drink but I have never heard of them.

The actual slaying of the pig is done by a professional "pig-sticker," a *böllér*, but four men must each hold a leg of the pig while the *böllér* sticks the knife blade into the neck and quickly severs the artery. After that, the hair is singed off, the animal washed and hung from a hook for dismembering. The *böllér* removes the head, the sides and the front ham; the men begin cutting up the different parts. He slits the carcass from top to bottom allowing the innards to be disgorged and the edible organs retrieved. Everybody at this point fortifies himself with large draughts of fruit brandy, *pálinka*. The women catch the blood in pans and take it to the kitchen where large frying pans are simmering with onions and paprika. They quickly prepare the first delicacy to be sampled by the guests – cooked blood. It is rich and thick enough to be eaten with a fork. With lip-smacking anticipation, everyone spreads some on bread, washes it down with *pálinka*. Everyone? Well, not quite. I managed to be otherwise engaged. It is pronounced delicious, glasses raised in congratulations to the cooks, more sips of *pálinka*, then back to the work of cutting up chops, spare ribs, hams and bacon. A 300-pound animal yields about 50 pounds of the various cuts and 30-40 pounds of bacon. Then there are the sausages and the jellied product called "headcheese" which the women make from the feet, head, tongue and heart. I am not completely sure what goes into the sausage: fat, certainly, and parts of some organs mixed with bread, and spices – salt, pepper, the ubiquitous paprika. There is a machine for shooting this mixture into tubes of the cleaned intestines. Later, some of the sausage is smoked to make the widely known and enjoyed *kolbász*.

Anna apologized that the mid-day meal, normally served about 1 o'clock would be delayed until 3 o'clock, and everyone was invited. The very thought of eating ever again was revolting to me, and everybody else appeared to be well fed and a little drunk, so nobody minded the delay.

The Hungarian appetite cannot be assuaged for long so everybody arrived at the table right on time. In a quick-change that rivaled the speed of time-lapse photography, the large kitchen had been transformed from an adjunct to the slaughter scene to a sparkling clean dining room, the table covered with a pretty embroidered cloth; china, flatware and wine glasses, napkins all in place, such was the housekeeping magic Anna could perform. She, who had arisen at 3 a.m., wearing a fresh dress, every strand of her beautiful white hair in place, cheerfully welcomed the guests and presided over the feast. That meal was a severe test of my firm resolve to accept the customs of the country with grace and equanimity, that is, not behave like a foreigner. The mounds of fresh pork, cooked in various ways, the fresh sausages, did not tempt me, to put it in the most delicate way possible. Nobody seemed to notice or care that I ate very little, mostly vegetables. I was grateful for the red wine. In the evening, a light meal was served, but I passed that one up giving as an excuse that I had eaten so much during the day.

Anna learned to cook between the two World Wars from her mother, whose style and recipes were early twentieth century. Anna's kitchen equipment was more modern than that in her mother's tiny village cottage, but her repertoire and cooking style were essentially the same as her mother's. My colleagues, at the gymnasium where I taught English, who were born in the late 1950s or early 60s, had more modern ideas about nutrition and food preparation, but still clung to some traditional practices and still used some of their mothers' recipes.

Hungarians eat a lot of pork, and they know many ways to cook it. Pork is also the source of "zsir," the lard used for all cooking and baking in traditional kitchens; therefore the pork roasts and chops one buys in the meat market have had all the fat carefully removed. It is the leanest pork I have ever seen. All the world knows about Hungarian Goulash (*Gulyás*), and all the world has its own idea of how to make it. That includes Hungarian restaurants in the cities and in the provinces. Károly Gundel, who founded in Budapest one of the finest restaurants in Europe early in the twentieth century, described it as a meat dish, usually pork, prepared with onions and paprika, containing cubed potato and small bits of dough – a "soup-like dish." The restaurant he established is no longer in the Gundel family but still bears his name, and is still one of the finest restaurants in Eastern Europe.

As in all of Europe, the cuisine has come under foreign influence. The wife of Matthias Corvinus, who reigned from the middle to near the end of the fifteenth century, was Italian and she and her retinue intermingled some Italian flavorings and techniques with the Hungarian. The Turks ruled Hungary for 150 years after the battle at Mohács in 1526 and influenced Hungarian cuisine enormously. One story regarding the remarkable growth of coffee houses in the seventeenth century is that after their defeat, the Turks exited the country so hastily that they left behind their huge stores of coffee beans, from which the Hungarians made coffee similar to, but better than, the Turkish coffee. Hungarian cooking lost some of its heaviness due to the effects of French cuisine introduced through the Royal Court at Vienna in the days of the Austro-Hungarian Empire.

In his mid-twentieth century Hungarian cookbook, Károly Gundel frankly states, "Most of the dishes described in this book would not be very easy to digest... especially if the dinner guests are not all Hungarian. The Hungarian dishes should be interspersed with lighter fare." However, in a more recent edition of his cookbook, Gundel cautions, "... you must use real Hungarian lard, green pepper, paprika, potato and onion... You can't obtain the same flavor if you use butter, oil or margarine instead of lard."

But things are changing. When I tried to buy olive oil recently and there was none on the shelf, the shop attendant offered me instead "*növény olaj*" (vegetable oil) and urged me to try it. He described its advantages, good taste, low fat, and a customer in line behind me added her own endorsement recommending it as superior to olive oil. Low-fat, even fat-free foods are beginning to appear in the supermarkets. And some frankfurters made from poultry are clearly labelled "No Pork" in English. But restaurant servings are still enormous and many foreigners, including me, find it impossible to finish an average-size entrée. A few restaurants will even give diners a "doggie bag" nowadays if they request it. However, I can well imagine that it might spark another revolution if anyone tried to bring *Nouvelle Cuisine* to Hungary.

V

LOCAL POLITICS

The street where the Kovács family lived had been recently renamed. Prior to 1989 it bore the name of a prominent communist, I was told, and people were not yet used to the new name. Therefore, I was advised to use both names when directing anyone, a taxi driver for example, to the house. When I asked János and Anna about the man for whom the street was formerly named, they both threw up their hands and shook their heads impatiently. János emphatically stated, "He was not a communist!" Anna said nothing, only turned her head from side to side as if this was all nonsense not worth talking about.

In the first years of the Hungarian democracy, the label "Communist" meant different things to different people, even as it once did and perhaps still does in the United States. When I arrived, Hungarians had not yet developed a lexicon of terms such as "fellow traveler," "Pinko," "radical left," to indicate various shades of Red. Politicians, public employees, and anyone whose position might be threatened by their political affiliation, were scrambling to identify themselves as Democrats and there was no in-between. If you asked about a public figure, "Is he a Communist?" in a room where there were at least two people, you could get chorused "Yes" and "No" replies.

A local election was held that summer to fill an office for which I could ascertain no American equivalent, something like a city councilman or alderman, perhaps. Anna showed me a campaign flyer extolling the qualifications of the candidate she favored. "Is he a communist?" I asked. "Yes," she replied, and added, "and he is a good friend, a very honest man." She repeated, with emphasis, "Honest man." At our evening meal that day, Anna told her husband about our discussion of the local election. Instantly, he contradicted her, "No, no, no! He is not a communist!" His tone was quite forceful.

Election day was a holiday and a festive occasion. János and Anna dressed up in their best clothes and marched off to the polls looking proud and purposeful. Anna's candidate won the election.

A few weeks later, on a Sunday afternoon, the successful candidate came to call, and Anna asked me to join them. Thinking they might be inviting me only out of politeness, I assured them it wasn't necessary, but their response made me realize that in addition to showing him off to me, they also wanted to display their American house guest to him. My participation in the conversation was limited, as I spoke so little Hungarian and none of them spoke English. I managed to congratulate him on winning the election. He was a very large man, obese in fact, with a fat face that almost swallowed up his eyes. He was also relaxed, pleasant, self-assured, and asked the usual questions about where I was from and why I came to Hungary. As the manager of a local state-owned factory and an office holder, he obviously had sufficient local government authority that the Kovácses valued his good will. Anna served their best brandy and pastry – her exceptionally delicious *sütemény* – in their bed-sitting room used for guests too important to be received in the kitchen. They talked and I tried to understand, making it a kind of Hungarian lesson, the way I sometimes listened to the radio to accustom my ear to the sound of the language. It was my impression that his political role was akin to the old-time "ward heeler" in America who kept the local community in line, that is, voting for the right party, and who in return had certain favors to dispense.

It was easy for me to understand this and relate it, accurately or not, to the small Southern town in America where I grew up. They didn't need "ward heelers" in such a small place as politicians performed that role directly. That János and Anna courted their official's friendship and favor was no mystery to me; in my hometown, staying in the good graces of influential people was important to one's sense of well-being, of belonging, and sometimes to one's livelihood. My grandmother's best friend was the Mayor's mother; my own best friend's uncle was the local judge; my father's best friend was the banker. The Mayor was generally thought to be corrupt; the judge was, as I now recall him, kind, but not very intelligent. The banker was reputed to be honest. Two out of three. Pretty good, I would say, for small-town America 50 years ago, perhaps even for today. In such a milieu, daily life is simple and secure, and the distant, complex politics of national government can seem irrelevant.

The system under which János and Anna had lived and prospered for forty years was dissolving and they were maintaining their equilibrium by clinging to the vestiges of the previous order that had served them well. Although they would certainly have been puzzled to be told such a thing, it was apparent that they lived by the advice of Voltaire's Candide – they cultivated their own garden. Of course they had the advantage of living some distance away from the capital city, the seat of government. It makes a difference as the Russians who live in Siberia used to point out.

The language problem made it difficult to discuss ideas with them, but we managed to exchange views on simple moral issues, and it was clear that although, like many Hungarians, they did not attend church during the Communist Era, they lived by the basic Judeo-Christian ethic. The only one of the Ten Commandments they obviously did not observe was the one against working on the Sabbath. They worked every day.

When I asked János about the current coalition government, he surprised me by how much he knew. He got out pencil and paper, our essential props for discussing complicated things. Although the arcane Hungarian grammar is all but impenetrable and the vocabulary unrelated to any other language, living or dead, *hála Isten* (thank God!), its alphabet is made up of the same basic letters as the English alphabet. They organize them differently and combine some to make additional letters, which results in an alphabet of thirty-eight letters instead of twenty-six. Simple drawings, geometric forms, charts and graphs, can go a long way toward making up for missing vocabulary. János printed out the acronyms and full names of the six major political parties in Hungary at that time, and explained the major tenets of each. The first democratic government, elected in 1990, was run by a coalition of three parties: the MDF (Hungarian Democratic Forum); the FKGP (Independent Smallholders); and the KDNP (Christian Democratic People's Party). He told me with complete confidence that in the 1994 elections, to be held two years hence, the MSZP (Hungarian Socialist Party, whose membership consisted mainly of the old Communist Party), would win the election.

János's obvious satisfaction as he made the prediction left no doubt in my mind where his sympathies rested. He obviously trusted the old regime under which he and his family had prospered. But he never openly expressed his personal political convictions to me. No matter how relaxed our conversation or how comfortable and open he was when discussing almost everything else, when it came to his personal political beliefs, he clammed up or seemed not to understand my questions. On the subject of the 1956 Revolution, for example, I could never get an inkling of which side he supported or of whether he was involved in any way. It is not likely that he could have remained neutral; he and Anna were both factory workers then and a primary element in the uprising was factory workers' demands for a greater voice in the management of their workplaces. However, most of the fighting took place in the capital, in Budapest, and it is possible that people in the provincial cities may have been able to avoid any active participation. His reluctance to reveal his personal convictions was frustrating, but it was probably a well-entrenched self-protective device often employed by of prudent people forced to live under repressive governmental systems.

The unwillingness to reveal past political involvement or beliefs that I found so frustrating in János was quite common. There may have been nothing to reveal, of course, but discretion may have become a conditioned response after years of living in a spy-infested police state. Only one person among my acquaintances voiced strong opinions on political matters, showed an interest in elections, in Parliamentary actions, and the performance of government officials; he opposed everything that was done, past and present, and despised all those in charge of doing it.

The one subject everyone was eager to discuss and on which everyone was in agreement was the state of the economy: it was terrible. Prices were rising, inflation was eroding the currency, and wages and salaries were not increasing commensurately. It was useless to call attention to positive signs, to point out that more consumer goods was gradually appearing in the market place; that was dismissed as of no importance since "no one can afford to buy them." The famed Hungarian reputation for gloom and doom seemed to be justified as they refused to see any evidence to the contrary. People from every level, working class and professionals, had the same complaints, even when many of my acquaintances began to acquire things they had never before been able to buy. This occasionally afforded me some inward amusement which I dared not express. During a visit with a neighbor, she complained lengthily about soaring prices, how hard she and her husband both had to work to provide for their two children, and how much easier life had been in the past regime. Then suddenly, she broke off this jeremiad, jumped up and said, "Oh, come and see my new dishwashing machine!"

In the weeks leading up to my first Christmas in Hungary, gloomy forecasts were on everyone's lips. "Nobody has money to buy anything!" they murmured sadly. "It is going to be a very poor Christmas!" When I went to Budapest on a shopping expedition, the streets, buses and trams were crowded. Although there was little in the stores to tempt the gift-buyer, customers competed fiercely to grab the most desirable items, and there were lines at the Cashier desk in many shops. Vendors in the hastily-erected street stalls were hawking machine-made garments, mostly of synthetic material, souvenirs, cheap jewelry. Romanian women stood in the street holding out embroidered linens, trying to catch the eye of anyone who passed by. People looked hopefully into the uninteresting windows, and went in and out of the shops. When I next heard the complaint that it was going to be a very poor Christmas, I described what I had seen in Budapest and said it seemed as if a lot of shoppers were getting ready for a happy holiday. "Oh, they are only looking. Nobody can afford to buy anything!" someone said, ignoring my remarks about the lines at the Cashier. Later a friend who heard this exchange said, with rare objectivity, "That is the way we Hungarians are. Every year we say it is going to be a very poor Christmas, that we have no money to buy anything. Then at the last minute we rush around and spend money like mad and have just the same kind of Christmas we always have." "Oh, just like we do in America!" I said.

The changes being brought about by democracy were only vaguely understood by the population, and their first brush with the new system was not reassuring. They were surprised and understandably frightened to discover that the removal of government control and restrictions, an essential element in the freedom most people wanted and expected, also meant the removal of the safety net they had come to rely on. Freedom of speech, and of religion, freedom of the press were lofty concepts that most people embraced but their effect on everyday life was not immediately apparent. The long-range significance of those ideals was not as visible to the average person as was the loss or potential loss of state-provided services and subsidies and the rising cost of bread, and other essentials. The former regime was "the devil they knew" while the new democracy was an unknown. They learned to manipulate the old system to fit their individual needs. There was a popular saying among workers, "He who isn't stealing from the factory is cheating his family." All free public services were fair game. The medical clinics overflowed with patients every day, many of whom had ailments as minor as a headache. Those who lived in poorly-constructed public housing, with thin walls and no insulation, kept their houses as warm as ovens in winter; they paid little or nothing for fuel. These abuses were tolerated by a government that was simply incapable of better management. If efficiency was in conflict with the socialist ideal, inefficiency had to be expected.

Government-owned apartments were sold to current occupants for almost give-away prices, but the new owners were shocked to discover what property ownership entailed – maintenance, cost of utilities, and above all, property taxes. Some new owners sold their apartments immediately at a handsome profit. I accompanied a friend to look at an apartment for sale. It was large, elegantly furnished, on the upper floor of a beautiful old building. The courtyard entrance was littered with trash, and the hallways were almost as bad; the elevator creaked and groaned but delivered us safely. In the course of the discussion, my friend asked about the "maintenance costs," and the owner was puzzled. She had never paid any; the government took care of the building. Until the apartments in a government-owned building were all sold, building service was provided as in the past. "And what about repairs? Suppose the elevator breaks down or a water pipe breaks, who repairs it?" She shrugged, saying she had no idea. It had never happened. When asked about taxes, she replied, "I don't pay any taxes. We never paid taxes!"

The election of 1994 pitted the Hungarian Socialist Party against the incumbent coalition whose leader, Prime Minister József Antall, died in December 1993. In the 1990 election, the first after the ouster of the communists, no candidate who had held office in the communist government stood a chance of being elected, so it was inevitable that the first democratically-elected officials would be inexperienced in government administration. It was remarkable that Antall, a relatively obscure historian who was chosen to lead that first democratic government, turned out to be a surprisingly talented politician. He rose to become what some observers called the most effective leader in post-communist Eastern Europe, and did so without resorting to the classically democratic strategy of endearing himself to the public. However, he gained public respect for his leadership and his honesty.

Antall was diagnosed with leukemia a few months after his election in 1990 and died late in 1993 leaving no obvious leader to replace him. Unavoidably, it had been his lot to deliver more bad news than good to the Hungarian people. Devaluation of the forint, increases in the cost of utilities, especially gas, for cooking and heating, and even rising food costs had made the administration unpopular with a large segment of voters. Those who tended to cling to the past were happy to be able to vote for the Socialist Party, and the accusation that the party leader, Gyula Horn, had been a cabinet officer in the last communist government did not tarnish him in their eyes. There were no doubt some who hoped that a socialist government might turn back the clock. Horn's opponents accused him of mistreating revolutionaries in the 1956 uprising; his response, at least that reported in the media, was surprisingly contained. He was a young army officer doing his duty. His supporters made much of the fact that as Hungary's Minister of Defense in the last communist government, he is credited with ordering the dismantling of the barb-wire fence between Hungary and Austria in 1989, thus presaging the fall of the Berlin Wall and the defeat of communism in Eastern Europe.

The explanation for the success of the socialists – they won the election in a landslide as János had predicted – seemed to be due to the misguided belief on the part of some that the old regime might return, and the disaffection of others with the moderate right wing coalition that had been in power for the first four years of democratic government. But whatever Horn's past political affiliation and persuasion were, it became obvious immediately that he was a canny politician. His party won enough seats to control the Parliament, but he wisely forged an alliance with the liberal SZDSZ (Alliance of Free Democrats) in order to minimize opposition to his legislative program, again demonstrating the truth of the old saw about politics and strange bedfellows. Privatization went forward rapidly after a rather slow start, and is expected to be completed soon. Hungary has attracted a great deal of foreign capital and support from other democracies. That most capitalistic of all institutions, the Stock Market, has opened in Budapest and is thriving. Hungary was the first former Soviet-bloc country to join the Organization of Economic Cooperation and Development (OECD), which has since become the Organization for Security and Cooperation in Europe (OSCE). The country is not headed for a return to the former regime.

NOTES FROM THE JOURNAL – A PERFECT DAY

The tiny Hungarian village of Pilisszántó. A sunny day in late June. Sitting under fruit trees outside a 200-year old house, bordered by flower and vegetable gardens and the vineyard further out, we ate from platters of traditional Hungarian food, washed down with good local wine, laughed and talked in Hungarian, English, German and French. Bowls and platters were replenished from time to time at the nearby outdoor fireplace where several men in the party prepared food throughout the day for the twenty-some friends and colleagues invited by Györgyi Rontó and her husband Dezső Holnapy, both Hungarian scientists, for a day at their place in the country. Among the guests were John and Mary Esther Jagger, scientists from Dallas, who were visiting me, and my friends Felicitas Ruccius-Koss from Germany and Peggy Chisholm, a Peace Corps volunteer from St. Paul. The numerous conversations going on at the same time in four different languages on a wide range of topics, were eager, rapid, sometimes loud, often with two or more languages in the same sentence. Nevertheless communication appeared to be flawless with everybody understanding each other perfectly. Long after the fire died down and the sun sank behind the wooded hills we sat and continued the polyglot conversation until the stars came out and we reluctantly said goodbye to our companions, our hosts, and to the end of a perfect day.

VI

NEW TEACHER, LEARNS

Toward the end of the training course the Peace Corps gave us our assignments; they told us where we would be spending the next two years of our lives. Most of us faced the day with a fearful curiosity, avid to know on one hand, and at the same time afraid of what we would find out. We assembled in the atrium on the ground floor of the college, the space where all large gatherings or entertainments were held. A map of Hungary had been drawn in the center of the floor, with the cities, towns and villages where Peace Corps teachers were going clearly marked. We stood around the borders of the map and when our names were called and our assignments read out, we each went and stood on the map at our school's location. The staff had informed us repeatedly during the training that no one, absolutely no one, would be going to Budapest, but that was still almost everybody's secret dream. The staff wanted to prepare us for the possibility of being sent to a remote village in the provinces, and to remind us that we had made a commitment to go wherever we were needed. When my assignment turned out to be a small suburban city only a 20-minute bus ride from Budapest, I could scarcely believe my good fortune. Like most good fortune, it was mixed, but the good far outweighed the, er, not so good.

The schools to which volunteers would go were required to appoint a "coordinator" who spoke English and was responsible for orienting the American teacher to the school, to the community, and by extension to the country. Soon after I learned where I would be going, I received a letter from my coordinator, ostensibly an introduction and a welcome to the school. But its tone gave me some concern; it seemed to suggest that he anticipated a social relationship rather than a collegial one. And he clearly expected a young woman whom he wanted to impress. The letter was all about him, vital statistics, hobbies, where he lived, and said nothing about the school, where I would live, how I would get there, or even when the school term would start. A photo was enclosed, showing a nice looking, bearded young man with a pleasant expression. My first impulse was to write back immediately and clear up his false impressions, and I began framing responses in my mind: Perhaps I should tell you that I am old enough ... No. No. Finally, I realized that my impressions might be mistaken and I had no right to assume what was in his mind, so I wrote thanking him for the letter and asking about the school, housing, schedules, and when school would start. I did not enclose a photograph, and never received a reply.

The question of transport was soon answered. Someone from my school (my coordinator!) would call for me by car on the appointed day. The Peace Corps staff had only sketchy, but reassuring, information about my housing: a private two-room, furnished apartment. The departure date was at the end of August, but nobody could tell me when school started.

As I began packing to leave the Kovacs's home, although I was not aware of it, Anna also began preparing for my journey. On the morning of my departure, she appeared with several large cartons, one containing canned fruit and vegetables in glass jars, very heavy. Others contained root vegetables, fruit, and cooked food, including two large boxes of homemade pastry, carefully wrapped. There were several kitchen utensils and other items she was sure I could not keep house without: a Hungarian coffee maker and four cups, saucers and spoons of the right size, demi-tasse; two large cocoa mugs; a paring knife; dishtowels, hot pads, dusting cloths. The bulk was astonishing and I didn't know how I was going to handle it. Ignoring my weak protests, János put everything in his car and drove me to the school were Zsolt, my coordinator, was waiting for me. We introduced ourselves; János transferred my baggage, including all the cartons, to the car Zsolt was driving – borrowed, I later discovered, as he did not own a car – proudly informed Zsolt that I could speak Hungarian (an exaggeration), and he and I said goodbye with the obligatory, but in this case, heartfelt, hugs and cheek kisses, both of us trying not to cry. The moment he left, I sensed that I had entered a different world.

The warm acceptance of the Kovács family had lulled me into the pleasant assumption that I would find the same welcome everywhere I went in Hungary. They had literally and figuratively clasped me to their bosom, made me an instant member of the family, and looked for things they could do to help me. They lived some distance uphill from the college where our training sessions were held, and

I rode a bus to and from classes. Occasionally, when I had to remain at the college later than the buses ran – they stopped running quite early – János insisted on calling for me and driving me home. This may not seem like a big thing, but automobiles were then rare in Hungary and gasoline, called benzene, was very expensive. Hungarians treated their cars the way a violinist treats his Stradivarius: they took them out only on special occasions, and I was fully aware of the magnanimous favor.

To say that Zsolt did not seem delighted to see me is an understatement; it was like going on a blind date and sensing from the first moment that you are not what the guy had in mind. He did nothing to disguise the fact that the mission to escort me to the school was an unwelcome chore. Unlike many Hungarians who speak English, he did not seize the opportunity to converse with a native English speaker. We had spoken very little in the flurry of leaving. Thus, it was only when I tried to make friendly conversation during the two-and-one-half hour trip, asking questions about the school, the town, the countryside we were passing through, that I realized my friendly overtures were not getting a friendly response. He answered my questions with no elaboration, and asked me none; we soon settled into a silent drive.

It was noon, lunch time, when we arrived at the school and we went directly into the cafeteria where Zsolt was visibly upset because he did not have a lunch ticket for me. After some moments of confusion, during which I insisted that I wasn't hungry (and indeed the aroma was not tantalizing) he thrust a ticket toward the woman behind the hot table and said to me, "You can have my ticket," implying that he was sacrificing his lunch for me, and not with very good grace. My protests went for nothing. He took the plate of stew from the woman and led me to a table on which there was a plate of sliced bread. Then he disappeared with a vague statement about having something to do. There was nothing I could do but eat the stew and bread; to sit there without doing so would have seemed outrageously disdainful. Zsolt returned with a bath towel, a bed sheet and a pillow case over his arm, and said he would take me to my apartment. Nothing was said about introducing me to the principal, or headmaster as he was called, or showing me around the school. He did introduce me to the doorkeeper, the woman who sat in an office at the main door and saw to it that only authorized persons entered the school. She was a short, stout, rosy-cheeked, grey-haired woman with a sweet face and a cheerful manner. He assured me that she knew everything about the school.

It would not be fair to say I was disappointed when I saw the apartment, because I had been told nothing about it, and if my hopes had been high that was my own doing. There were two rooms, one of which was quite large, the other quite small, tiny really, plus a tiny kitchen, tiny bathroom and tiny entrance hall. In the large room were two couch-beds, used everywhere in Hungary as couches during the day and beds at night. They sat squarely in the middle of the room, and had been stripped down to their striped cotton ticking. No pillows were visible; they were inside the bed, where pillows and bed clothes are stored during the daytime. Also in that room were two small desks, a large wardrobe, a very unsteady gate-leg table and 4 straight chairs, two with red vinyl seats and two with black. A light fixture with three bulbs, two dim and one burned out, hung from the center of the ceiling. The windows were covered with dingy off-white lacy panel curtains, and on each side were skinny draperies of a thin synthetic fabric in a color that is very popular here; I call it "angry orange." The color yellow, in shades ranging from deep ivory to deep orange, is used everywhere. One soft, paler-than-lemon shade is sometimes called "Maria Theresa Yellow" (harking back to the days when Hungary was part of the Hapsburg Empire) and is a popular choice for the outside of houses, especially those finished in stucco, as many houses are. Stucco, composed mainly of cement and sand, has the charm of being both fire-resistant and cheap. The floor of my new home was covered wall-to-wall in a rug made of some ersatz fibre in a nondescript color – well, no, it wasn't nondescript. It was the color of dirt.

The second room was just wide enough for a bed-couch on one side and a small desk on the other, with barely room to walk between them. The desk was close enough to serve as a bedside table. There was a built-in closet with shelves for folded garments, no rods for clothes hangers. The floor covering was the same as in the larger room, and the light fixture was similar, only higher up, and held only one bulb, 25 Watt. Neither room contained a lamp, or for that matter a table on which a lamp might stand.

In the kitchen, a sink and a stove stood side by side against one wall, with room to stand between them and the other wall. There was an outside window. The small refrigerator, which could not be fitted into the kitchen, stood just outside the kitchen door in the tiny entrance hall. There was a bathroom with tub, wash basin, and toilet with a pull chain for flushing – no cabinet of any kind, no shelf, no mirror. The floor was covered with large, loose (not attached) squares of thick, heavy linoleum, the color of milk chocolate. Some of the squares extended beyond the floor and were folded against the bottom of the wall, giving the impression of an uneven baseboard. At first glance, the entrance hall appeared to have a parquet floor, but a closer look revealed that it was linoleum patterned with a parquet design.

This was a typical apartment in what Hungarians called a "*lakótelep*" and translates as "housing estate;" in the United States the word would be "project." The construction was said by some to be "typical socialist design" but one Hungarian friend said "these damned communist buildings." There were twenty or thirty units in that *lakótelep*, and the only variation was that some were 10 storied, and some were only four storied. My two-room apartment was on the first floor (one flight up from the ground floor) in a ten-storied building across the street from the school. Individual apartments came in three standard sizes, one-, two-, and three-room, plus kitchen and bathroom. Hallways were narrow and dimly lit, and the use of ersatz materials throughout was as ingenious as it was tasteless. In some cases it was pure trompel'oeil. It was several months before I realized that what I thought were dark brown baseboards at the bottom of the walls where they met the floors were in fact only strips of wide, brown plastic tape!

It could have been worse. There was hot and cold running water, luxuries that I have gone without at times in my life; there was electricity and there was a gas stove, which I have also lived without. It was mid-afternoon, and Zsolt was racing me through the apartment, pointing out things at breakneck speed, in a hurry to be off. It was Friday, and he announced that he and his family were leaving for the week-end. The week-end! My "coordinator," designated as my guide and mentor through the settling-in process, he who was supposed to "orient" me, was going away on Friday afternoon and return on Monday. What would I do in case of an emergency? Oh, call Antal. Who is Antal? Here's his number. Does he speak English? No. Who is he? He's the man who takes care of things. There were no dishes, cooking utensils or implements in the kitchen. He said I should buy whatever I needed, and the school would reimburse me. Buy? Where? I needed a tea kettle or anyway a pot to boil water, and at least one knife, one fork and one spoon. And food. Where would I buy bread? Milk? He waved in the direction of the school and said there was a market and a place to buy household articles very near. Could I walk there? To the market, yes; to the "*háztartásibolt*" (household needs store, something like a hardware store), it would be necessary to take a bus. Which bus? Where did I get tickets? Not on the bus, tickets could be bought only at the bus terminal. I asked if he would just walk with me to the store before we parted, or ride with me to the place where I could buy utensils, and he very reluctantly agreed. He said he had a date to take his 3-year-old daughter walking that afternoon, and we would have to hurry.

Hurry we did. At the household needs store, I got a tea kettle and the basic utensils I needed, a knife, fork and spoon. The paring knife Anna had packed for me, and the "Survival Tool" (knife, bottle opener and other small implements) that a friend had given me before I left the United States, were my only food preparation implements for several weeks. At the state-owned supermarket, called an ABC (pronounced Ah-Beh-Tseh) I bought bread, milk, cold meat and cheese, and at an open-air vegetable stall, I got some fruit, carrots and cucumbers.

There are no pilot lights on the gas stoves in Hungary so I bought, for the equivalent of $15, a flint lighter. I could have bought a lot of matches for that amount but I could not find matches. Later I discovered they were kept under the counter and one had to ask for them. My dinner was tea, and some of the food Anna had insisted over my strong objection that I bring. I was chagrined to remember how resistant I had been to bringing those cartons. Before falling asleep, I reminded myself that in the past I had converted several unpromising spaces into comfortable, even attractive, living quarters, and vowed I would do the same here.

There was no telephone in the apartment, nor any hope of getting one; Zsolt did not have a telephone in his apartment, and when I asked if there were public telephones, he said there were, "But good luck finding one that isn't out of order." János had access to a telephone at the factory where he was temporarily working as a guard, and he insisted that I should call him when I arrived to let them know I was all right. So the next morning I went in search of a public telephone. There were several in the area around my building, but I could not decipher the instructions for making long distance calls; it didn't matter because none of the telephones I tried were in working order. Finally, I took the bus to Budapest, went to one of the big foreign hotels where there was a telephone desk and an operator to assist with long distance calls. Her main function was to handle international calls, but she did tell me how to make a toll call within Hungary. I finally reached János and told him I had arrived safely and all was well and then we were cut off; nothing I did restored the connection.

Estimates of private telephone service in Hungary at that time ranged from 10% to a probably-inflated 20%. In what was probably an attempt to cheer up those people waiting for telephone lines, a public announcement had been made that by the year 2000, at least 30% of the population would have telephone service. The Kovács family had been on the waiting list for 17 years and were glad they had only three more years to go. The waiting period was then 20 years.

Before returning home, I decided to console myself with a visit to the famous Gerbeaud Cukrázda (Pâtisserie-Confectionery) on Vörösmarty Square, where it has stood since 1870, having been opened in 1858 by a Swiss family named Kugler. It was sold to Émile Gerbeaud in 1884, also Swiss, who renamed it and gave it the cachet and the luster it retained through two World Wars and decades of a communist regime. Its three rooms, each with a different decor, are more like the public rooms of a palace than a place to have coffee and pastry. The soaring ceilings, crystal chandeliers, paintings hanging on brocade-covered walls, and marble topped tables, some with art nouveau-curved brass legs, some with copper neo-classical patternbook-like legs, and others with goat-footed brass legs, create a setting that is both elegant and comfortable. In the tradition of the European coffee house, you could sit for hours over a cup of coffee, talk with a companion, read, write, or if you are fortunate enough to get a window table just look out at the fascinating Vörösmarty Square. There, in good weather, portrait painters, musicians, breakdancers, even a few jugglers gather throughout the day. The focal point of the square is the huge marble monument commemorating the writer Mihály Vörösmarty, who is depicted sitting in a chair at the apex, looking down at twenty-four figures on the plinth who are reciting his famous "Szózat" (Appeal). During the communist era, Gerbeaud was run by the state, as it continued to be until it was sold to a German hotel-restaurant chain in 1996, with the understanding that the Cukrázda would be continued for ten years. The exterior of the building has been beautifully restored, and the upper floors turned into business space. So far the interior decor and furnishings of Gerbeaud are little changed, but something must have been lost in the translation regarding the understanding that it would remain a Cukrázda. The menu has been significantly enlarged to include salads and more sandwiches, and unbelievably, they now serve alcoholic drinks! That will no doubt increase the profits, but its Old World charm has gone, along with the peaceful aura. It is crowded and noisy, and the overworked waiters simply dash off if you are slow in ordering, and practically push customers away from the table if they see an empty cup or glass, as others are waiting. That afternoon in 1992 will stay in my memory and I will always be glad I saw Gerbeaud before it was "renovated."

That week-end, I read C.P. Snow's "A Coat of Varnish," a magical escape from my surroundings, and also a reminder of a very different period in my life. The book was set in 1976, the same year I met Lord Snow in the House of Lords' bar. During a visit to London, a friend, Lord Ritchie-Calder, invited me to a session of the "Lords." We were in the bar later when Lord Snow came in and joined us as the two men were friends. There is a scene in the book set in that bar, and I realized that he was probably working on that book when we met; it transported me temporarily from my dreary surroundings into a brighter time and place.

Also, that week-end, I made a feeble effort at cleaning the apartment and storing my possessions, inspired by the discovery of a reasonably good Czech-made vacuum cleaner on the closet floor. The biggest accomplishment of the week-end, however, was writing a letter to Anna in Hungarian confirming what I had told János on the telephone, and thanking her for her many kindnesses, with extra thanks for the food and other things she had insisted that I bring with me. I made out a list, in Hungarian, of the things I needed in the apartment: lamps, tables, a mirror among them. At the end, I added a "Wish List," things I had little hope of getting: washing machine, television, and telephone.

On the first day of school, a sunny September morning, opening ceremonies were held outdoors at 8 o'clock under a cloudless blue sky. In the warm sunshine, dressed in bright summer colors, teachers and students greeted their colleagues, their classmates, and each other, as if they were happy to be back in school. It was impossible, in that setting, not to feel optimistic and hopeful. The headmaster introduced all the new teachers including the "American Peace Corps English teacher." Perfunctory applause followed each introduction. No special interest, no noticeable curiosity in the American. Earlier that morning, I met the headmaster and he asked me to come and talk with him after the meeting. He gave me my teaching schedule, hand-written, which indicated the day, hour, class level and room number of my classes, 16 hours each week. (I had tried to find my classes on the composite schedule posted in the teachers' room but my name wasn't there. Later I discovered why. They had used the name "Béke" which means "Peace," because at the time the schedule was made they did not yet have the name of the Peace Corps teacher. I was sorry they had to change it; I rather liked it.) The headmaster was an English teacher and still taught 4 hours per week. He told me he would be going out of the country in a few days for six weeks and would like for me to teach his classes during that time; he would give me the texts and discuss the lesson plans later. It was something of a surprise to learn that I would be responsible for 20 hours teaching plus the necessary preparation, while I was still wondering if I could manage 16 hours. The English as a Foreign Language (TEFL) training we had been given in Szekszárd was the only teacher-training I ever had. The Peace Corps made the assignment, I assume, on the basis that as a writer I knew the English language. Having broken that news to me, the headmaster asked, quite perfunctorily, if the apartment was all right, clearly expecting a perfunctory reply of "Yes." It was fine, I told him, but I would need a few more things. He said I should make a list of what I needed and give it to him for his approval, after which I could buy the things and the school would reimburse me. It was his turn to be surprised when I gave him the list I had prepared over the weekend; he was quite impressed, not only that I had already done it, but that it was in Hungarian. It was obvious that he had no idea how pressing my needs were. I pointed out my "Wish List," saying I would understand if those items were impossible, but wanted to indicate that they would be very nice to have. He looked at it and – it was a day for surprises – said, "The washing machine and television are no problem. We can give you those. But a telephone is out of the question." My joy at getting a washing machine and a television went a long way to compensate for my disappointment about the telephone.

Although the headmaster seemed to think he had solved my problems, and I could see that he was ready for me to leave his office, I had one more important request, a reading lamp. It was impossible to read, write, or do lesson plans at night under those dim lights suspended from the ceiling, I explained. He looked a little exasperated, thought for a moment, then reached over and unplugged his desk lamp and handed it to me. When I demurred, not very strongly, he insisted, saying, "I never use it." And that was the only lamp I ever got! It made me feel better about the extra teaching load he had so casually assigned to me which, as it turned out, I enjoyed. He taught the advanced classes and with those students, it was possible to have interesting discussions comparing the cultures and social customs of our countries. Most other students were not at that level.

It was apparent that he had no idea what was involved in setting up a household, as few Hungarian men would; after all, that is the woman's domain. Although Hungary's standard of living, especially in the last years of the communist government, was higher than in the other "Iron Curtain" countries, consumer goods were nevertheless scarce. There was never enough to supply the demand; therefore, sales promotion was unnecessary. Window displays or counter displays were not used to help shoppers locate particular items. In fact, it could sometimes seem as if displays were deliberately meant to mislead customers, making a shopping expedition seem more like a treasure hunt. Add to that my handicap of speaking very little Hungarian and having no clear idea of what things should cost, or even being certain about the value of the different pieces of money, not to mention the difficulty of transporting heavy china and hardware by public transportation. I was paralyzed. Where and how could I even begin? It was clear by that time that my coordinator had washed his hands of me, and that I could expect no further help from him. The answer came in the second week of school when a beautiful young woman, a former Russian Language teacher who was being "recycled" to become an English teacher, introduced herself, first name only as was the custom. She said she had a car and could take me shopping for household equipment. My mixture of surprise, relief, and gratitude made me almost inarticulate. (An even bigger surprise awaited our acquaintance.) In two shopping excursions, we bought the basic items – dishes, pots and pans – and some large pieces of black cloth to cover the couch-beds in the room I was using as a living-dining-work room. It actually seemed possible that the flat could be made livable, perhaps suitable for guests. But whom did I know well enough to invite?

The obvious place to look for potential guests would be among my colleagues, none of whom had invited me to their homes, even for a cup of coffee. For a while I was too busy to notice: setting up the apartment, advising friends, family, and business correspondents of my new address, studying Hungarian, not to speak of turning myself into an English teacher. Just learning my students' names, trying to pronounce them correctly, and keeping the Gyöngyvérs, the Gergelys, the Gábors, and the Piroskas straight was daunting. There were usually two or even three students in each class with the same first name and that meant learning the last names too in order to distinguish between them. For various reasons, not all of them positive, but not all negative either, some of those names are permanently engraved in my memory: Fülöp, Mincsovics, Bresztyenszky, Szoboszlay, Kovalcsuk, Somogyi, Vaczlavik, Dósa, Egri, Köpf. Their variety indicates the rich ethnic heritage of the Hungarian people whose ancestry is rooted in a multitude of far flung regions throughout Eastern Europe and even Asia. Eventually, I learned my way around town, and improved my ability to communicate with people in the community. The experience made me feel like a child again, learning a new word every day.

About that time, an incident occurred that cheered me up considerably – I was able to use the Hungarian language well enough to help another foreigner. One morning, as I started to cross the main road on which the school was located, a large produce truck pulled up to the curb in front of me and stopped, blocking my way. The driver, a goodlooking, blonde young man jumped out of the cab and came up to me holding out a paper with the name and address of a fruit market on it. He did not speak, only thrust the paper in front of me. I assumed he could see I was a foreigner who probably did not speak Hungarian. So, I began speaking slowly in Hungarian to say that I did not know the name on the paper, but that there was a fruit market nearby… and I realized he was not understanding a word I said. "My God, my Hungarian is really poor," I thought, and started to apologize, speaking even more slowly, "I'm sorry I do not speak Hungarian well, but I am an American…" At the word "American" his eyes lit up, and he said, in perfect English, "You speak English?" "Yes," I replied, "Aren't you Hungarian?" "Oh, no," he said, " I don't know a word of Hungarian. I am German, but I speak English." Then as I repeated in English what I had started to tell him in Hungarian, I looked up the street and saw a Hungarian man approaching. So I asked him if he knew the place and he told me where it was in Hungarian, which I translated into English to the German who drove off. I hope he found it!

When a staff member at the Peace Corps office asked me how I was getting along, I said I was enjoying the teaching, and that the students were either charming or interesting or both. But my colleagues, I told her, apparently thought I went up in smoke at the end of the day, for no one had shown any interest in how I spent my free time, or suggested sharing any of it.

That soon changed a little, but not much. The headmaster asked me several times if I was very busy, and thinking he was concerned that I might be bored, I always said yes. And, in fact, I was very busy, although I had no social life. Then, once when he asked that, he rather hesitantly said, "Well, I - er - thought that if you were not too busy I would - er - like to invite you to dinner some time." Greatly surprised, I said, "Oh, of course! That would be very nice. Certainly I have time for that!" We settled on a date two weeks hence. About a week later, he asked me whether I preferred an evening or a mid-day meal. Then I remembered that "dinner" usually meant mid-day when Hungarians have their main meal. It took a while for me to get over assuming "dinner" was in the evening. I said, "Whatever your wife prefers." He looked a little baffled at this and said, "Oh, yes. All right. I will ask her." And I had a feeling he had not told his wife about inviting me. That was not at all unusual, as I learned later. Hungarian men issue invitations and tell their wives after it is settled, in the same way one might tell the cook, "There will be an extra person for dinner on Saturday." A few days later, he told me we would have dinner at a restaurant in the evening and set the time they would call for me. They lived in the building next to mine, and since he did not have a car, we would be going to a local restaurant by bus. It seemed simple. But I began to feel uneasy, as if it were a rather difficult and awkward undertaking for him. Was his wife, who did not speak English, reluctant to entertain a foreign woman who did not speak very much Hungarian? Or, was she just angry at being ordered to prepare dinner for a stranger? I had not met her so I had no basis for any conclusion and only felt uncomfortable, but I was not at all prepared for the way things turned out.

It was pouring rain, which can put a damper on any evening, especially one involving bus transportation. And I was surprised, puzzled, dismayed even, when he called for me without his wife, but with his very pretty teen-age daughter who, he said, spoke some English. When he introduced her he made no mention of his wife's absence. As we walked under umbrellas to the bus stop and then rode to the restaurant standing in a crowded bus there was little opportunity for conversation. After we were seated in the restaurant, he and his daughter spoke together in rapid Hungarian for the first few minutes. It was a typical Hungarian restaurant that offered two menus, one listed dishes that were already prepared and could be served immediately and the other listed those that would be prepared after the order was placed. His daughter asked if she could order something that was ready to be served immediately and if she could order it when we placed our drink order, because she had to leave. She was looking after a friend's dog while the friend was out of town and had to go and take care of the dog as soon as possible. He agreed to that. Her meal was served with our drinks and she demolished it before we ordered our meal or finished our drinks. She made no effort to practice her English. As soon as she left, he said, in a very unconvincing way, that his wife was sorry she could not join us but she was ill with the "flu." My imagination immediately conjured up an image of her saying, "You can take that foreign woman to dinner if you want to, but leave me out, Buster. I want no part of it." He relaxed amazingly after his daughter left, and seemed almost like another person. As we began to talk, I realized that he was a very intelligent and perceptive person, and in spite of all my foreboding it turned out to be a very pleasant evening. His wife, whom I met later, was a very gentle, kind and somewhat shy woman. Although I never understood what happened that evening we went to dinner – perhaps she really did have the "flu" – it did not at all foreshadow our future relationship. She was exceedingly gracious and hospitable to me during my two years at the school.

The only other invitation I received during those first months of the school year was from Zsuzsa an attractive young colleague in the English department whose desk was next to mine in the teachers' room. She had been very friendly and helpful to me from my arrival, and one day as we walked to our classes together, she rather tentatively said that if I was not too busy and could find the time she and her husband would like to invite me to dinner sometime. I accepted enthusiastically, saying I would be delighted. A few days later she suggested an evening, and I agreed. After all, my calendar was hardly overcrowded. But a few days later she said we would have to postpone it, and after one other postponement, I went to their home for an excellent dinner and most enjoyable evening that included her husband and two beautiful, bright, thoroughly charming boys, ages six and three. Postponement of invitations is not unusual; social engagements seem always to be tentative. In my early days in Budapest, I once asked a British friend to go somewhere on a Sunday afternoon and she said she had another engagement. "But, it is with Hungarians," she added, "and may be cancelled. You never know." There were many occasions later when I remembered that conversation.

It turned out that I had a friend there, waiting for me in a way, but neither of us knew about it. Before I left New York, I had some Hungarian lessons with a young man, a Budapest-born journalist. At our last session, he gave me the name, address, and telephone number of his brother and sister-in-law and urged me to call them when I got to Budapest. "But I am not going to Budapest," I said. He waved that aside, saying I would certainly get there eventually. When I began to think about finding friends, I looked up their name in my address book and to my surprise saw they did not live in Budapest – they lived in the very suburb where I was living! And only one street away from me! We were neighbors! Then I really looked at the first names and saw that the woman's name was that of my Good Samaritan friend, whose last name I had never heard. The next morning, I asked her if her husband had a brother in New York and her face lit up. "He told us he had given our telephone number to a Peace Corps teacher, and my husband said I should ask if it was you, but I said, 'Oh, no, it couldn't be. The world is too big.'" She, her husband and two children remain among my favorite people in Hungary.

At first no one at the school, the headmaster included, had any idea what to expect of an American Peace Corps teacher. From its name they were not even sure it wasn't a military organization, very off-putting to begin with. If I had known how little they knew about me, their stand-offishness would have been more understandable. I assumed that the Peace Corps had furnished the school with a dossier or CV or at least a brief biographical sketch that would give them a few facts, but that was not the case. This came to light when the headmaster asked me a question – one of those routine things that would be included in any resumé – and I was so surprised that I blurted out, "Didn't the Peace Corps tell you anything about me before I came?" Only my name, he said.

Thus it was revealed that I, a complete stranger, had arrived to be a colleague of, and teach the children of, people who had spent their lives in a government system that mandated keeping strangers at a distance until they were certifiably harmless. Fear, suspicion, caution, and mistrust were standard behaviors when dealing with foreigners. Moreover, I was by Hungarian standards an "old woman," who could easily be the mother of most of my colleagues, the grandmother of the students, and that created further confusion as to how I should be received. After retirement, women in Hungary become housekeepers, baby sitters, and general factotums for their married children. Wasn't I needed at home? And how does one treat a colleague or a teacher of that age? It is also highly probable that the trait I think of as "that Hungarian pride" influenced their attitude. They bridle at the slightest suggestion of patronization or condescension. As a country, as a people, they have suffered greatly throughout their history but they resent pity. Anyway, if Americans wanted to help them, where were they during the Revolution of 1956? I was to hear this question more than once.

One colleague who became a close friend told me that after the headmaster made the announcement at a faculty meeting that an American Peace Corps teacher would be at the school in the fall semester, she went home and said to her husband, "I don't think I can handle this." When I pressed her to tell me what she was feeling, why it seemed to be such a challenge, she could not remember or was too tactful to tell me. "What did you expect me to be like or to do?" I asked. "Did you think I would say things like, 'Don't you know any better than that?'" By then, we knew each other well enough that we both laughed. All she would says was, " I think I may have been worried about my accent." Later she told me that

I was not anything like she had expected an American to be. Still later, after she had met several of my friends who visited me, she said, "I once told you that you were not anything like I expected an American to be. Well, your friends aren't anything like I expected Americans to be!" Dispelling stereotypes between people of different cultures may be one of the greatest achievements of the Peace Corps.

The school had devised a team-teaching system for language classes. Hungarian teachers taught grammar which they could explain to students in the Hungarian language, and the native speakers (there was also a native German teacher on the faculty) were responsible for speaking, pronunciation, and comprehension. Close coordination between teamed teachers was vital to insure that lesson plans were correlative. It was hard to find time during the school hours when both were free to meet, so we had to get together after school to go over plans for the coming weeks or next semester. These sessions also served to acquaint us with each other and to acquaint me with Hungarian educational philosophy and practices. At the end of the semester we met and agreed upon each student's final grade. Those sessions opened my eyes to an attitude about grading that may exist in the United States somewhere but I never heard of it. Considerations other than performance in class and test scores entered into the final grade determination. As we debated whether to give one student the top grade of 5 or the next highest of 4, which I favored, the other teacher said, "Oh, a 5! He needs a 5 because he wants to go to university!" The concept of need in relation to grades had never before occurred to me. Nor had another concept. "You can't give him a 1," I was told, when I proposed that grade for one student. "His father will beat him if he brings home a poor grade."

The quite perceptive headmaster observed that my coordinator did not relish his assignment, and urged me to bring any problems directly to him. He had so much to deal with that I was reluctant to do this but he insisted and I soon found out that it was the only way to get things done. He introduced me to Antal, a nice looking, quiet, dignified man, and said he was the person who would handle any repair problems I had in the apartment. Antal was the school's building caretaker, engineer, repair man, and superb gardener who kept roses blooming in front of the school most of the year, and who carried on his belt a bunch of keys the size of those worn by the castle keeps in Shakespeare's plays. He brought me a large bookcase, a washing machine, and eventually a television; he installed a mirror and a shelf in the bathroom; removed some shelves from one closet and put in a rod so I could hang up my clothes. The washing machine was a mixed blessing.

There were no drain pipes for such appliances in the building, so washing machines had to be squeezed into the bathroom where they could drain into the bathtub. My bathroom was so small that once the washing machine was installed, one could get into the bathtub only by climbing over the washer. The motor of the washing machine, like all the others in my building, was too powerful for the housing, and you could always tell who was doing laundry. When any machine went into the Spin Cycle it sounded like a freight train was coming through the building, and unless it was heavily loaded, overloaded in fact, it danced all over the bathroom. There was a huge gash inside my bathroom door made by a former tenant's machine that ran wild. But the clothes came out very clean.

As that first Holiday Season approached, I though of having an Open House on New Year's Day, an informal gathering like those I remembered from my Virginia childhood. A large bowl of eggnog, and maybe one of punch, stood on the sideboard or dining room table, with stacks of cups of the right size, a plate of fruitcake, and sometimes cold meats, cheeses, nuts. People came in, whole families including children and grandparents, drank to the New Year and soon moved on to the next place where they would do the same thing. When I told a friend I was thinking of doing this, she was doubtful about it. In the first place, she pointed out, there wouldn't be other places to move on to, as that is not the custom here, and those who did come would stay for several hours. Therefore, you cannot, as you might at home, invite everybody you know, because there won't be enough room. As it turned out, fate intervened, and prevented me from going through with my plan by something that rarely happens to me – I got sick. Peace Corps volunteers had been given all the appropriate inoculations before coming to Hungary, plus the necessary boosters after arriving, and we thought our immune defenses were impregnable. But apparently some Hungarian virus was not aware that it was supposed to back off in the presence of immunizations against small pox, "flu," polio, tetanus, and even the super serum, Gamma Globulin, and it pounced.

Unpleasant as it was, and I was sick for almost two weeks with vomiting, diarrhea, and associated manifestations, it had some quite beneficial side effects. The young, female Hungarian doctor, who had recently joined the medical staff of the Peace Corps, came to see me as soon as the school notified her of my illness. She did not like the idea of my being alone, without a telephone, and wanted to take me to a Budapest hospital immediately. It might have been tempting if I had not already had the experience of visiting a friend in a Budapest hospital and seen how many patients were in one room, and how far away the toilets were, the latter a significant factor considering my symptoms. Caring for a patient outside of Budapest made more work for the doctor, who clearly preferred to have me in a nearby hospital, but she accepted my decision with the grace I later learned was characteristic.

Unbeknownst to me, Dr. Margit (she was called and referred to by her first name which was not Margit plus "doctor") went through my building and found a neighbor with a telephone who would be willing to come and check on me every night at 9 p.m. Later, Dr. Margit telephoned the neighbor to inquire about my condition and determine whether she should visit me before she went to bed. The neighbor happened to be a teacher at my school, with whom I had only exchanged greetings in the hallway. Within a very short time, everyone at the school knew about my illness, and the doctor who visited me every day, found herself answering the door for neighbors and colleagues bringing gifts of food, flowers, and other things.

Dr. Margit fit no stereotype I might have imagined of a European, female, communist-educated doctor: six feet tall and slender, beautiful, with sparkling dark eyes and dark hair down to her waist, wearing a mini skirt and high-heeled shoes, which looked just right on her. It was she who said, when she first entered my *lakótelep* flat, "No wonder you are sick, living in this damned communist building!" She insisted that I must eat something, went to the market and bought what she thought I should have, then prepared food and disposed of it when I did not eat it, and washed the dishes. She filled the refrigerator with soda and things she thought I might want later, and put away the gifts of food that had arrived. Now THAT's a House Call.

The Peace Corps hires local doctors to handle volunteers' medical care only if the medical training of the host country meets American standards. Dr. Margit was well-trained at Semelweiss Medical School in Budapest. She later interned briefly in England and worked five years in a Paris hospital; she spoke French as well as English. In addition to her superb training, she has that gift of all good doctors: the minute she walks into a sick room, the patient feels better.

That was my only illness in the six years I have been in Hungary. It may have immunized me against all the local "bugs;" goodness knows it was powerful enough. It certainly immunized me against any feeling of isolation or rejection. The suspicions, fears, or whatever that made my colleagues and neighbors wary and slow to be friendly with me disappeared as soon as they saw me as a person they could relate to, a sick woman, alone and needing help. They could deal with that. No people in the world are more compassionate to the suffering than Hungarians, especially the women. They, themselves, have suffered greatly but they want no sympathy or anything that smacks of it: they prefer to do the helping, just as they prefer giving to receiving.

After my recovery, my colleagues and neighbors had completely reversed their attitude toward me. If I only hinted at some need or help, it was instantly at hand. One night about 10 p.m. the husband of a colleague appeared at my door. He was an electronics engineer who commuted to a responsible job in Budapest and often worked long hours. His wife had told him that I could not get CNN on my television set which I should have been able to do, and sent him to my flat to make the adjustment that evening as soon as he got home from work! Another neighbor, hearing that I was having trouble with an electrical connection came by one Saturday morning to take care of it. For my second Christmas there, he helped me select, and then transported to my apartment a Christmas tree, set it up and attached the tree lights which his wife found in a shop and bought for me.

Invitations poured in. One of the earliest is especially memorable. Kati, a teaching colleague, invited me to accompany her to the Museum of Applied Arts (Iparmüvéseti Múzeum) in Budapest. This was my first visit to a major Budapest museum—in all, there are 192 museums in that city. Designed by Ödön Lechner and Gyula Pártos and built in the 1890s, the building's red granite facing and ceramic tile roofing were prepared in the famous Zsolnay porcelain factory of Pécs. It is one of the most important art nouveau buildings in Hungary, and is also said to be an example of Oriental-Hungarian Secessionist architecture. Whatever the style is labeled it was a stunning initiation into a museum-viewing in Hungary. Kati also invited me to dinner at her home where I met her brilliant husband András, and her charming and intelligent children, Eszter and Zsombor.

After I left the school, they continued to invite me to special events, such as the *Szalagavató*, the dance program given in late winter by the students who will graduate in June, and the graduation ceremony, the *Ballagás*. And I still participated in planning the East-West student-exchange program, arrogantly, and I hope facetiously, called "Fit for Europe." It brought high school level students in former communist countries together with their peers in Western Europe in order to ease their future integration into the European Community.

NOTES FROM THE JOURNAL – CONCLAVE IN KRAKOW

The young immigration officer at the border was obviously bewildered. Slovakia had been an independent nation for only three months, three very cold months beginning January 1, 1993, not a heavy foreign tourist season. It was understandable that he panicked when confronted with a bus load of Americans carrying passports that identified them as being members of something called "The U.S. Peace Corps." "That sounds military," he was surely thinking. We tried to explain that our purpose was the same as that of the chicken that crossed the road – we just wanted to get to the other side. We were on our way to Poland. He went off to consult and returned with an older, perhaps more experienced, colleague and after a delay of about an hour, they allowed us to cross their border. Our ancient bus groaned up the rolling hills, the beautiful rolling hills of Slovakia, rising in places to 6000 kilometers, at a pace of ten or fifteen miles per hour. At the Polish border it took the Slovakian guards longer to let us out than it took the Poles to let us in. It was nice to be welcomed by Poland. Our destination was Krakow were we met with Peace Corps volunteers serving in other former-communist countries: Ukraine, Bulgaria, Albania, Russia and the Baltic countries, to compare experiences, exchange information, and explore the possibility of setting up joint programs.

We arrived after midnight, expecting a hotel, but found ourselves in a standard communist guest house. Each room had four double-decked bunk beds to which eight guests were assigned in order of registration without regard to gender or traveling companions. Not knowing about this system, we made no effort to approach the desk in the company of our friends. By random chance, seven of us assigned to one room were women. The eighth person was a young man who had arrived earlier from Bulgaria, also there for the Peace Corps conference. He was already in bed but awake and we introduced ourselves, but it was too late for small talk. Our program began at 8 o'clock the next morning in another part of the city so we went to bed immediately.

The next morning we were stunned to discover that the currency exchange office did not open until 8 o'clock and none of us had zlotys for even a cup of coffee. Then our good fortune in the room assignment came to light. The young man from Bulgaria had arrived the day before in time to change money, and generously treated us all to coffee.

At conference sessions we heard about the life of Peace Corps volunteers in other former-communist countries and became aware of how well-off we were in Poland and Hungary. Our colleagues from Albania, Ukraine, Bulgaria, Russia, and the Baltic countries were ecstatic over the abundant hot water in our hostel and confessed they had to quell the urge to steal toilet paper and other such goodies that they never saw in their countries. And they almost swooned over the plentiful food that could be bought everywhere and without coupons! Very soon, we residents of Poland and Hungary remained quiet, saying little about our living conditions somewhat embarrassed to reveal our comparably luxurious lifestyle. We had no success in establishing joint programs. It was still not possible for people in some of those countries, Albania, for example, to travel in and out of the country without special dispensation.

Unlike Warsaw which was almost leveled during World War II, Krakow miraculously escaped devastation by bombs, but Wawel Castle, the finest surviving piece of Renaissance architecture in Poland, was desecrated by the Nazis who set up their headquarters there. From the 10th century, the castle has served both as both a cathedral and a fortress. Its 71 rooms are said to contain paintings and furniture from the 16th century when it was largely rebuilt, including a magnificent sequence of 16th century tapestries commissioned by the royal family. I cannot vouch for the furnishings and tapestries because the promise of a tour of the castle never materialized. On a later tour, we visited the large Renaissance *Rynek Główny* (main market square) one of the largest and most distinctive market squares in Europe in the heart of the *Stare Miasto* (Old Town). The green belt of the Planty gardens surrounds the *Stare Miasto* and the Wisla River skirts one corner. There we heard the unfinished trumpet call that sounds on the hour from the taller red tower of the richly decorated Kościól Mariacki cathedral on the northeastern corner of the square. The call is cut short to commemorate the legendary 13th century trumpeter struck in the throat by a Tartar arrow as he warned the town of an attack. Then we were told we would visit the castle but we stopped off at a small museum, Zbiory Czartoryskich, where we were shown a treasure of which the city is most proud, Leonard da Vinci's

Lady with the Ermine. That painting has always repelled me for some reason, even if the ermine is a symbol of chastity, or perhaps because of that. Fortunately, the museum also has Rembrandt's *Landscape with the Good Samaritan*. As it got later, it became obvious that we would not have time to see the castle, and sure enough by the time we got there it was too late for a tour.

We were invited to climb the Zigmond Tower – quite a climb, I have forgotten how many steps – to the large bell at top. There is a superstition that if one rubs the bell's clapper while making a wish, the wish will come true, and I never pass up an opportunity to court good fortune. The Trevi fountain has received many pennies and lira from me, and once in Odessa I went down very steep steps and crossed a narrow sandy beach to throw a one-kopek coin into the Black Sea. The superstition is that by doing so you will surely return to the spot where the coin was tossed. When I reached the water, and looked into my change purse, all I had was a two-kopek piece! With some foreboding, but hoping it might mean I would return twice, I threw in the two kopeks. As yet, I have not returned, but that was less than 10 years ago, and it could still happen. So I climbed to the top of Zigmond Tower, rubbed the clapper of the large bell and made my wish. It has not yet come true, but my hope still lives.

We did visit Krakow's Cathedral, next door to the castle, where Poland's Kings were crowned and buried and where Pope John Paul II was once the archbishop. Outside the cathedral stands a statue of Tadeusz Kościuszko, the Polish patriot who became an American Revolutionary soldier in the late 18th century and later died resisting Russian invaders of Poland. We were not able to visit the Jagiellonian University, where the distinguished astronomer Nicolaus Copernicus studied in the late 15th century. It is the second oldest university in Eastern Europe after Prague's Carolinum (Charles University).

Before I left Hungary, my friend Dezső Holnapy told me to telephone his Polish friend, Tomas Boche'nski, when I was in Krakow. I am never sure how people feel about hearing from a friend of a friend who has just arrived in town, so I took the precaution of writing him a note to say I would be there and told him where I would be staying. When I arrived, there was a letter waiting for me inviting me to visit them any time – for lunch, dinner, tea or any other time – and to telephone them at any time of day, late or early! As I found out, they are indeed very good friends of Dezső Holnapy and his brilliant, charming wife, Györgyi Rontó, a well-known Hungarian biophysicist. Boche'nski called for me on my second evening there in his new Peugot automobile and drove me to his family's large apartment in an old, substantial building, on a street where there were many like it. On the way to his home, he told me two very important things. First, about his friendship with the Holnapys. He and Dezső are both engineers who were among the avant garde in introducing computers into the engineering field in their countries. They met at a professional meeting and found that they liked each other in addition to having much in common professionally, and they enjoyed seeing each other at meetings and conferences. There came a time, I believe in the 70s, when the economy of Poland was very bad, food and medicines were scarce, and Tomas had two small daughters. Being aware of the situation, and with no preamble, the Holnapys wrote to the Boche'nskis and asked if they would like to send their daughters to Budapest where life was better at that time to visit them until the Polish economy improved. This gesture from someone who was only a professional acquaintance touched them deeply and they gratefully accepted the offer. The girls went and stayed with the Holnapys until such time as things improved at home, which sealed the friendship between the families for all time. From that story, I understood why Desző was so certain I would be warmly welcomed by his friends solely on the basis that I was a friend of the Holnapys.

The other story he told me was quite remarkable in a different way. It was in the form a message I was authorized to deliver to Györgyi and Dezső. His wife, he said and as the Holnapys knew, had been blind for a long time following eye surgery, and three weeks before my visit she had surgery on one eye that restored the sight in it! This had just occurred as the bandages had been removed the very day I was visiting them! They were all very excited about this, and had not had time to let their friends know, so I was authorized, requested actually, to deliver the good news! It gave me great joy to be favored with such a happy mission.

Mrs. Boche'nski spoke only Polish and Russian so I had to dust off my Russian but we managed quite well. A cousin was visiting them, and one daughter and a 5-1/2 year old granddaughter live there. So we had a convivial evening beginning with some very good Polish vodka, a kind I had not seen since I left the United States, followed by an excellent meal and good conversation. They showed me a photograph of their former home, designed by one of Poland's best architects which had been confiscated during the communist years and turned into a school. It was sad to see the "before" picture, a veritable mansion, and to see the "after" picture, a dilapidated structure with several small buildings scattered on the grounds. I asked if they expected to have it returned to them but they said there was no plan in Poland to restore property to the original owners as there was in some other places, East Germany, for example. They were quite unemotional about that, saying it would be unusable by them in its present condition and too expensive for them to restore.

It was my good fortune to arrive just when the family had an important reason to celebrate, but they appeared to be generally happy people. They expressed optimistic expectations for the future of Poland, and dismissed their past misfortunes as if they were scarcely remembered. The difference in their attitude and that which prevailed among the Hungarians I was encountering in those days was striking; people in Hungary were usually very pessimistic. We parted as warm friends well met, and for me, in happy anticipation of carrying good news to my Hungarian friends.

The Nazi concentration camps of Auschwitz and Birkenau are located 60 kilometers from Krakow, and numerous trains and buses go there every day. A number of people in our group stayed over one day after the meeting to make the trip, but I was committed to return to my teaching duties. My feelings about this were very mixed. It seems ghoulish somehow to visit those places; I am not clear about what it accomplishes. But it may be a duty, penance of a kind, that this generation owes to those human beings who, in today's world which we call civilized, were subjected to almost unimaginably inhumane horror. A visit there may be a silent prayer that human beings will in time cease to feel that they must every now and then make other human beings suffer.

VII

SCHOOL DAYS, SCHOOL DAYS

In the ten-minute break between classes, bedlam broke out in the hallways. Rock music blasted from the P.A. system; students squealed and shouted to each other; boys and girls rushed into each others' arms and stood embracing or fondling; some sidled into the toilets to smoke a forbidden cigarette. At least half of the student body raced to the canteen to buy sandwiches, candy bars, soda, pastry, potato chips. Not all of them succeeded in reaching the counter before the class bell rang or before the stock was depleted, but those who did and who next came into my classroom brought food and drink along. No, this was not East Bronx or Elm Street High. It was a Hungarian *Gimnázium* (high school) in 1992, one of those institutions which in the 19th century were known for the high intellectual level of the faculties and students, comparable to the best schools in West Europe. Graduates of Hungarian gymnasiums were often admitted to the best universities in Europe, including those of Germany and Austria. That era produced a remarkable number of brilliant Hungarian scholars and scientists.

But when I went to teach English in the suburbs of Budapest, the gymnasium of the previous century no longer existed. Schools had embraced democracy with a vengeance, or so it seemed, and the students had their own interpretation of what democracy was: it meant unbridled freedom. And like people in all other democracies, including the United States, they were having trouble defining the limits of that freedom. Although it was well-known that I did not allow eating and drinking during my classes, they never stopped trying, and never stopped assuring me that other teachers allowed it. "I am not television," I told them, "that you can watch from a couch while eating and drinking. I am not even taped. I am coming to you LIVE!" This served not only to get their attention and have them put away their snacks, but it led into a discussion of the word "live," a difficult English word for foreigners. It is spelled one way, but has two pronunciations, and at least three different meanings. "I live in Hungary." "We caught a live rabbit." "The broadcast was not taped, it was live." Whenever possible I tried to segué from reprimands into instruction as if that had been the purpose all along.

In appearance, they looked just like American teenagers, and remarkably like each other. In dress, they were definitely classless and very nearly genderless. Boys and girls wore blue jeans, T-shirts, and athletic shoes, often with designer labels. Hair length also was uni-sex, shoulder length or longer, occasionally very short; even a "Punk" or a "Mohawk" showed up now and then. (One bit of graffiti seen on a wall near the school said, "Punk is not dead!") Earrings were standard for young women and a single one in the ear of a male student was not rare. They listened to the same music as American teenagers, had similar film preferences – sex and violence predominating – smoked the same cigarettes, and used some of the same four-letter English words, though not so often or at least not so publicly. Movies and television may or may not influence morals, but they are indeed homogenizers of fashion. Most of the students had television, refrigerators, and washing machines at home, and more than one-third of Hungarian families owned an automobile. Although the legal driving age began at seventeen, I never heard even the eighteen- or nineteen-year-olds speak of driving a car. Some mentioned that they were taking driving lessons, but it was rare for anyone that age to have access to the family car. A student driving to school would have been unthinkable, probably not allowed.

After the fall of communism in 1989, the education ministry repudiated the system that had been introduced in 1949 when Hungary was ruled by the Soviet-trained Mátyás Rákosi. Not only was the curriculum Sovietized then, but university registration was denied to children of former "elites" (high ranking officials, estate landowners, aristocrats); preference was given to children of Communist Party officials and of the working class, the new "elites." Since a gymnasium education was essential preparation for university registration, this ruling also affected the make-up of the gymnasium student body. When I arrived in Hungary such restrictions no longer existed. My students came from professional, academic and working-class families. Not even residence location mattered; students could apply to the gymnasium of their choice. The majority of my students lived in the community, but some came from other places, and traveled by bus, metro (subway) and *villamos* (tram) as much as two hours each way. They were between the ages of 15 and 19, born between 1973 and 1977, and started to school between 1979 and 1983. Thus when Hungary underwent the radical change to a democracy in 1989, they were still in primary school. If they were somewhat disoriented by the changes that were taking place in their schools, along with those in the political, social, and economic life of their country, it should not be surprising.

The changes in Hungary's education system throughout the twentieth century were a direct result of the cataclysmic events in the political, economic, and cultural life of the country: World War I followed by the communist regime of Béla Kun, the authoritarian regent Admiral Miklós Horthy, and the ignominious Trianon Treaty of 1920 that deprived Hungary of three-fifths of her land and one-third of her people, World War II, German occupation, Russian occupation, Mátyás Rákosi, Imre Nagy, János Kádár. They all left their mark. Not all of the changes have been unwelcome. Today's gymnasium curriculum is still a demanding one but bears little resemblance to that of the nineteenth century which followed the Austrian and German models, and included six or eight years of Latin, three years of Greek, mathematics up to integral and differential calculus, and thorough grounding in Greek, Roman, and Hungarian history, and in Magyar literature.

In 1949, the communist government, nominally headed by István Dobi but controlled by Mátyás Rákosi, revised the Hungarian education system in the service of creating a "new socialist man." The teaching of Russian language was made mandatory from the fifth grade to the universities. It was optional from the third grade. They removed sociology and psychology from the middle school curriculum, and introduced a falsified history of the Soviet Communist party. Engineering and technological subjects were given priority. Hungarian history was de-emphasized and tailored to conform to the current party line, with alterations from time to time as the line shifted. Some aspects of history were ignored or presented in distorted versions, including events that occurred during and after World War II, notably the Russian liberation of Hungary from Germany in 1945. When the 1956 Revolution occurred, the approved history texts depicted it as the result of reactionary elements gaining the upper hand and threatening the bases of the socialist system, the established government, not as a popular movement in which most of society became active, that is to say, not as a Revolution.

After 1956, János Kádár became head of the government through an arrangement with the Soviets and under circumstances so devious that even today the details are not fully known. Before the country's borders were closed, about two hundred thousand people fled to the West. Kádár announced a radical break with the past but continued to punish and terrorize those who resisted the political system. Retribution for 1956 lasted for years but the regime had two faces; even in that fearsome time, some improvements were instituted. In 1962, Kádár ended the restriction on university registration by children of former "elites" and others who were not communist party members. All young people were then eligible to register if they met the academic requirements, but preference was still given to children of party officials and of the working class, often regardless of qualifications. The results of such a policy were unavoidably mixed. Social and economic leveling of a society cuts two ways – as it increases opportunities for people on the lower level, it reduces them for the former privileged class. One of the most intelligent and cultivated women I know was a university student during the time of the restriction. Assuming that she was from an intellectual family, I asked her how she was able to get into the university. "What are you talking about?" she said. "I was in the preferred group; my father was a butcher, we were working class people!"

When Mikhail S. Gorbachev became the leader of the Soviet Union in 1985, all the satellite, or so-called "Iron Curtain," countries were affected. Of greatest significance to Hungary was Gorbachev's declaration that each socialist country had a right to go its own way, thus removing the fear that Soviet tanks might again roll through the streets of Budapest if Hungary deviated from the party line. In March 1988, the Hungarian Socialist Workers Party that had dominated the political life of the country fell apart. Their leader, János Kádár, was removed as its head, and others took the reins of the party, among them a reform communist, Imre Pozsgay. On the basis of a study conducted by the Hungarian Academy of Sciences, Pozsgay broke with his colleagues, and proclaimed that the 1956 action was in fact a popular uprising against abuses by the leaders of the party. It was, he affirmed, a Revolution. The effect of that proclamation was to dislodge instantly one great block in the wall of dogma built by Hungarian communism, and the way was cleared for teaching history truthfully. A cascade of political events followed. The party announced its own dissolution and reconstituted itself as the Hungarian Socialist Party. The constitution was revised to legalize groups opposing the ruling party, whether they called themselves parties or not. Hungary officially became a multi-party state. In the Spring of 1989, Hungary began to dismantle its barrier to the West; the electronic warning system on the Austrian-

Hungarian border was removed, presaging the downfall of the Berlin Wall in November, 1989.

A new minister of education was appointed, Ferenc Glatz, a historian who abolished the mandate that Russian language and Marxism be taught in the schools, and removed from the schools' textbooks that conformed to the distorted communist version of history. New textbooks were commissioned, but were not available by 1992. History teachers used photocopied material from selected sources, more reliable than the previous textbooks, but some of which reflected the teachers' own biases. The majority of gymnasium teachers at that time had been born in the 1950s and 1960s, a period when all education and acculturation was controlled by communist doctrine. Those teachers had seen the best years of Hungary's economic life. Born after the horrors that followed 1949, they knew only what their parents or grandparents told them of the Stalin-style show trials featuring confessions extracted by terrifying tortures, not only of Hungarians but also of Western businessmen accused of conspiring against the socialist state; or the cruel dictatorship of "Stalin's best pupil," Mátyás Rákosi, who instituted a reign of terror through the AVO, the State Security Division, later the AVH, that reached into every sphere of life, its major task being the discovery and destruction of opposition to communist rule.

Most of my colleagues, both teachers and administrators, were university students between the mid-1960s and the mid-1970s, years that have been called Hungary's economic "Golden Decade." In those years salaries grew annually by three to four percent. Real wages and the consumption level of the population were three times greater at the end of the 1970s than they were in 1956-57. Growth of production after 1968 was double the world average, and between 1972 and 1982 Hungary's agricultural growth was the second highest in the world after the Netherlands; it was third in the world in per capita grain and meat production. Many of that generation recall their university days as a very happy time of life, and in the lean economic years of the early 1990s one often heard the almost prayer-like invocation, "Bring back Kádár!" It was seldom a real wish, but only an expression of discouragement, something like "God help us!" After hearing it from one of my colleagues several times, I challenged her. "If Kádár was so great, why did you go to all that trouble to get rid of him?" She looked at me as if I were a half-wit, and patiently explained. "Because we had no freedom of speech, no free press, and were constantly afraid of the secret police!" We both laughed. But I often wondered what the teen-agers who had little or no memory of the Kádár era thought when they heard their teachers and others voice that wish. It called to mind the efforts in America to eradicate racism by desegregating schools. Some people reasoned that if children started in kindergarten and went all the way through high school with classmates of other races, any vestiges of prejudice would disappear. Therefore, the problem of racism might be solved in 12 or 13 years. That estimate did not take into account that children who lived in previously prejudiced and segregated societies would be taught by teachers from those societies and continue to live with parents whose beliefs were not changed overnight by a decision of the Supreme Court. Now, more than 40 years after segregated schools were declared unconstitutional, the United States is still wrestling with problems of racism.

The interpretation of a well-known fairy tale by a fourth-grade teacher in Hungary amply illustrates this phenomenon. It was told to me by the mother of the child involved. His class wanted to perform a drama as a program for their parents at the end of the school year, a common practice. Her son was given the assignment of selecting and directing the play. When she told me he had decided to do a dramatization of "The Ugly Duckling," I spontaneously exclaimed, "Oh, that's fantastic!" My outburst puzzled her. "It's so anti-communist," I explained. She wanted to know why I considered it so. "Because it is a tale of individual triumph over the group," I told her, "and a plea for tolerance of differences in people. Although communists preach tolerance they do not practice it, and the subordination of the individual to the group is a basic tenet." She told her son what I had said and he related it to his teacher. "You will be very interested in the teacher's reaction to your comments," his mother later told me. "She said that was not the point of the story at all. She explained that the message of 'The Ugly Duckling' is that we must all remain in our own group, with our own kind."

That incident is not likely to have much influence on my friend's son who, as his mother was, is encouraged to think for himself. Books are available to him at home and he is already an omnivorous reader who does not hesitate to express his own ideas freely. Once I asked her how she had gone through the standard elementary and secondary schooling of the 1960s and not been taken in by the rhetoric of the time and by the perverted versions of history dispensed in the classroom. She said she brought her books home and her parents read them. When they read something they knew to be incorrect, they told her the true story. The home environment greatly influenced the attitudes, behavior and beliefs of people born in Hungary after 1945.

Literature, television, radio and all communication media were controlled during the communist era, although censorship seems to have been less rigidly enforced in Hungary than in some other countries. Classical children's literature found its way to Hungary: Aesop's fables and Hans Christian Andersen's fairy tales are generally well known. Old Hungarian fables have survived through generations, but they did not laud individual effort or even personal valor of ordinary people. Many are about goodhearted kings and loyal hardworking peasants. The rather eccentric "Good King Matthias" (Mátyás Király) is the subject of many stories with a moral message. He travelled around the country in disguise, frequently bestowing gifts and honors upon worthy peasants he encountered who pleased him by their diligence and loyalty to the throne. The message: a peasant had only to do his duty, cultivate his fields and pay homage to the king, and some lucky day his disguised sovereign might appear, observe his essential goodness and reward him. It is easy to see how The Good King could be replaced by The Good Party. But the communists did not leave it to chance. Between 1949 and 1953, an abundance of literature was published, written with government sponsorship, that was mainly anti-Western, especially anti-American propaganda. In addition to the written word, anti-American myths and rumors were circulated, one of the more amusing being that Coca-Cola contained a mysterious ingredient whose effect upon humans was unpredictable, possibly dangerous.

One Hungarian friend told me of being at a teen-age party in the 1960s in a home where the father had recently been on a trip to Western Europe and had brought back some Coca-Cola. The young male host found one bottle in the refrigerator and daringly offered everyone a taste of it. Before my friend accepted, she telephoned the mother, not to ask permission, but to tell her what she was about to do so her mother would be prepared for whatever happened. The trepidation she described about drinking Coca-Cola in the 1960s was similar to that experienced by young Americans at that time when they were offered LSD or Marijuana. Now in Hungary, cola drinks are so popular that the Coca-Cola and Pepsi-Cola companies are locked in a metaphorical toe-to-toe contest over the hugely profitable Hungarian market that looks even more promising for the future.

The change in government that occurred in Hungary in 1989 was to some people like an exploding fireworks display that ended with the word "Freedom" spelled out against the night sky. They thought it was beautiful, but they were not sure what it meant. Not only students but the entire population was finding it difficult to define that new freedom. The heady reaction of the young people is not surprising. Some of them went a little wild, and interpreted "democracy" as license to behave as they wished anywhere, anytime, including the school classroom.

The student body of the late 19th century gymnasium as it was described by John Lukács writing in BUDAPEST 1900 (Grove Weidenfeld. New York. 1988) bore little resemblance to that which I stood before in the late 20th century. And the faculties of the Hungarian gymnasium a century ago had changed at least as much. Lukacs wrote, "Many of the gymnasium teachers were doctors of philosophy. Others were humanists and literary men (sic) of respectable stature. The level of their training and competence, not to speak of their dedication, was at least comparable to that of senior professors at the most reputable American universities now." He also praised the high standard of the curriculum. However, Lukacs's high praise of the curriculum and the faculty did not imply an endorsement of the system which he described as one "…where the unilateral emphasis was on the discipline of brain work and not on character." and the "students were haunted by the fear of being suddenly called on, of being inadequately prepared, and of receiving a consequent poor or failing mark at the end of the semester." There were, he said, even student suicides during the weeks in June preceding final examinations. He deplored the rigorous application of the curriculum, with its almost impossible demands, the severity of which led to cheating and prevarication and the youthful conclusion that such acts were inevitable conditions of survival in a world with rigid, senseless rules.

Any fear instilled in students by a rigorous curriculum and demanding teachers was gone by the time I arrived, but a few vestiges of the 1900 climate remained. While the consequences of receiving a poor or failing mark seemed to be of little concern to my students, cheating and prevarication were commonplace, and pretty much taken for granted by teachers as well as students. Cheating was considered as giving or receiving help and done with little or no effort at concealment. My refusal to tolerate cheating – when I saw it happening during a written exercise, I moved the student's seat or took away the notes that were being clandestinely referred to – was treated with indifference. A shrug or slightly condescending smile was the only reaction. This idiosyncratic foreign teacher, they seemed to be thinking, what strange notions she has! If a student hesitated slightly when called upon to recite or answer a question, another student or several others responded correctly in audible whispers or even aloud. They never accepted the explanation that it did not help a student for others to call out the answer, that oral response is a necessary learning technique.

Standard textbook English becomes boring to advanced students, especially the brighter ones, and occasionally I introduced them to other writing styles. A brief experiment with Shakespeare's Elizabethan English was less than successful, even with those who had read or seen his plays in Hungarian. Modern radio and television scripts which I photocopied and assigned roles for class readings were quite popular. Risking their derision, I even dared to give them for reading and interpretation some of the mottoes, adages, that were framed and hung on the walls of my own long-ago classrooms. Those admonitions from my earliest public school years have stayed with me; I can still picture in my mind their exact location on the classroom wall. No doubt they would be jeered at by American students today, but I hoped the Hungarian young people would be so absorbed in concentrating on the syntax and examination of the metaphorical roots that they might overlook their fustiness. Two that I wrote on the blackboard challenged their knowledge of English grammar and evoked some interesting interpretations: "Play the game; never mind the score," and "If a task is once begun, never leave it till it's done. Be the labor great or small, do it well or not at all." Calling their attention to the grammatical forms – imperatives, conditionals, subjunctives, contractions – I could only hope the messages would penetrate subliminally and stay with them through the years as they have with me. If they found them ludicrously old-fashioned, their derision never showed.

The classes that never failed to delight the students were those in which we sang. American folk songs and Christmas carols were favorites. Some were well-known to them in the Hungarian language and it was easy and fun for them to learn the English lyrics. They never got tired of singing along to Woody Guthrie's taped "This Land is Your Land." In one class we wrote, with everyone contributing suggestions, several revised versions in which we substituted Hungarian place names for the American ones, for example:

> This land is your land, this land is my land
> From Nyíregyháza to Margit Island
> From Békéscsaba to Nagykanizsa
> This land is made for you and me.

Another song they liked which proved useful in teaching synonyms and antonyms was "Down By the Old Mill Stream" in a version my generation knew and loved in high school. They enjoyed the music and even seemed to find the grammatical insertions amusing. The version we started out with was:

Down by the old (the old not the new) mill stream (not the river but the stream)
Where I first (not the last but the first) met you (not him/her but you)
With your eyes so blue (not green but blue)
Dressed in gingham too.
It was there (not here but there) I knew (not thought but knew)
That you loved (not hated but loved) me true (not false but true).
You were sixteen (not fifteen but sixteen)
My village queen (not the king but the queen)
Down by the old (the old not the new) mill stream.
And we ended, dragging the words out slowly: "Not - the - ri - ver - but - the - stre - a - m."

Then as an exercise, we varied the lyrics, substituting other appropriate English words: "Down by the old (not the young but the old) mill stream (not the ocean but the stream) When I first (not the second but the first) met you (not them but you)." All students were urged to make suggestions. It conveyed the idea of synonyms, antonyms, and alternate English words without the drudgery of memorizing definitions.

One of the most satisfying rewards of my teaching experience came when I began to hear students singing those songs in English as they went through the hallways between classes.

The student government organization was a year old when I arrived. The progressive headmaster hastened to introduce democratic institutions into the school immediately following the inauguration of a democratic government and a revised system of education. It was a home-made variety of student government that bore slight resemblance to any such organization I had known. It was modelled loosely after the United States government with a president, a vice president, and a senate comprised of representatives from each of the four classes. Duties and responsibilities of officers were not clearly established and students did not willingly accept nominations. The honor of holding office was somewhat diluted by the low esteem in which authority figures were held. Officials in their society had been hated and feared, and teenagers desire above almost everything else to be popular and well-liked. When a student had been reluctantly persuaded to run for office, all campaigning was done by others; the candidates never admitted they wanted the post, and did not seem to know whether their supporters were friends or enemies, whether their leadership ability was being recognized or if they were being made the butt of a practical joke.

In truth, the student council was more of an ornament of democracy than a reality, but it served some useful purposes, and the mere introduction of the idea was an important step. The president acted as the external representative of the school and that gave the position prestige. The president also became the leader in planning student activities within the school and for cooperative arrangements with other schools and external organizations, thus eliminating the formerly necessary participation and subsequent domination by faculty members. The absence of established guidelines made it necessary for elected officers largely to define their own responsibilities and privileges, but the young men who were presidents in the two years I was there rose to the position with remarkable poise and judgment. There was no female candidate for president either year, but there was at least one female senator.

Perhaps the most significant effect of the student council was that it provided a model, albeit incomplete and hazy, of a system of responsible self-government. This was at a time when the country's new government was struggling to bring about the radical transformation from a one-party dictatorship to a democracy. Hungary was the first country in history to attempt to go directly from a state-controlled economy to a free market society in which private enterprise was not only allowed but encouraged and expected to drive the economy. Mountains of legislation covering private property and all it entailed, accession, transfer, taxation, in addition to such matters as education, social welfare, human rights, everything touching the lives of the people, was piling up in the parliament and none of it pouring out as fast as the country's citizens had expected and hoped for.

Efforts to engage the interest or at least arouse the curiosity of students in the historic and dramatic changes their country was going through met stubborn, sometimes belligerent unconcern. "I am not interested in politics," said one of the brightest. Another shrugged, "What difference does it make? Everything will still be the same." Hungary has been promised happy tomorrows in exchange for hard work today by too many invaders, occupiers, puppet rulers, monarchs, and elected leaders for them to embrace any new system with enthusiasm. Most troubling of all was their inability to envision their own role, to conceive that their ideas and opinions could affect future events. They seemed to be unmoved when I said, "In a couple of years you will be voters!" The voting age is 18. "In twenty years your generation will be running this country!" They could understand the language – and that was my job – but I wanted them to comprehend the meaning, to overcome their feeling of powerlessness.

It was impossible to know whether the reluctance to express their hopes for the future indicated lack of imagination, fear of being considered naive by their peers, or merely lack of ambition, indifference. It could not be lack of imagination, I decided. A six-year-old boy in a family I often visited showed me some pictures he had drawn of space ships and beings from another planet. In a confidential whisper, he told me that he had looked out of his window very early one morning and seen a space ship land in the field across the road and that is what he drew. Only he, no one else, he assured me, had seen it. No lack of imagination there.

It was suggested to me that the reluctance of young people to talk about themselves or to express opinions might be a hangover from almost three generations under communism, during which they were always under the watchful eye of the police, the State Security Division. People became very guarded in their conversations and instructed their children from an early age that they must not talk with strangers, and must never discuss with anyone, not even with friends and neighbors, personal or family matters. Everyone was viewed as a potential informer. Interrogating children with feigned friendliness was one technique used to obtain information. By questioning a young child, one might discover that father had a shortwave radio under the bed, or some other forbidden possession. It could be a difficult habit to break as they grew older, even after the radical change in government and the subsequent curtailment of police power. This might explain why teenagers and adults still feel considerable guilt about open expression of ideas, hopes, and beliefs.

The students at my school were not representative of the country as a whole. Although not all would go on to the university, the fact of their admission to the gymnasium placed them in the upper level of students in their age group based on educational achievement and intelligence.

In 1995, *Reader's Digest, Hungary* (*Válogatás*) commissioned a study of the beliefs, values, and expectations of young people throughout Hungary. The group surveyed was between the ages of 15 and 24, which includes both gymnasium and university-age students. That group also included the first generation to come of age in the post-communist period. The results, published in the September 1995 issue of *Válogatás*, surprised many because they indicated that, as the heading of one local English-language newspaper editorial phrased it, "The Kids are Alright." (sic)

In answer to questions about politics, the majority thought the current government was left of the current population, which they considered to be more conservative than they themselves. Most defined themselves as left-liberal, but 24 percent said they were strongly conservative, and a majority thought the country would return to a conservative government within the next five years. Seventy-three percent thought NATO membership would be a good thing for Hungary. (When a referendum on the NATO question was held in November, 1997, 85 percent of the more than 50 percent of eligible voters who voted said "Yes.") Most surprising was that of this third generation brought up in a "Godless communist" society, 46 percent said they considered themselves to be religious. However, only 11 percent said they went to religious services regularly.

They were asked why they were proud to have been born in Hungary, and the greatest number give as their reasons the culture, science, and sports; a large number were proud of their history, geography, and natural resources. Many were just proud to be Hungarian for general non-specific reasons. Another question in the "Have you stopped beating your wife?" category was, "Why are you ashamed to have been born in Hungary?" Many did not answer that one; the few who did cited ethics, spiritual qualities, the economic situation, and the general difficulty of life in Hungary.

As for the future, 65 percent said they expected to marry and have children, 17 percent said they intended to have more than three children. Only 2 percent said they wanted no children. The majority were "fairly optimistic" about the future.

The young people in this survey represent the population that will shape the values, beliefs, and culture of Hungary well into the next century.

NOTES FROM THE JOURNAL – EAST LONDON CAMPGROUND

Students and teachers from seven former communist countries (Bulgaria, Estonia, Hungary, Lithuania, Poland, Slovakia, and Ukraine) met for ten days with their counterparts from England, Greece, and Norway, plus one student from Australia and one teacher from the United States. Camping out in England for ten glorious days in June, and never a drop of rain! It seemed like a miracle! (The 1993 Wimbledon Tennis matches were played during that time without a single postponement, truly a miracle!)

The Bulgarian students were from a school that emphasizes the French language and were more comfortable with French than with English which was the common language of the group. Within the first few hours, they discovered that I understood their French and instantly incorporated me into their group, calling me "Madame" throughout the entire ten days. They had brought tapes of Greek music with them, and after dinner on the first evening they urged me to join them in front of their tent where we danced to the music. It was my first lesson in Greek folk dancing which turned out to be lots of fun. We had several dance sessions after that and I spent more time with the Bulgarian students than with the Hungarian, which was all right because there were quite a few Hungarian teachers and only two with the Bulgarians.

A great deal of my time, however, was spent working on the taping of the winning songs that had been submitted during the previous year in a song-writing contest. The lyrics had to be written in English as well as the language of the composer, and I was one of the judges of lyrics, and wrote the commentary for the tape of the winning songs. Writing the introductory narrative to the cassette explaining what it was all about and an introduction to each song giving the name of the composer and the performer was pretty simple. The difficult part was rehearsing the charming boy and girl from Eastlea School who read the material for the tape. Not only did I have to teach them the pronunciation of Hungarian, Lithuanian, Greek, Bulgarian, Norwegian, Estonian, Polish, Slovakian, and

Ukrainian names but I also had to clean up their pronunciations of some ordinary English words, since their East London accents were very authentic. I did not want them to lose the accent, but did want to be sure each word was understandable. The final tape was better than I expected it to be.

At twilight on the last evening, I strolled through the campground with the headmaster of my school, Béla Tóth, and the faculty member responsible for the Hungarian delegation, József Bendik, viewing the peaceful, orderly area. The Bulgarian students were, as usual, playing music in front of their tent and teaching Greek dances to their new friends from other countries. At another tent, a guitar player accompanied a mixed group – Estonian, Norwegian, Greek and Slovakian – singing in the common language of the camp, English, songs that they all knew. The sound of music and song floated through the air, soft as the warbling of birds returning to their nests at the close of the day. The scene symbolized the harmony that had characterized the past ten days during which young people and a few older ones from 12 different countries, all with their own language, customs, and beliefs, took turns cooking and serving meals, danced, sang, talked, and went sight-seeing together in perfect communion. Béla, József, and I spoke of our good fortune – the weather, the logistics, and especially the pervasive good will. Béla, looking out across the campground said, "It is a microcosm of a peaceful world!"

VIII

BEYOND THE CLASSROOM

L anguage teaching in a classroom has certain limitations, and the inability to have real conversation is a major one. It was my goal to have every student say something in English in every class, but in the larger classes, where there might be as many as twenty students, this was not always possible. Some were extremely timid about speaking a foreign language and had to be prodded to say even a simple word. Others who were ready and willing to speak were bored when so much class time was devoted to encouraging the slower ones. For this reason, and one other, I decided to organize an English conversation group. The other reason was to provide a setting in which those students who were able to converse in English would feel more comfortable expressing their thoughts, ideas, and opinions.

Lukac's well justified concern about students' faulty ethical orientation was overshadowed in my mind by the fear that they might be missing one of the essential needs of adolescence, the romantic imagination. Straightforward attempts to stimulate their imagination seemed to have been hopeless. Asked "Where would you spend your summer vacation if you could go anywhere in the world you wanted to, money no object?" most said they would "go to Lake Balaton" where they usually went. "Money is no object!" With that prodding, a few mentioned Paris or London. The question, "What would you like to find yourself doing twenty years from now?" brought such replies as "I'll be married," or "I'll have a job." It was pointless to ask, "How has your life and that of your family changed in the last 5 years?" There was no reply at all. A line from Vachel Lindsay's poem "The Leaden-eyed" came to mind, "Not that they starve, but starve so dreamlessly." I dared not ponder the opening lines of that poem: "Let not young souls be smothered out before they do quaint deeds and fully flaunt their pride."

Besides teaching English, I wanted to help them find something that would light up their imagination, perhaps even move them to do a "quaint deed" or two, or at least think about it. Literature used to provide the ideas that set youthful hopes and aspirations ablaze but now young people in Hungary, as in America, are more likely to spend free time looking at television programs or playing computer games than in reading books. It is not a question of availability. Book stalls abound throughout the country; bookstores and libraries are plentiful. When deprived of television or computers, as when traveling on the Metro, passengers often read books, and as on the New York subways, the most popular fare is paperback books with lurid covers. They do not light up the kind of imagination I had in mind.

Science fiction is popular with some young Hungarian readers. Isaac Asimov was the favorite author of one of my students. Imre read every Asimov book he could find in either Hungarian or English. They all read romantic novels set in the sixteenth and seventeenth centuries when the Turks occupied Hungary because those books are on the reading lists of Hungarian literature classes. Many tell of heroic Hungarians who resisted and successfully outwitted the oppressors or died gloriously in the attempt. But there was no evidence that the readers dreamed of or yearned for adventure as the young Christopher Columbus is said to have done when he haunted the wharves of Genoa pestering the sailors to tell him stories of their travels. And popular character-building children's stories such as the one about a young Abraham Lincoln walking miles to return a borrowed book would be incomprehensible to them. This is undoubtedly a sign of the times, at least in part. The world seems much less mysterious and romantic when scenes from the remote corners of the earth are flashed into our living rooms every day, and movie adventures depicted by Hollywood's special effects creators surpass anything the young mind might imagine.

With no more than the announcement to my classes that beginning on a certain date, once a week after school, my apartment across the street from the school would be open to anyone who wanted to meet with others for the purpose of speaking English, a Conversation Group was launched. The enthusiastic response surprised me; I was prepared for the possibility that no one would be interested. Part of the attraction was no doubt due to my specifying that it would not be a class, no attendance record would be kept, no text used. It was to be a social gathering which I suggested they view as a visit to an American home. The only rule was that everyone had to speak English. Also, some saw it as a chance to get together with their friends, and there were very few places in the community where that was possible. There was a disco, but it was too expensive for most of them, and the majority were too young for discos anyway. There was no bowling alley, skating rink, or even movie theatre. School events were the center of their social life.

Housing space was and for a long time had been inadequate in Hungary, especially in Budapest and its surrounds, and was rigidly controlled during the communist years. The amount of space allotted to a family was based on family size, a bedroom for each two persons. Every room was used for sleeping. A family of four, two parents and two children, would normally live in a two-room apartment, consisting of two rooms, kitchen, bath and toilet. One teen-age male in my class was an only child and he shared the bed-living room with his grandmother. Entertaining friends at home in the evening was out of the question for most young people. One of my first culture shocks came when I observed that seats on public transportation vehicles became the equivalent of the American living-room couch. Boys and girls snuggled together, and girls often sat on their boy friends' laps on the tram or bus when plenty of seats were available. They have no inhibitions about public display of affection, and some of them can make even French lovers on park benches seem almost sedate.

We drank Coca-Cola and other soft drinks, ate "junk food" which they loved and sang American folk songs. It did not take long for them to be at ease enough to discuss subjects that would not have come up in the classroom and probably – almost certainly – not at home. At first their questions tended to be about customs and behaviors in England and the United States, and soon progressed to more sensitive topics such as AIDS, contraception, the polite way to ask for the toilet, and how often one's underwear should be changed. We also talked about some of the differences between British and American English, and the differences in the way Hungarians, Americans, and the British react to jokes, cartoons and other forms of humor. What is extremely funny in one country may be merely puzzling in another.

That underwear question might seem to be incongruous but it came about in a perfectly logical way. The school participated in a student exchange program that brought students form Western Europe and England to Hungary and sent Hungarian students on return visits several times during the school year. Guests were always housed in the homes of students in the host countries. Proposed for discussion one day was the question: What are some problems that arise when one is a guest in a foreign home, and when one is the host of someone from a foreign country? At first, no one could think of any problem, but after some prodding and heavy thought, one young man hesitantly said that he did once have a small problem when a foreign guest was staying in his home. The guest did not bathe regularly and his family complained, not to the guest but to the student, about his friend's body odor. Hungarians, like Americans, are strong believers in regular bathing. We all wanted to know how he handled his problem. "We took him swimming," he said. Hoping to broaden the topic without seeming to play censor, I said that clothing worn repeatedly without laundering, as may occur when traveling, can also be a source of unpleasant odor, especially in warm weather. Immediately, someone blurted out, "How often should one's underwear be changed?" A couple of quick intakes of breath and a few titters were heard, but the question was seriously considered. Various opinions were expressed, some serious, some facetious but no unanimous agreement was reached. However, it was obvious that they were glad to hear each other's comments, and enjoyed the mildly titillating aura created by the discussion in mixed company of a somewhat taboo subject.

At that time, the HIV virus was almost unheard of in Hungary, not that it did not exist, but it was rarely mentioned. And if the subject came up someone was sure to dispose of it immediately with the statement that there was no AIDS in Hungary. A few people in the medical field were beginning to be concerned and to disseminate information about the disease but the general public preferred not to hear about it. Soon after I arrived at the school I asked a colleague who appeared to be the most worldly-wise faculty member whether the students were given any sex education. It made him so uncomfortable he could scarcely answer me. He looked around the room as if he might find the answer lying about somewhere, shook his head as if to jolt his brain into action, and finally said, "We tried. We invited a lecturer to come, scheduled it after classes, and announced that time and place on the bulletin board, but nobody came."

The number of reported cases of AIDS was low, but immigration into and migration across Hungary was surging. It was only a matter of time before the virus would find its way here. Young people seem always to be ahead of the general population in learning about things that affect the whole society, and I had no doubt that the students knew a great deal about AIDS, but they obviously welcomed an opportunity to discuss it with an adult.

The subject of drug abuse was almost as unwelcome among my colleagues at school as AIDS, but in discussing the transmission of the HIV virus, the use of drug-injection needles was unavoidable. None of the students in the conversation group had given me reason to believe they were using drugs, but I was quite sure that some others were at least experimenting with marijuana, and many students drank beer and wine. Hungary is a wine-producing country and one gets the impression that consuming wine is almost a patriotic duty. Wine is offered to guests or drop-in visitors as casually and as often as coffee or soft drinks. Beer and wine drinking by teen-agers is accepted as a fact of life. A few of the older students occasionally boasted about having been drunk or "high" at a party the previous night or on the week-end, and I suspected that "high" meant drugs.

School parties were very popular among the students, and were held frequently, it seemed to me about once a week when school was in session. Parties were nominally chaperoned, that is, members of the faculty came to the school on party nights and had a social gathering of their own in the teachers' room. On a very few occasions I joined the group in the teachers' room during a student party, but I never saw a faculty member go near the party area where refreshment tables were set up and students danced to recorded or live music. When I passed through the party area on the way out, it was obvious that some students were drunk or well on the way. If the school authorities knew about this – and I am sure there were proscriptions against it – they ignored it. Perhaps there is something to be said for condoning it in a protected setting. School parties ended in time for students to travel home by public transportation. Nobody was going to drive an automobile or ride home in one afterwards, as would be the case in other countries, in the United States, for example.

What was not possible for me to condone was students appearing in class under the influence of alcohol. This was rare, but it happened, and there was one chronic case. The student was incapable of making progress and his behavior was so disruptive that it impeded everybody's progress. My efforts to have some action taken failed. The class master to whom disciplinary problem were supposed to be referred bluntly stated that she did not want to deal with it, because nothing could be done. So convinced was I that this could not be true that I went "over her head" and took it up with the headmaster. He was, as always, most courteous. He thanked me for bringing the problem to his attention, said he had previously received reports regarding that particular student, but did nothing.

When I visited the school about a year after leaving, two of my former colleagues drew me aside to tell me they had been thinking and talking about me lately. They said they remembered my concern about drugs, and the school had recently had its first student death resulting from a drug overdose.

Now that American films and television programs are widely viewed throughout Hungary, English language students are exposed to many frequently-used terms and expressions not given in language textbooks. They pick up the profane and the obscene with surprising ease and are more likely to be stumped by euphemisms than by what we call "dirty words." A case in point are the various American euphemisms for what in Hungary is called "toalett," a word that is understood and acceptable everywhere. The British "W.C." is also used in Hungary but you would never get to the right place pronouncing it as the British do. Hungarians say "vay-tsay." Expressions like "Ladies' Room" and "Men's Room" strike them as imprecise and "Bathroom" as downright misleading. In Hungarian homes, the bathroom is where one takes a bath, and the toilet is in a separate room. Since my vocabulary of current euphemisms is out-of-date, I could only tell them the ones that were being used a few years or many years ago, such as "john," "can," "the library," and the British "loo,'" plus such circumlocutions as "May I please wash my hands?" or for women, "I must powder my nose." They found them fairly amusing, but the one that really put them in stitches was by far the most used when I was their age, "I have to see a man about a dog."

Some of them were adept at remembering appropriate and polite expressions also. One or two of the boys always came into the kitchen and helped by opening the soda bottles – opening bottles is a "man's job" in Hungary – and also got out glasses, put chips into bowls and such things. Once I said to one who had been very helpful, "Thank you very much for your help, Imre." He, a 16-year-old, second-year student, gravely replied, "It was my pleasure."

As I had announced at the beginning, the conversation group was not a formal class, so no one had to give notice whether they would attend, although some voluntarily let me know when they could not be there. It eventually settled down to 10 or 12 more or less regulars. That was a good group for conversation and everyone had a chance to talk; it was even better on those rare occasions when only two or three showed up. On one memorable occasion, there was a very large group, more than I had chairs for!

Seven students from a Ukraine gymnasium in the city of Belaya Tserkov near Kiev, were visiting the school for a week. Most of them spoke English, and the students with whom they were living asked if they could bring them to the conversation group. So I expected seven extra students, and in recognition of their being strange to the group, made photocopies of the English Language lyrics to some American folk songs for which we had tapes, and asked one local student to bring a tape player. Of course I bought more soda and snacks than usual. But not enough for the crowd of more than thirty that trooped into my tiny living room that afternoon. When word got around that the foreign visitors were coming, many local students came, some for the first time. We played cassettes and sang – the former-Soviet visitors knew all the tunes and many of the words. Nearly everybody sat on the floor and several had to share each copy of lyrics which made a degree of intimacy unavoidable. Almost immediately the atmosphere became very warm and friendly and conversation in English, Hungarian, and Russian flowed freely. After all, study of Russian language was mandated in Hungarian schools for 40 years prior to 1989, and in Ukrainian schools for even longer. They were all studying English so communication was no problem.

That gathering was a notable success due to the very cordial interaction between students of two countries that had not too long before felt less than friendly toward each other. It was much talked about the next day which was the visitors' last full day at the school. In the afternoon, the Ukranian students made an unscheduled visit to my classroom to get my autograph on American paperback novels they had bought in Budapest. Presumably the autograph of an American teacher in a Hungarian school was an acceptable substitute for that of the American author.

The ceremonies and festivities attendant upon graduation from the Hungarian *Gimnázium* are very different from those celebrating graduation from high school in the United States. School officially ends sometime in early June, but the Senior Class festivities begin in late January or early February with a performance – drama, dance, or music – for their parents and other guests. In the weeks preceding this event, classes are a shambles; students ask to be excused to rehearse or just do not come to class. They are so involved in the preparation for that evening it would be impossible for them to concentrate on the lesson anyway. This offended me a bit by implying that my class was not a top priority. After I attended my first "*Szalagavató*," as the performance is called, I understood its importance to them. It was a dance program and began with an old Hungarian folk dance. A number from *Hair* an American musical of the 1960s, followed and both were impressively performed. Hungarian students might be expected to do the centuries-old folk dances well, but they also caught the mood and spirit of the piece from *Hair* perfectly! Next came an original dance choreographed by one of the students, very modern, and surprisingly good. The highlight for me was a gorgeously costumed, and very lively "can-can;" the output of energy was extraordinary! After that, the audience was ready for the final number, a Viennese waltz, performed with the grace and beauty usually attributed to Franz József 's court in the old days of the Austro-Hungarian Empire. The gowns may not have cost as much as those worn by Viennese countesses, but those titled ladies were surely no more beautiful than the lovely young girls wearing diaphanous pastel colored, bouffant-skirted costumes. Instead of fancy, elaborately decorated Empire uniforms, the young men wore elegant, emphatically unmilitary dinner jackets. They swept across the wooden gymnasium floor with the stately grace of courtiers and their ladies gliding across the marble floors of the Hofburg Imperial Palace.

The program seemed a perfect metaphor of the transitional period the people of Hungary were living through – a mixture of the old and the new, the traditional and the experimental. How could one even think of the term "leaden-eyed" in connection with these young people after this demonstration of their clear perception about their life and times.

One day before the actual graduation ceremony, the *"Ballagás"* there were no classes. It was the day of the "Mad Ball" or the *"Bolond Ballagás,"* when students wore ridiculous outfits, somewhat like dressing up on Halloween. This is a kind "Roast" of the school and the teachers, a time when students may satirize the school as an institution and individual faculty members if they want to. An outdoor picnic on the school grounds was included in the day's program.

That night before the *"Ballagás"* the graduating students who would be the center of attention at the next day's ceremony got little if any sleep, and the third year students almost surely had none. The graduating seniors spent most of the night paying tribute to their teachers of the past four years by serenading them under their windows. They requested permission to do this, and asked each teacher to set the hour for their appearance. No one had prepared me for this custom and I had a social engagement in Budapest that evening. They assured me it was no problem; the serenading goes on all night, and they would come at whatever hour I set. Late in the evening after I returned home, they arrived, carrying lighted candles, and as I had been told to do in recognition of the tribute,

I placed a lighted candle in the window to burn during the serenade. Not all the graduating students knew English, of course, so they sang a couple of Hungarian songs and then those who could do so sang for me, in English, "My Bonnie Lies Over the Ocean," pronouncing it "Bony." I made a note to teach them another song for next year.

While the seniors were going through the community serenading their teachers, the third-year students were decorating the school with fresh flowers. The next morning flowers were everywhere: the fence around the school area was festooned, the gate was completely covered in fresh spring flowers, and the pathway from the gate to the front door was bordered on both sides with iris, tulips, stock, lilies, narcissus, daffodils, lilacs, everything that was in bloom in the middle of May. Inside, the building was decorated throughout with more Spring flowers. Bouquets were tied to the stairway banisters and sprays covered open wall spaces. Garlands were strung along window sills; nosegays decorated doors. The junior class had most certainly worked all night long; the school was transformed into a flower garden. The classrooms were also filled with flowers and teachers were invited to specific rooms. One student in the room I went to made a speech thanking the teachers for their excellent teaching and apologizing for having been inattentive and other flaws during their four years. Then each teacher received a gift from the students. Mine was a large dark green ceramic wine pitcher which I treasure.

The name "*Ballagás*" which is translated as "Commencement Parade" comes from the song "*Ballag már a vén diák*" (The Old Student is Walking). The graduating students walk through the classrooms bidding farewell to their school, and through the Teachers' Room (*tanári*) to say goodbye to their teachers. No student should miss this ceremony and the system is designed to insure that all who attend the school for four years can participate. If, as John Lukács wrote, there were in the late 19th and early 20th century some suicides among students during the week preceding final examinations, that possibility has now been eradicated by the custom of holding the commencement parade on Saturday morning before examination week. This was confusing until I learned that diplomas or certificates of graduation are not passed out at that ceremony. They are presented individually, may even be mailed, to the students following the successful completion of the examinations. Once I grasped the significance of this it seemed an inspired concept. All students join their classmates of the past four years in the social affairs and ceremonies associated with graduation, and if they fail an examination, it can be taken again later, and after it has been successfully passed the student receives the certificate of graduation. Thus, no one is embarrassed by the public revelation that he or she failed an examination and is at the last minute excluded from the ceremony after the family has gone to the effort and expense of preparing for the event.

Two years as a Peace Corps teacher went by so fast and kept me so busy that when they ended, I realized my interest in Hungary had not yet ended. There had not been time for many things I wanted to see and do. So I moved to Budapest where I rented a flat near the central Váci Street and only a couple of blocks from the Danube River. When the fall school term began, some of my former students who were still at the gymnasium came to visit me occasionally. I asked about their new English teacher, a young Hungarian man who had just graduated from the university. One said, "He is a very good teacher, but..." and paused as if he was at a loss for words. Thinking I knew what stopped him, I prompted, "It must be nice to have a teacher who is of your own generation." That unloosed his tongue. "Oh, no, that's just it! He's not like us. You were like us!" That may be the finest compliment I ever received.

In 1996, I attended the *"Ballagás"* of the first class I taught, those students who entered the gymnasium in 1992, the year I arrived. The school building and area were, as at the first commencement ceremony I attended, transformed into what appeared to be a flower garden in full bloom. Lilacs and tulips were especially bountiful that year and the Junior Class had outdone themselves with festoons of lilacs dripping from the upper and lower window sills, from door lintels and frames, and tied with ribbons to stairway banisters. Daisies, ferns, tulips, and iris were attached in clusters to the walls. It is customary for family and friends to present graduates with bouquets of Spring flowers, roses, lilies, gladioli and whatever is in bloom, which the students hold in their arms as they parade through the school. Even some of the tallest, strongest young men seemed to have more flowers than they could comfortably carry. My attention, however, was riveted on one of my favorite former students, one who I thought might be among those most likely to "do quaint deeds." She carried only one very large bouquet, composed of purple and white turnips, carrots, broccoli, kohlrabi, curly lettuce, radishes, artistically arranged and surrounded by leafy vegetables in a variety of shades of green! Although I could take no credit for her, I wept with pride. It was an emotional experience, moving and somehow rewarding, just to be there and to stand with the other teachers in the *tanári* when the graduates marched through.

The graduating students did not expect me, and the light in their eyes, the happy smiles of many were all the reward I needed for my effort to be present. Some of them reached out to touch me as they marched past, one or two threw a kiss, and one young woman paused for us to exchange the Hungarian cheek kisses. That graduating class was special, not just for me – all secondary school graduations in Hungary were special that year. It was the first year that all graduating students had gone through the entire four years of secondary-school education under the revised democratic system.

NOTES FROM THE JOURNAL – THE ŐRSÉG: BEHIND THE BACK OF GOD

The Days of the Flowers (*Virágzás Napjai*) convention in the Spring of 1994 was held in the village of Őriszentpéter in an area called "The Őrség" on the westernmost border of Hungary. It is so remote that people who live there used to say it was situated "behind the back of God." It was a place I had long wanted to visit so I was thrilled when my friend and neighbor, Anikó, invited me to attend a four-day meeting there devoted to the arts and the environment.

In spite of its lush forests and rolling hills, The Őrség did not attract early settlers. Its soil is poor, mostly clay, winters are harsh, and it rains so much that earlier houses were built around a courtyard with adjoining porches so neighbors could talk with each other. But in the 10th century, it was a vulnerable outpost that had to be guarded, and the Magyar tribal leader sent his best soldiers there to defend the border. As compensation for this hardship assignment, those who went and their descendants were exempt from taxation and other exactions associated with serfdom. Many of the inhabitants today bear the same names as the original 10th century soldiers. Their isolation afforded them a measure of autonomy and The Őrség became a largely self-governing community, remote enough to ignore and usually to be ignored by the central government. That situation changed when the communists came to power in the late 1940s. Its proximity to the West made the area a possible escape route for Hungarians who wanted to leave the country. It had never been easy to traverse, but then the government actively discouraged travel to and through it. Maps were not available and there were no street or road signs – still true when we went there in 1994. The community that had for centuries been a barrier against invaders from the outside was turned into an obstruction in the path of insiders who wanted to get out. Today, The Őrség is still a guard post, but a different kind. Because of its isolation, much of its medieval architecture and life style have been preserved – electricity came only after World War II, and the soil is still tilled by plow horses – it has become a guardian of Hungary's past.

Some of the earliest settlers used the clay soil to produce excellent pottery that has almost disappeared, and built what came to be called "bun-topped houses," with rounded thatched roofs that had one short side where the roof did not come all the way down to the top of the outer wall. This left an opening for the smoke from the pottery ovens to escape. The tiny village of Pityerszer is now an "open air museum," where some of these houses can be seen in their original state.

Anikó said we would travel in her car and told me to meet her in the parking lot between our buildings in the afternoon of the day the convention opened. When I arrived in the parking lot, I was surprised to see two other people with her, a couple from England, Tony and Mária (I will call them). After hasty introductions, we stowed our luggage, and departed as quickly as possible. There was no hostelry for large groups in Őriszentpéter so meeting participants were housed in private homes. We hoped to arrive in time to find our accommodations and attend the opening program that evening. On the way I found out that Mária, who had a beautiful British accent, was actually Hungarian. She had moved to England with her mother in 1956 when she was a young child. Her mother had died recently and Mária had come back to Hungary with her British husband to visit the place where she and her mother had lived, Nagykanizsa, about 60 kilometers south of Őriszentpéter. They were intelligent, attractive and very charming, and I began to enjoy the expedition immediately in spite of the rain that had set in and showed no sign of letting up. We arrived later than we planned, and I was worried that we might miss the first event of the evening, which I particularly wanted to see. It was billed as a film based on a play by Thornton Wilder, but nobody said which one. We went directly to the building where the film was shown, a large wooden structure that served the purpose of a City Hall, or more accurately, "Village Hall." The program indicated that it was the "Mayor's Office."

We were greeted at the door by the film's director, Péter Sülyi, and someone found seats for us in the very crowded room where a screen had been set up at one end. The title of the film was "*Itt a Földön Is,*" ("On Earth as it is in Heaven"), "Thy will be done," from The Lord's Prayer being understood. I am not sure which Wilder play it was based on, but it might have been a one-act play called "Pullman Car Hiawatha," which, like the film, takes place on a train. The only similarity is that they are both about a woman dying on a train before it reaches its destination. The photography by András Dér was well done and the interesting film seemed very short in spite of the uncomfortable seats and limited vision - the screen was too low. After the film, a buffet supper was served at the neighboring village day nursery, but we asked if we could go first to our lodgings and were guided there – we would never have found it otherwise. A very cheerful, pleasant woman directed us over several one-lane roads to a place where she said we should park the car. With no house in sight, we took our bags and walked down a narrow path covered with pebbles that were slick from the rain, then turned off into a field of wet, knee-high grass. The house was on the other side of the field. It wasn't far we realized later, but it seemed so under the circumstances. However, the trek was quickly forgotten when we saw what a very nice place it was, a whole house with two bedrooms, a spacious kitchen-living room with a small enclosed porch attached. The bathroom had everything that was necessary including a hot-water tank that Tony later coaxed into operation. Our guide showed us where the light switches were, how to turn on the stove, and gave us keys. By then, it was about 11 p.m., and we were very hungry, so we hurried back to the school house were supper was served. Having risen at 5 a.m. that morning and taught a full school day before starting the trip, I was hoping the day would end after we ate, but it was not to be.

A reading of the poetry of József Attila, an early 20th century avant-garde poet whose work (and suicide at the early age of 32) has inspired several generations of young poets, was scheduled to follow the supper at the school, but it was decided to move it to a more intimate setting, the home of a well-known Hungarian actor. He was a member of the organizing committee for the meeting, but was performing in Budapest at that time and was not present. So the whole group moved in a caravan, as only the leaders knew the way, and we soon arrived at the large modern house nestled in the woods with no nearby neighbors. We sat in roomy armchairs, and on upholstered couches, or fat pillows on the floor. It was indeed not only a more intimate setting but a great deal more comfortable. The "reading" turned out to be a recitation by the actor Fenyő Ervin, who had been in the cast of the film shown earlier in the evening. His knowledge of Attila's poetry was remarkable. He recited for almost two hours, and never looked at a note! Unfortunately, my own appreciation of the performance was somewhat dampened by the fact that I had been up for almost twenty hours.

It was after 2 a.m. before we finally fell into our beds. The next morning we slept until 8 a.m. which did not give four people much time to take turns in the bathroom, get dressed, have breakfast in a strange kitchen, walk through the weeds to the car and get to the school house for the morning program. We were a little late. We had missed the first part of a chorus concert by school children, but were in time for a long dissertation on the environment, a philosophical commentary on how man sees himself or should see himself in relation to his environment, given in rapid-fire Hungarian. Even with Mária and Anikó interpreting for me in discreet whispers, I missed most of it.

At lunch that day, Mária said she and Tony wanted to go to Nagykanizsa, and suggested that if Anikó and I did not want to miss the program, she and Tony would like to borrow the car and drive there the next day, Sunday. Having looked at the program, I said I would prefer to go to Nagykanizsa, whereupon Anikó said if we were all going she too would like to go. And that simple decision led to what was for me one of the most moving episodes of my years in Hungary.

The rain stopped and the next morning was sunny and clear. We still got lost a couple of times but finally got on the right road. It was obvious that the city of Nagykanizsa was very important to Mária, but I felt that I should not ask why. She telephoned to someone there before we left the village, and at least twice on the way we stopped for her to telephone again. She said someone would meet us in Nagykanizsa. When we reached the city, Mária directed us to the place where we were to meet a woman who had been a lifelong friend of her mother. Obviously following a plan she and Mária had worked out, she told us to park the car, and led us on a walking tour through what had been before World War II the Jewish Quarter of the City. She knew the area very well and identified many buildings for us. ("That's where the bakery used to be. Do you remember it, Mária?") She told us about some former buildings that had disappeared, and new modern structures stood in their place. We came to a wooden wall with a locked gate, also wooden, wide enough for an automobile to drive through. Our guide had a key and opened the gate for us to walk in, then locked it behind us. She led us into a building and up a flight of stairs to a room where Jews had secretly held their religious services during the German occupation and the despotic reign of the Hungarian fascistic Arrow Cross that between them wiped out most of the Jewish population in the entire country, Nagykanizsa included. I learned that Mária's mother had been married in the 1940s and had two small daughters. Her husband, who was in poor health, and the children were sent to Auschwitz. It is not known how the father died, but the little girls were among a large group of children that were taken on a boat out into the midstream of a river where the boat was blown up. Mária's mother who was in good health was sent to a labor camp where she survived by having the strength to walk several miles to a factory each morning, work twelve hours, and walk back to her barracks every evening. After the war, she married again and Mária was born, knowing only that she had two half sisters who died at Auschwitz. Her father died while she was a small child and after the 1956 Revolution she and her mother escaped to England.

We went back to the car and drove several kilometers out of the city to a synagogue and the cemetery surrounding it. Workmen were industriously constructing a tiny synagogue out of the ruins of what had obviously been a much larger one. The workers told us that the membership of the synagogue then numbered 30, whereas there had been 2000 members before World War II. The small new structure, nearly complete, was very modern, with simple almost severe design, but it was hard to see how such a small membership could afford even that. They said that donations by people from other places, including the United States, made the rebuilding possible.

We walked out into the park-like cemetery, the gravestones, monuments, and markers neatly lined up between and beneath many old, very tall trees. An *"allée"* of chestnut trees, so tall that their tops met, formed a woodland Gothic cathedral down the middle. As I strolled at random enjoying the peace, the trees, the order, I realized that Mária was methodically going up and down the rows and reading each marker. At one she suddenly stopped. We sensed that she had found what she was looking for and the rest of us went to join her. "Here it is," she said. It was a memorial plaque, engraved with the names of her mother's first husband, and Mária's two half sisters, and the simple statement that they had died in Auschwitz in 1945. She was seeing it on behalf of her mother who had never been able to do so. Her quiet grief was more for her mother than for the people she had never known, but it moved all of us to silent, painful memory of a terrible time in the world when human beings suffered unbearable horror. I understood why she had been so intent upon visiting Nagykanizsa. Her husband put his arm around her.

We got lost again on the return trip but eventually found our way back to Őriszentpéter. The "Days of the Flowers" conference was turning out to be quite different from what I had expected. Each day's program was enticing, but I wanted to see more of the area. The next day I suggested that we skip a cello concert and go to see more of The Őrség, especially the medieval churches. To my surprise, and delight the others agreed.

First we went to Ják, a small village on the western edge of Őriszentpéter to see the church built in 1256 and still in use. One of the best examples of

Romanesque architecture in Hungary today, it is also an example of the "conspicuous consumption" of the nobility of the middle ages. It was built by the Ják clan whose wealth is displayed by carvings of stone frogs, dragons, leering lions – one with a human head in its paws symbolizing man in the grip of evil – on the walls and in every nook and corner.

On the door of the Romanesque church at Vellemér, smaller than the one at Ják but prized by art historians for its 14th century frescoes, a sign told us where to find the woman in the village who keeps the key. She welcomed us warmly and came with us to open the door. Although it was a bright day, I found the frescoes too faint to see and soon gave up and went outside and talked with the woman who opened the door. She was waiting to lock it again after we left.

Like all people who live in isolated communities she was pleased to talk with an outsider, but her knowledge about the church and its history was very limited. Anyway, she was more interested in finding out about me than in telling me about the church. My companions stayed for a long time there, and when we left, we drove through the villages and saw other churches from the outside including the Protestant ones built by the early German settlers. Religion in the area had a contentious past. In the 17th century Counter-Reformation Protestant churches were appropriated, Lutheran bibles had to be smuggled in (in wine barrels, they say) and some Protestants were massacred by Catholic mobs. But today's interdenominational climate was evident as conference music programs were scheduled in both the Catholic church and the Reform church of Őriszentpéter.

In the poor villages where no rich medieval noblemen built churches and the citizens could not afford to build one, they made do with a belfry and the towers of wood and thatch are still standing in several places.

The conference program was so rich with instrumental and vocal concerts, lectures, drama and discussions that I felt guilty about missing much of it. On the last day, sunny, no rain, I dutifully attended an outdoor lecture on a plan for people to work together in 12-family units to produce organic food. It did not have much relevance to my life and went far toward assuaging my guilt about skipping some of the others.

On the way home, Anikó drove and Mária, Tony and I sang English and American folk songs, Ben Jonson's "Drink To Me Only With Thine Eyes;" "Down by the Old Mill Stream"; and a particular favorite of mine in which the sunflower is a symbol of enduring love: Eben Eugene Rexford's "Silver Threads Among the Gold," the last lines of which are:

For the heart that has truly loved never forgets
But as truly loves on to the close
As the sunflower turns on her God when he sets
The same look which she turned when he rose.

We got lost on the way home and arrived quite late, but nobody seemed to mind.

IX

HOME BESIDE THE DANUBE

L iving in a foreign country under the aegis of an American agency is a decidedly different proposition from living there on one's own. During my two years as a teacher with the Peace Corps, the school gave me a furnished apartment, including utilities. Health care and a living allowance for food and other necessities were provided by the Peace Corps. Embarking on a longer stay in Hungary as a private person with no official connection challenged my adaptability, resourcefulness and personal courage in ways that went far beyond the challenges I encountered during the first two years.

It might have been somewhat easier in another city, but as far as I was concerned Budapest was the only place to live in Hungary, putting me into agreement with about twenty percent of the Hungarian population. Ever since Buda, Pest, and Óbuda were fused on the last day in 1872 to form the capital city of Budapest, it has been home to approximately one-fifth of the country's population. That resplendent city suffered severe damage in late 1944 and early 1945 when the Soviet troops entered Hungarian territory and were opposed by the occupying German forces and their fascist allies, the Hungarian Arrow Cross. After fierce tank battles in the Transdanubia area around Lake Balaton and a six-week siege of Budapest, the retreating Germans blew up all the bridges across the Danube River connecting Pest and Buda and destroyed bridges throughout the country, even those across small streams. They dismantled and carried away most of the factories of Budapest, and confiscated anything movable – machines, wagons, carriages, foodstuff, works of art, the gold of the Hungarian treasury – to take away with them. That which could not be carried away was wrecked or made unusable; railroad tracks were uprooted or otherwise ruined; roads were demolished, factory buildings and other structures were damaged or destroyed.

The Budapest bridges were rebuilt with remarkable speed using the original drawings, except for the Elizabeth Bridge, built at the turn of the century and for many years the largest arched bridge in the world. It was replaced in the early 1960s by a modern suspension bridge. Most of the damaged infrastructure, some factories and official buildings were also replaced or repaired. But many large, sturdy old residences that had escaped undamaged or with only external scars were neglected and poorly maintained although they continued to be occupied. Some of those same buildings were at the center of the fighting during the 1956 Revolution and their exteriors were further damaged and scarred but the need for housing was such that only essential repairs were made and people still lived in them.

My only comparable previous experience was in Tokyo with my foreign correspondent husband, having arrived there very soon after the Japanese surrender that ended World War II. The residential areas had been almost entirely destroyed by fire bombs and it was a long time before rebuilding could begin. Quite a few large old houses built of stone or other substantial materials survived the bombings but were made untenable by damage to power and water lines throughout the city. Journalists were not officially part of the occupation forces and did not have access to army housing or authorization to purchase food and other items at the army commissary; therefore, we had to compete with the general population for housing and consumer goods in a market where shortages of everything made people desperate. We finally rented a house that had no electricity until we managed to "acquire" a transformer and have it installed on an electric pole in the street near the house.

The housing situation that existed in Budapest after 1989 was certainly not as bleak as that in Tokyo in 1945, but it was daunting. Many old mansions that were formerly one-family residences had been converted into flats to accommodate several families. Most of them were constructed in an era before electricity and running water were standard in residential architecture, and those amenities had been superimposed upon the original structure later with more of an eye to the practical than to the esthetic value. And then, when big houses were divided into flats, wires and piping had to be re-routed and the result was likely to be inconvenient and insufficient and sure to be unsightly. No effort seemed to have been made to conceal or even camouflage pipes and wiring. One wonders if, because of their modernness, they were left exposed as a status symbol, recalling the story that some people in the United States put their first electric refrigerators out on the front porch and left the door open and the light on at night to impress their neighbors.

Following Hungary's conversion to democracy in 1989 the influx of foreign capital brought an influx of business people and foreign personnel, who further strained the already inadequate housing resources in Budapest. Large corporations, embassies, and well-heeled entrepreneurs could pay high rents and thus pick off the best houses and apartments. Coming along in 1994, with no official connection and without entrepreneurial-level affluence, I was discouraged at every turn, assured by everyone that it would be impossible to find a comfortable place at an affordable price. Thus I started the search already prepared to make compromises, to accept something that was less than ideal. My first tour with a rental agent to look at available places not only reinforced that resolve but convinced me that I must go even further and be prepared to settle for something that was not even within shouting distance of ideal.

One of the first flats I saw was in a large, solidly-built old mansion just off a broad tree-lined boulevard, obviously once a single-family home that had been divided into smaller units. The exterior needed cleaning, sandblasting, not a drawback as far as I was concerned; the layers of dirt and pollution gave it a patina of age and dignity. The trash in the courtyard and hallways, on the other hand, gave it an air of neglect. At first glance, it was an astonishingly attractive place. The living room was furnished, over-furnished, actually, with antique furniture of the 19th century, so much that there was scarcely room to walk through. Beautiful oil paintings hung on two long walls from ceiling to below eye level, and the floor was covered with oriental rugs. French doors along a third wall led to an outside balcony. Even though it was dusty and littered with the possessions of the departing tenant who was packing to leave the country, even though it had not had a good cleaning or airing for some time, my first thought was, "What a find!" Then we entered a doorway in the fourth wall that led to the kitchen. The agent pointed out the conveniences, stove, tiny refrigerator but I was so beguiled by the living room that I could not focus on it for a few minutes. When I really looked at it I saw that the stove was only a two-burner hot plate, no oven, that I would have to kneel to reach into the refrigerator, and that something seemed to be missing. Oh, yes. A kitchen sink. "There's no sink!" I blurted out. The agent didn't bat an eye, "Certainly there is," he replied smoothly, "right there, in the bathroom." And, indeed there was a sink in the bathroom. One had only to cross the large living room to reach it. Reluctantly, I passed on that one, but it prepared me somewhat for other places I would be invited to consider.

One place I saw was so sparkingly clean and neat I almost took it without further examination, which would have been a mistake. It was very modern, as the bachelor-owner pointed out with particular emphasis on the shower curtain. Hand-held showers are standard bathroom equipment in Hungary, and rarely ever is there a rod or other framework on which a shower curtain could be hung. The owner of that apartment was eager to display its cosmopolitan accouterments such as, in addition to the shower curtain, a built-in bar in the living room. Aside from the fact that I really did not need a bar in the living room, that not-very-large room turned out to be also the dining, sleeping, working room. In other words, with the addition of a small bathroom and tiny kitchen, that was it. When he led me out to a minuscule balcony with a glorious view of the Buda Hills, I began to think perhaps the dollhouse dimensions of the place might be tolerated. But sanity returned as I recalled that we reached the building by climbing uphill on foot. Even if one had an automobile, which I did not, there was no road, so all groceries or other packages would have be hand carried uphill in all weather. And there were sure to be at least a few days every winter when the hill would be covered with ice. It was with a tinge of regret that I said No to that one. But it was with no regret whatsoever that I passed up the next one.

The man who owned that apartment described himself as a theatre director, and indeed, the place did suggest a particular kind of stage set, perhaps an Italian bordello of the early 20th century. The kitchen, at the entry, was small and clearly inconsequential. No pots or pans, no cooking utensils were on view. Next there was a small foyer-size area that he called the living-dining room. A small round table with three chairs – the kind that were seen in early 20th century ice cream parlors – sat at the end near the kitchen. At the other end was a red plush sofa and two matching overstuffed chairs crammed together around a tiny rectangular table. It suggested a waiting room. The real centerpiece of the flat was the bedroom. It was larger than all the rest put together, and the very large bed in the center of the room occupied most of the space, leaving only room on one side for a small red-velvet-upholstered love seat and two matching chairs arranged around a dainty coffee table. The bed itself was covered in a brilliant red satin coverlet with ruffles cascading to the floor. There were paintings on the wall which I glanced at and quickly glanced away when I saw that they were all the same genre – female nudes in various poses. It embarrassed me to look at them in the presence of the male rental agent and the male owner.

Eventually, I rented an apartment that impressed me so much from its general appearance that I agreed to take it without asking the right questions or making a very careful inspection of it. I prefer to think it was because I was exhausted after a long day in which I had seen so many places that my perceptions were dulled, rather than admit it was just stupidity. The spacious entrance hall lit by a ceiling light with a pseudo-Tiffany lampshade misled me from the start. True, the very ornate wall paper patterned with deep red flocking was a bit too much, but the oriental floor covering and the elegant wooden hall-tree made up for it. In the living room wooden shelving covered one long wall; nice rugs on the floor; a radio, tape and record-player combination; a television set that the owner said was new (not true); attractive upholstered couch with two matching chairs, and a coffee table, or "smoking table" as they are called in Hungary. A small white ceramic fountain stood near the windows; it was electrically operated to produce a gentle spray of water over the artificial ivy arranged in the bowl of the fountain. Its saving grace was that it could be turned off. In the corner there was a built-in bar with a hanging lamp over it and on the wall behind it shelves for glassware. I saw immediately that with a slightly raised chair, the bar could be a desk and the shelves used to store stationery supplies. That corner was probably the deciding factor, since I seem not to have explored the rest of the place very thoroughly.

In the large bedroom, what looked to be at least a king-size bed stood with its ornate headboard centered against the back wall. Although the resulting appearance was of a wide one-piece bed, it was two Hungarian-style couch-beds joined together. Each one had a compartment for storing bedclothing, very practical. There was a small table of white lacquered wood on each side of the bed, and a chest of drawers opposite the bed, also white lacquered. One side of the room was all closet with mirrored doors. The outside wall was all windows with several large potted plants in front of them.

In the bathroom the large tub made me think of a small swimming pool, deep enough that an inside ledge served as a step to make the entry gradual, or it could be a seat. I described it to friends as a bathtub that seated three, or if they were all good friends, four. All the fixtures – wash basin, toilet, bidet, tub – were blue. Painted on the blue tile walls were woodland scenes. In such an opulent bathroom, how could I have failed to notice that there was a water bucket sitting on the wide rim the bathtub. Not only did I miss that, I also failed to notice that several things that should have been there were not – no towel rack or even a tiny hook to hang up a robe or towel, no medicine chest or supply cabinet, not even a shelf, and no electric outlet for a hair dryer.

The kitchen was large; there were two windows overlooking a courtyard, and even a breakfast alcove. A built-in upholstered banquette ran along one side and one end of the table, which seated four or in a pinch, six. The refrigerator was behind a beaded curtain; a large eat-in-kitchen would surely have a good refrigerator, I must have thought, as I glanced in its direction. Only when I moved in did I discover that it was so low I had to kneel to get access to it, and that the door to the tiny freezing compartment was broken off. The counter space between the stove and sink was not even wide enough to hold a dish drainer, a critical concern when dishes are washed by hand. There was no oven thermometer, so baking was impossible for me. Later I discovered that few Hungarian women have oven thermometers. Their delicious pastry is obviously the result of some secret Hungarian female legerdemain.

When I went to bed the first night, my attention was called to the water bucket on the rim of the bathtub by the sound of dripping water. The electric water heater, on the wall above the bucket, was turned on by the flow of the water, and automatically went off when the water was turned off. Only this one did not go off completely but continued to drip, so I heard water dropping into a metal bucket all night. I also discovered that those elegant white lacquered bedside tables contained no lamps. The very fancy chandelier of pink and white crystal that hung in the middle of the ceiling did not give enough light to read by but I tried anyway, and saw that I had to get up and cross the room to switch the light off, return to bed in the dark, and of course repeat the procedure if I had to get up in the middle of the night. So I brought the one table lamp from the living room to the bedside table and looked for an outlet to connect it. None. No electric outlet on the entire long wall behind the bed! The nearest outlet was across the room too far for the lamp cord to reach and there was no extension cord.

During the first days, I made a list of items to be discussed with the landlord: a cabinet or shelves and towel racks for the bathroom; lamps for the bedroom and extension cords to connect them; repairs to the water heater and the refrigerator. They were the main things; there were several smaller items. He looked the list over and agreed to take care of everything. He explained that it was not necessary to repair the water heater, that the bucket was there to solve that problem. When I complained that it was unsightly, he was unmoved, and when I added that the dripping noise interfered with my sleep, he said that would be easy to fix, and proceeded to fold a thick piece of cloth and put it in the bucket, saying it would muffle the noise. No lamps or extension cords ever came; the refrigerator was never repaired; no towel racks or hooks were installed in the bathroom. Appeals to the rental agency had no effect. The rental lease stipulated that either the landlord or the tenant could cancel upon giving the other 30-days notice, but I was reluctant to go through the trauma of finding and moving into another place and convinced myself that in spite of all the difficulties, I could make a comfortable home there. My Hungarian friends supported this idea by telling me I was lucky to find it; they assured me that it was better than most rental flats and that the same or worse problems existed everywhere. So, I undertook to make some improvements myself. I bought a reading lamp for the bedroom and an extension cord, also two towel racks, which a friend volunteered to install. Every month when I paid the rent, I reminded the landlord of his promises, and he always agreed saying he had not had time, but he did nothing and for every repair or improvement I made, something else would break down or go out of order. First the hanging lamp over the bar, my work center, ceased to function. A new bulb did not fix it; the fault was in the wiring. In reply to my frantic call, the landlord came and repaired it – at least four times. It would work for a few hours and then go out again. Finally he came one Sunday and spent the day re-wiring in places where furniture including heavy bookcases had to be moved; then it was fine. But soon after that the same thing happened to the light in the entrance hall. Since that wasn't necessary for my work, my call was not quite so frantic. It was several weeks before he came to repair it, after which it promptly went out again. Eventually, an electrician came and re-wired the hallway.

It was August when I moved in, and when cold weather came, I discovered that the gas radiator that heated the kitchen and the entrance hall did not work. After several unsuccessful attempts to repair it himself, over a period of several weeks, the landlord finally sent someone to repair it. While it was out, I used the stove oven to heat that area – no need for a thermometer to do that.

It was exacerbating enough to have so much of my time taken up with breakdowns and outages and inconveniences in the apartment, but as if he wanted to add to my discomfort, every month when I paid the rent, the landlord said he was raising the rent and asked for more than the lease stipulated. Ignoring his requests, I reminded him of our lease, and told the rental agency about it. They assured me that he had no right to ask for a higher rent. Standard two-year rental leases in Hungary at that time contained a clause stating that the rent amount could be re-negotiated after one year if the Hungarian rate of inflation exceeded 10% during that year. At the time my lease was signed, the inflation rate was running between 24-28%, so it was a fair and reasonable provision, but it was neither fair nor legal for the landlord to raise the rent before one year had elapsed.

With all its drawbacks that place had some quite desirable features. It was , near Moscow Square, about halfway up the *Vár* (Castle Hill), and so within walking distance of Buda Castle which now houses the National Library, the Hungarian National Gallery and the Museum of History. Also on the *Vár* is the gorgeous Matthias Church (*Mátyás templom*), the "Coronation Church," originally built in the 13th century and renovated through the centuries in various architectural styles until the late 19th century when it was reconstructed in its present neo-Gothic style. Across the street from the church is the Budapest Hilton Hotel – wait a minute. Hilton Hotel? Yes. It was designed to incorporate ruins of a 13th century monastery, and from its lounge on the first floor can be seen one of Budapest's most satisfying views. Over the monastery ruins and across the Danube River the fantastic (that is the only word for it) Hungarian Parliament Building is framed in the window that forms the lounge's fourth wall. Whenever possible, I always take visitors there, and when I lived nearby I used to walk up there just to sit alone and contemplate the scene. What led the Hilton organization to that happy architectural design is an interesting story, but it is enough to say that it is one of those remarkable inspirations with which a capitalistic enterprise occasionally stuns the non-capitalistic world.

In the apartment, the abundance of book shelves was a joy as were the radio-tape player and the television set for music, weather reports, and some news. Occasionally, I could even get CNN on television. So, in spite of everything, I might have remained there except for an incident that finally made it impossible.

Early one evening I was doing laundry in the bathroom when the telephone rang. My phone rang so seldom in those days that it was startling. Quickly drying my hands, I rushed to answer, hoping the caller would not ring off before I got there. It wasn't necessary to hurry. Very few people had extension phones in Budapest so everybody patiently let the phone ring a long time before giving up. A man, speaking English with a very heavy Hungarian accent, did not give his name but started out by apologizing for disturbing me and said he was a former tenant in my flat. Then I recalled that I had found a new unopened package containing three pairs of men's socks on a closet shelf, and immediately asked if he was calling about that. But, no, that is not what he wanted. He said he had written a letter to Berta, the landlord's wife, addressed to my apartment, and he wanted me to deliver it to her. I said that I would of course be glad to deliver it, that I occasionally got mail for them, and that I had that very day given Andor, the landlord, some mail that had arrived for them. "You gave it to HIM?" I could hear the alarm in his voice. "You gave my letter to HIM?" A light began to dawn. "I gave him mail today that arrived over the last two weeks. When did you mail your letter?" He sounded relieved, and said, "I wrote it about 4:30 this afternoon. And I did not mail it; I put it into your box." I assured him that I had not taken it out of the box. With great urgency in his voice, he said, "Don't give it to him: give it directly to her." I said that I almost never saw her; it was Andor who came to make repairs or met me at the rental agency to collect the rent, and I had no idea when I would see her again. Still, he insisted that I should hold it until such time as I could hand it to her in person. This made me very uncomfortable but I did not know how to extricate myself at that point.

Greatly to my surprise, the next time Andor came to make a repair, she came with him. Reluctant as I was to become involved in what appeared to be something clandestine, my instincts were all against giving her the letter in front of her husband, so when he went out of the room at one point, I handed it to her without a word. She seemed only slightly surprised and put it into her handbag. I thought that was the end of it but a few days later, I received another call and another letter. Again, I protested that I did not expect to see her. But again he insisted that I hold the letter until I saw her, and again she appeared at the apartment on some rather flimsy errand and I gave her the letter. She asked me if he had given me his address, which he had not, and I suggested that perhaps I should give him her telephone number if he called again, and she looked frightened and said, "No, No." After a few weeks and several letters, Andor called me one day and without any greeting or lead-in, said very peremptorily, "Don't give my wife any more letters from ____" and named the man as if he knew him well. I tried to tell him that I had been dragged into that role against my will, but he hung up before I could do so. That provided the impetus I needed. No matter how difficult it would be or how unlikely it was another place would be better, it was clear that I had to move.

In spite of the gloomy predictions of my friends, I did find another and better place. It had the same amount of floor space but was more efficiently designed; there were three rooms in addition to the kitchen and bath, so I could have a separate work room that also doubled as a guest room when needed. It was owned by a young couple, both employed, who had moved with their young daughter to a single-family house in a Budapest suburb. The wife came each month to collect the rent, and always asked if everything was all right, if anything needed repair. At first, there were some (apparently usual) problems with the hot water supply and with the electric wiring, which her husband came and cheerfully repaired; if it was something he could not fix, they sent a professional to take care of it. The rent was the same as I paid at the first place, and the stipulations in the lease were the same. Although the inflation was beginning to decline it was still well above ten percent, so after the first year, I expected to renegotiate the lease. Instead of that, however, when the owner came to collect the twelfth-month payment, she said in an off-hand way, "The rent will be the same for the next year; we do not plan to renegotiate." This was so unexpected that I could hardly murmur a "Thank you." Afterwards, I decided that I should be prepared for a really hefty increase if I wanted to renew the least at the end of the two years. As it turned out, I did want to renew the lease and I told her so several months in advance. This was necessary because foreigners must have written evidence of an assured domicile in order to apply for a residence permit. And without a residence permit, one is a "tourist" with a limited stay of three months. A residence permit, therefore, eliminates the need to leave the country and return every three months. The following month, I again told her that I needed a new lease, and asked if we would have to visit the rental agent. She said that would not be necessary, that we would handle it personally. Then I said we should discuss the rent. She said, "Oh, yes, sure." But did nothing. Finally, as the expiration date on my residence permit came closer, one day when he was there, I tried to make him understand the urgency. "You know, I must have a new lease in order to apply for an extension of my residence permit." He also said, "Oh, yes, sure." But I persisted. "When will I get it, and how much will the rent be?" "Oh, the rent," he said. "What would you like to pay? Whatever suits you suits us." After a speechless moment or two, I said, "It's your apartment! I can't set the rent." And he repeated, "Yes, you can. Whatever suits you, suits us." So I was forced to set my own rent. Instead of going through a methodical calculation, taking the rate of inflation into account, I simply suggested an increase of 10,000 forints. He agreed immediately and seemed pleased. Afterwards, I figured out how that related to the past year's inflation and realized that it amounted to about 16.5 percent increase, whereas inflation had been between 20 and 25 percent. Their attitude is baffling and very "un-landlordish" in any culture I know about. My only guess as to their reasoning is that they are happy to have a tenant who enjoys the apartment and takes good care of it.

When I first looked at the apartment, they were clearly concerned about renting to a foreigner who might leave on very short notice, and whose Hungarian language was not fluent enough to make discussion easy. They insisted on a payment of three-months' rent in advance – two months' security and the rent for the upcoming month. One-month security is usual, but I agreed to their demand with only slightly raised eyebrows. Our negotiation took place with a rental agent and that may have been his recommendation. When I asked where and how I would pay the rent – all bills, rent, gas, electricity and telephone are paid in cash – the wife said she would come each month to collect it. That, I presumed, was a way to be sure that everything was in order, that I had not absconded with the furniture, set the place on fire, or painted the walls some hideous color. One serious drawback to living in well-kept rental quarters in Hungary is their practice of covering the walls with expensive wall-paper which makes it impossible to hang pictures. They do not want their tenant to hang pictures, apparently, as there are no moldings from which they might be suspended. This is, for me, a serious deprivation. The beautiful view from my living room window makes up for that somewhat but not entirely. And there is one wall in the living room covered with a poster scene from a tropical island, somewhere in the Caribbean, perhaps. That appalled me at first and I asked them if I could have it removed. The woman looked deeply hurt and said, "Oh, don't you like it?" And although she reluctantly agreed that I could remove it, I did not have the heart to do it, and I have learned to like it, or at least got used to it.

The fact is that we have become friends. They frequently bring me simple gifts, and on trips to the States, I bring their young daughter something from America, a place from which any gift seems to be a treasure. I have visited their quite large home in the suburbs on a spacious lot with fruit trees, and even a small swimming pool. One could not ask for a pleasanter landlord-tenant relationship.

From my apartment, it takes about five minutes to walk to the Belgrade quayside of the Danube River that extends from the Szabadság bridge to the Erzsébet bridge, where boats arrive from and leave for Vienna. The yellow Baroque Serbian Church stands across the street in a walled churchyard where seasonal flowers and shrubs bloom beneath acacia and linden trees. The gate is locked, and for additional protection, anyone who approaches or only passes by is threatened by a large dog with a loud, deep-throated bark, except on Sunday

morning from 10 a.m. to noon when he is banished during church services. That
is the only time visitors can enter the church or the churchyard. Around the corner
on Papnövelde Street is the twin-towered University Church with a clock in each
spire. Bells ring on the quarter-hour with a soft resonance that gently reminds and
does not disturb. They ring louder on the hour, and fifteen minutes before services
--Mass on Sunday morning and Vespers every evening. And they ring very loud
and long once a day at noon as in Christian churches throughout the world since
1456. This daily pealing of the bells reminds Hungarians of János Hunyadi's great
victory in July 1456 when he defeated the Turks at Nándorfehérvár (Belgrade,
today) and stymied the Ottoman expansion into Europe for nearly a century.The
clocks frequently stop running or show the wrong time, but the bells ring
faithfully at the correct times.

The renewed extension of Váci Street, south of Elizabeth Bridge, the location
of some of Budapest's most elegant designer boutiques, parallels the street I live
on. There are six or eight movie houses within walking distance, as are the Gellért
Hotel, the Taverna, Astoria and Korona hotels, the superb Apostolok and
Százeves restaurants and many others. Even the Opera House on Andrássy Street
is near enough to walk to in nice weather. And the superabundant City Market
(*Vásárcsarnok*) is within not only walking but grocery-carrying distance! When
friends see the place and find out how much rent I pay (Hungarians always ask,
just as they always ask how much you earn), they say it isn't possible. They have
almost convinced me that I am only making it up.

NOTES FROM THE JOURNAL – VACATION IN, WELL, CROATIA

When I heard Hungarians say they were going to Croatia on a vacation even before the United Nations peacekeeping force arrived there in 1992, I thought they were either insane or just joking. So it was a great surprise to find myself on Croatian soil while the Bosnian War was still going on. Not that I planned to go; it came about quite unexpectedly.

A few days after I moved into Budapest, my friend Peggy telephoned and asked me how I would like to go to Trieste for a long week-end, the next week-end, that is, beginning the day after tomorrow! Before I could ask her what she had been imbibing or protest that I had not even unpacked, she explained. She and another friend had planned the trip several weeks ago, bought the tickets, made reservations and an emergency had arisen at home and her friend had to leave for the United States immediately. Knowing that I am usually agreeable to traveling at any opportunity, she immediately called me. I didn't hesitate. "Wonderful idea!" I said. "Trieste," I thought. "Hmmmm. Italy. I must get some lira." American Express was the place I turned to for all currency transactions in those days. The clerk looked surprised and said she wasn't sure they had any lira, but she managed to scrape up 55,000, about $35, and I took it all.

We arrived after midnight on Friday and the next morning went to the Tourist Office near the train station to inquire about renting a car, thinking we might drive around the area, and perhaps go to Ljubljana to visit a friend. There were no rental cars available – they had all been taken, but we could not have gone to Ljubljana anyway. The tourist agent said we could not drive a rental car into Slovenia from Trieste – something to do with insurance. He urged us to take a boat trip along the Istrian Peninsula, saying that it was the most interesting way to spend a day or two in that area, and gave us a brochure describing the trip. An Italian boat, the "Marconi" went from Trieste to the island of Lussinpiccolo in the Adriatic Sea, and stopped at several places along the way. We did not want to go all the way, so we bought tickets as far as Brioni, planning to disembark there, have lunch, go for a walk, and re-board the boat on its return from Lussinpiccolo.

When the boat pulled out the next morning, it went North in the Gulf of Venice to pick up passengers at the small ports of Grado and Lignano. At Grado, Slovenian immigration and passport control officers checked our papers. Our next port of call was the Slovenian port of Piran. As we moved through the Gulf of Venice towards the Adriatic Sea, we began to understand the unique character of this multinational Peninsula jutting out from the southern end of Slovenia. The western edge of Croatia lay peacefully along its coast, largely unaffected by the Bosnian War or by the fighting that was still going on between ethnic Serbs and Croatians in Krajina.

When the Kingdom of the Serbs, Croats and Slovenes was stitched together after World War I from the provinces of Croatia, Dalmatia, Bosnia, Herzogovina, Slovenia, Vojvodina, and the independent state of Montenegro, and re-named Yugoslovaia, its jigsaw geography made the gerrymandered voting districts in the United States look almost reasonable. And when Slovenia and Croatia declared their independence in 1991, and established their new national laws, border controls, and currencies, the imponderables multiplied.

We did not get off the boat at Slovenian Piran, but when we stopped there, Croatian officials came aboard to check our papers. We thought that was for the next port, Croatian Umag, but we passed that up and went directly to Brioni and discovered that, in spite of its Italian-sounding name, we were in Croatia. We disembarked along with several other passengers who went off on a tour of the national park. We chose to go immediately to the rather nice looking hotel near the water's edge, with the idea of having lunch there. We assumed that such a modern-looking hotel would accept credit cards or if not, American dollars. So we confidently went into the dining room and ordered lunch, which was delicious and well-served. When our bill came, we were shocked to be told that they did not accept credit cards or American dollars, or any but the local currency, Croatian Kuna! All right. Where do we exchange money? Unfortunately (they were most apologetic) the hotel's money exchange window did not open until 3:30 in the afternoon, more than two hours later, and there was no other place in Brioni where currency could be exchanged. We offered them Hungarian forints, which they dismissed with barely a gesture, as if to say, "Surely you are joking." Between us we had only a small amount of lira after paying taxi fares in Trieste and buying the boat ticket to Brioni, but after they were convinced we had no other way to pay, they agreed to accept lira. We emptied out our handbags and pockets of all the lira we could find, including the smallest coins, and dumped it on the table. We suspected it was not enough, but they seemed satisfied.

We headed for the national park, the thickest woodland area we had seen along that coast, and the only one that seemed to have a variety of very large, old trees. For many years the forests on that peninsula like all of the Dalmatian coast was denuded by the Venetian boat builders, and by thieves, poachers, and poor peasants who cut down trees and sold them to boat builders or any other willing customer. Reforestation was difficult because young trees were easier to cut down that large old ones, so they disappeared before they reached the majestic proportions of ancient trees. In recent years, there has obviously been more success with replanting as we saw many clumps and clusters of young trees, but the coastline remains mostly barren. As soon as we entered the dark shade of the park, we drank in the smell of the cypresses and pines, enjoyed the occasional sunlight filtering through the leaves of poplars and beeches, relieved when we came to the dense, cooler spots where the tall, thick branches of plane trees, chestnuts and the older cypresses blocked out the strong sunshine. Since it is a National Forest, it is protected from desecration by marauders of any kind, and there were many large, old trees.

When it was time for the exchange window to open we hurried back to the hotel to buy kuna. We had no idea how much we would need, and asked the agent if we could pay for our boat tickets back to Trieste with kuna. He assured us that we could do so, and we bought enough for that.

When the boat returned from Lussinpiccolo, we lined up with the other passengers who had stopped off in Brioni, but when we reached the deck, the officer demanded our tickets. Only then did we realize that we should have bought round trip tickets. The agent in Trieste had not mentioned that fact. We said we would like to pay the fare to Trieste in cash. This was obviously not the proper procedure; but he reluctantly let us board, implying that we could pay our fare on the boat. This slight hold-up in boarding annoyed or at least aroused the curiosity of the other passengers, all of whom seemed to be Italian or, anyway, European – we were the only Americans – and we slunk to our seats, feeling that we had "let the side down" as the British say and trying to be as inconspicuous as possible. Our efforts were in vain. As soon as the boat left the dock, a stentorian announcement reverberated through the boat which we understood even though it was in Italian. Would those two passengers who do not have a ticket please report to the Captain. He refused to take our kuna, saying we had to pay in lira. We told him we had bought kuna, not lira, in Brioni to pay the boat fare, which we understood was acceptable. But not by him. He agreed, with some reluctance, to take American dollars. Spurning America dollars was something new in my experience, but later I heard what seemed a plausible explanation for it. In some of the newly independent countries few people outside of banks felt confident about calculating the exchange rates. And all currencies, including established ones, were undergoing such volatile fluctuations in the Bosnian war zone that it was risky to accept any currency except the one used by the business enterprise making the transaction. At that point, we realized that the kuna we had bought in Brioni was useless to us as we were on our way to Trieste. We asked the Captain if the boat would be stopping at any other Croatian port. He shook his head. Our crestfallen expressions must have touched his heart; he then said he could pause at Umag, where there was a shop right at the dock, and he would give us 3 minutes there to dispose of our kuna. When we pulled into Umag, we stood beside the Captain who had a gangplank laid down for us, and as we raced down it, he called, "Three minutes! You have three minutes!" I don't know whether he held a stopwatch in his hand, but certainly in my imagination he did. By this time, other passengers on the boat had lined up at the rail on that side to see what was happening, and as we ran towards the tiny kiosk, I felt sure they were saying, "These Americans! Wouldn't you know they have to shop!" There was almost nothing in the place to buy – whiskey and cigarettes, mainly, which neither of us wanted, some very cheap, commonplace souvenirs and postcards. We bought a few postcards, and ran back in something close to three minutes, still stuck with our Croatian currency. We hastened to our seats and sat very low in them hoping people would turn their attention to something else.

We had seen so little of the Istrian Peninsula and since we still had two more days, we decided to get off in Slovenian Piran which we had heard was a very pretty and charming port city. We had been given passport approval for entry into Slovenia earlier in the day at Grado, and we decided our currency situation couldn't be any worse there than any other place on the peninsula. The other passengers probably said whatever in their languages means "Good riddance!" as we departed, but the Captain, who either was a chivalrous Italian or was only amused by the whole event, bade us a smiling "Goodbye," and urged us to return for another trip sometime, as if we had made his day.

Our first view of Piran confirmed what we had been told. It was a beautiful town at the edge of the sparkling water, with flowers everywhere, and pastel colored buildings reminiscent of Southern California coastal towns. We chose a small but attractive pink stucco hotel and literally threw ourselves upon their mercy as soon as we approached the desk. It was Sunday, the banks were closed, we had only American and Croatian money and we were in Slovenia. The clerk responded immediately and soothingly; the hotel accepted credit cards so paying the hotel bill was no problem. But local restaurants would insist on Slovenian tolar. So the hotel gave us enough tolar in exchange for dollars so we could pay for dinner. Suddenly life was simple and the peninsula was paradise, and we just dropped our bags in the room and hurried out to look around. The Town Square, quite nearby, was round, not square, and had been turned into a roller rink. In the middle stood a prominent statue of Giuseppi Tartini, born in Piran in 1692, and surely the only virtuoso violinist in the world to preside over a roller rink. Preparations were underway for some kind of performance and we made a dinner reservation at a restaurant named Mario's with outside tables from which we would have a clear view of whatever was about to take place in the Square.

When we returned after dark for dinner, the rink was brilliantly lighted and a roller-blade exhibition was just starting. Groups of school-age children were there and more still arriving, all dressed in colorful costumes. There were several adults who appeared to be professionals. We decided it was a performance by recognized roller-blade experts in which the young ones were a kind of chorus line, but they were all very good. The dinner was delicious, and we enjoyed the roller-blading floor show. The only disappointment came at the end of the meal when we order Espresso, and they informed us that they served only Turkish coffee! No Espresso in a restaurant named "Mario's!" It reminded me of my indignation when I could not buy Pelligrino mineral water at a D'Agostino's Supermarket in New York! What's in a name? As Juliet Capulet asked, sighing over Romeo Montague! We settled for the Turkish coffee, ignoring the sludge, and chased it with another glass of wine.

The next morning we were at the bank when it opened, very unsure of how our request would be received. We wanted to exchange Croatian kuna for Italian lira in a bank where the local currency was Slovenian tolar, and we were not optimistic. But we were wrong. Like everyone else in Piran, the bank teller was most helpful and understanding. When we had disposed of our kuna and received enough lira for the return trip to Trieste, we also wanted to buy stamps to mail postcards, but didn't know how much they would cost. At the post office, we showed a clerk the cards we wanted to mail, and she obligingly calculated how much we would need, so we went back to the bank, and got enough tolar for cards plus a visit to the coffee shop where we sat at an outside table and addressed postcards. Peggy couldn't resist the water and went for a swim while I continued to sit and tried to gather my thoughts about our "weekend in Trieste" so far.

When large nations break up into smaller sovereign states, the rest of the world takes note of the geographical, geo-political., global significance. And if this occurs, as it usually does, in the course of military struggle, at least part of the world mourns the mayhem and carnage, and attempts to aid refugee migrations; they may decry human rights violations and all the other monstrosities, the strange fruit produced by the violent copulation of nations at war. But little thought is given to those fortunate people on the outskirts of the fray, whose houses are not looted and burned, whose men do not die, whose women and children are not raped and murdered, who are spared the most gruesome ravages of war. Yet they are not entirely spared. Imagine what it must be like to wake up one morning in the same house you were born in and have lived in all your life, to find that you are now the citizen of another country, that the documents certifying ownership of your home and other possessions are no longer officially registered with the government in control, and could be considered invalid, and that all the money you possess, even your life savings is in a currency no longer valid in your new place of abode. Their lives will never be the same again. All their anticipations, dreams, and hopes for the future of their children have vanished, and in their place there is nothing but fear and uncertainty. Our brief, sometimes amusing, efforts to cope with hastily drafted travel restrictions, new currencies, ill-informed border guards, can make us indifferent to the plight of those people who, in comparison with others who live with terrifying war on their doorstep, are not thought of as victims.

Under a cloudless blue sky, beside clear water sparkling in the golden sunshine, I was enveloped in a serene gold and blue world. As my thoughts turned to the hell that was so near, a shadow was suddenly cast over it all as if the sun had gone behind a cloud. Southward along the Dalmation coast and to the east of us were places named Dubrovnik, Sarajevo, Mostar and Banja Luka, where families, lives, homes, schools, churches, courts of justice, were disappearing, or had already been destroyed, some by the very same people who had created them, in their struggle to hold what they believed to be their rightful piece of the earth.

The cloud turned darker, and then came the guilt, black, black guilt. A quotation from Alexander Pope's "Epistle to Dr. Arbuthnot" in his "Essay on Man," came to mind. Written with a very different meaning, it aptly described my feeling, "Thou stand'st unshook amidst a bursting world."

NOTES FROM THE JOURNAL – HUNGARIAN CHRISTMAS

On Christmas Eve in predominantly Catholic Hungary, Baby Jesus comes to bring the Christmas tree and presents to children. On that day, everything in Hungary stops soon after midday; everybody goes home. All public transportation ceases; all businesses, offices, shops and retail markets are closed, and children must be taken out on some excursion so "Baby Jesus," like Santa Claus, can arrive in secret. Early on December 24th, I took a bus from Budapest to Budaörs and brought the two children of my friends, Dóri and László, to Budapest. We had an early lunch at McDonalds, the restaurant of their choice, then took the last tram of the day to the Kempinski Hotel on Deák Square. There, they stood open-mounted in front of the enormous Christmas tree in the middle of the lobby. The gingerbread house beside the tree was large enough for a small child to walk into except it was wisely protected by a gingerbread fence. It was bitterly cold but we walked along Váci Street viewing the Christmas decorations, more elaborate that year, my third Christmas in Hungary, than I had seen in any previous year. The attempts at public decoration in stores and along the streets my first Christmas there had evoked more pity than joy. The sparse, worn, flimsy, tarnished ornaments, tired festoons, suggested the gallantry of a proud, wrinkled old lady garbed in the shabby finery of better days. There were no lights that year; I remember it as the Christmas without lights. But that third Christmas was a very different scene. Decorations began to appear in store windows some time in November; lavishly ornamented trees sprang up in the squares, garlands on lampposts, and lights! Christmas lights everywhere, even if some were blatantly commercial. The wide arch of lights anchored to the rooftops on either side of Váci Street spelled out not a holiday greeting, but the name of the company that provided it, "Tungsram Electric Company." To the children it was beautiful. Public transportation had ceased long before we had seen our fill, and we walked back to my apartment, not very far away. There, the children helped me finish decorating my tree, which their father had brought and set up for me several days before. Their mother had given me lights for it when I told her I had been unable to find any in the market. Baby Jesus doesn't bring trees to grown-ups, so we have to do our own.

The children's father came and drove us back to Budaörs where, sure enough, Baby Jesus had arrived and left a beautiful tree and many presents underneath. The children's grandparents on both sides were there, and after the ceremonial lighting of the real candles and sparklers on the tree, we made a circle, held hands and sang the traditional old Hungarian Christmas hymn. I could only hum along but the first lines in English are, "The angel from heaven has come down to you, shepherds, so you can hurry to Bethlehem to see him."

X

TO MARKET, TO MARKET

Two years after Hungary installed a democratic government committed to converting the economy to a free market system, very little change was visible. Privatization was very slow in getting started. This was discouraging to the population that optimistically, albeit unreasonably, expected the blessings of democracy to descend upon them immediately. One blessing that did appear immediately was the freedom to criticize the government, and that they embraced with exuberance.

People in the streets rarely smiled or even had a pleasant expression on their faces. Moreover, they were annoyed by the cheerfulness of others, particularly foreigners, and did not hesitate to let it be known. "Americans smile all the time," they said, "it can't be sincere." In truth, Hungarians had little to smile about. Prices were rising steadily, inflation was soaring, thus eroding the value of the forint, and salaries were not increasing fast enough to keep pace. Sympathetic as I was with Hungarians about the delayed free enterprise, it turned out to be auspicious for me. It was my good fortunate to arrive on the cusp, you might say, just before the turnaround began to take place. Therefore I was able to experience the market place as it operated under the socialist-communist system, then watch the transition that took place in the next five years.

The difference between a centrally-planned economy and a free-market system is easily discernible; the most unsophisticated customer entering a retail establishment for the first time knows right away which system is operating. Planned economies function for the people in name only in reality for the convenience of the State. Little or no consideration is given to the convenience, preferences or taste of the customer. The missing element is competition. In a free-market system where competition abounds, pleasing the customer must be the first priority if a business is to succeed. In a planned economy it is always a sellers' market. The first clue is the sales staff. Their attitude is that they are doing you a favor to let you buy something. My first realization that I was no longer in the world of the free market came in a shoe store. Seeing several pairs of shoes in the window, I went in and asked if a particular style was available in my size. A pretty young woman stood in the middle of the shop observing her fingernails, and without lifting her eyes, replied, *"Nincs!"* (Hungarian for "We don't have it.") Coming so newly from a culture where the "hard sell" is inevitable, I stood silently waiting for her to offer something else. "But how about this beautiful pump?" for example. However, she never uttered another word and I turned and walked out. Later I learned that she was probably telling the truth, that the window display, which consisted of less than a dozen pairs of shoes, was probably the entire stock. In any case, salespeople had no stake in moving merchandise. Their earnings were the same whether they sold anything or not, and it was easy to say *"Nincs!"* Selling something was work, not much, but more than simply taking the money and handing over the merchandise. They had to write out a slip, which the customer took to the cashier, paid for the article, then returned to the salesperson with the receipt showing that payment had been made. Only then was the purchase handed over, and handed over it was. There were no bags or wrapping paper. Everyone carried a shopping bag that held all purchases – shoes and strawberries, cheese, fish, sweaters, fruit – unless, of course, you remembered to bring several bags.

The State-run ABC (pronounced, Ah, Beh, Tseh) was the main outlet through which food, and some household necessities were sold; every municipality had one. The size of the store and range of stock depended on the size of the population it served. The quality of merchandise in these stores was reasonably good but limited in both quantity and variety. No effort was made to present the stock attractively or even to place it conveniently. Shelving was haphazard; neighboring items often had no relationship with each other. And there were few clues to guide the shopper. Moreover, the lighting was dim which not only added to the difficulty but the gloomy atmosphere dampened one's spirits; nearly everybody sighed deeply as they came in the door, picked up a basket – hand-carried basket, no shopping carts there – and started down the first aisle.

On my first ABC visit, I was reminded of a reverse experience when I accompanied a Russian visitor on her first trip to a large American supermarket. She stopped inside the doorway openmouthed, looked around scanning the wide, brightly-lit aisles and the endless shelves and cases of canned and packaged goods, frozen foods, fresh produce, bottled drinks, glassed-in meat cases, and could not take it all in. "I am angry! Angry!" she cried. "When I see all this. So much. So much. And I think of our empty stores in Moscow!" She was very near to tears.

My reaction to the Hungarian stores was not anger but sadness. And yet I was also aware of the advantages in that system. Uniform prices and the absence of competition eliminate comparison shopping, haggling, or promotional hocus-pocus of any kind. It means no advertising, no coupons, no sales, no price wars, and, of course, no choices. Customers may compete savagely for the most desirable goods but finally they must take whatever is available. When the State owns all means of production and distribution as well as all raw materials, it not only controls prices, it controls consumption. Overproduction is rarely a problem.

To people living where every sense is bombarded with advertising every waking hour, on radio, television and signboards, in newspapers and magazines, ballparks, supermarket receipts, and now even in theatres, the absence of advertising may sound like a consummation greatly to be desired. But shopping for a specific item in a foreign country, without signs or window displays (much less "Yellow Pages") can be an intensely frustrating experience. It was useless to ask local people where to buy ordinary items, a can opener, for example, or a screwdriver, or shoelaces. Apparently some things were passed along from generation to generation and nobody had to go in search of them – can openers and screwdrivers, probably. But shoelaces? Someone suggested that I try a *háztartásibolt* (household needs); another said perhaps in a *vasedény* (cookware, dishes); even the ubiquitous Keravill stores were suggested. There seemed to be one of those on every street. They looked like hardware stores in the United States, but that is misleading; they were very specialized. That name Keravill is an acronym which defined the nature of the merchandise originally sold there: "ke" stood for *kerékpár* (bicycle); "ra" for *rádió*; and "vill" for *villamos*, meaning electrical. They sold accessories and replacement parts for bicycles, radios and radio parts, and electrical equipment, but no shoelaces then or now. However, they have changed. Their stores are now beautifully lit, the windows decorated with lamps, refrigerators, laundry machines, microwave ovens and electronic apparatus of all kinds. Their neon signs and advertisements leave no doubt about where they are and what they sell.

In a household goods store, I did find a complete set of screwdrivers, one of every size, such as a carpenter or a cabinet maker might buy, but they would not sell me a single one. A Hungarian friend came to help me with some household repairs and brought with him a large, well-stocked tool box. Surely he knew where small tools could be bought. "Where can I buy a screwdriver and pliers?" I asked him. He shrugged and shook his head in an "I don't know" gesture, and insisted on giving me one of each from his box. I found a very flimsy plastic can opener at an ABC and it lasted until good ones began to appear two years later. Now they are plentiful. I have heard that shoelaces are also available now, but no one has told me exactly where and I haven't persisted. I brought a considerable supply with me on my last trip to the West.

It took a while but after a few experiences, all frustrating but enlightening, and some hilarious, I began to understand how to solve my many shopping problems. My friend Peggy had a rug on her kitchen floor that I admired and she told me I could buy one just like it in a little shop next door to her building. All I had to do was turn left as I exited through the gate that separated the courtyard of her building from the street. Following her instructions I walked the entire block but did not find the shop. After turning back twice and scanning all the store windows, none of which displayed rugs, I gave up. The next time we met, I told Peggy there was no such store, and she repeated her original directions, "Next door, the first entrance you come to after turning left outside the gateway to my building." "But that's impossible," I protested, "that shop has little girls' dresses in the window!" She nodded vigorously, "Yes, yes! That's where they sell rugs!"

A visitor to Hungary who stayed in my apartment when I was out of town had a similar experience looking for coffee filters. My coffee maker was the kind that required paper filters and the supply ran out while I was away. My friend, whom I call a "world class shopper" because she is very good at ferreting out things in the market place, had to concede defeat in her search for coffee filters. When I returned, she was most apologetic and said, "You must have brought them with you; I looked all over Budapest and they don't exist here!" In my new-found wisdom, I smiled knowingly and said, "I'll bet you didn't look in the stationery store!"

I had finally figured out the logic, or at least I had concocted my own version of how a planned economy works, and it served as my shopping guide: The most efficient way to produce and distribute consumer goods is to reduce to a minimum the number of production facilities, thus reducing the delivery points of raw materials; and, further, to reduce the number of distribution centers in order to keep shipping and transportation costs to a minimum. Therefore, a factory which receives cotton yarn or cotton fabric can produce many unrelated articles all made of cotton, and in the same spirit of efficiency ship them to the same distribution outlets; this reasoning also applies to paper goods. Hence, little girls' cotton dresses and rugs in the same shop; coffee filters and writing paper in stationery stores.

Beginning in the 1960s, the communist government allowed small private businesses in which family members only could work. Hiring outsiders was considered to be exploitative; or, to put it another way, only members of the family could be exploited. Among those private businesses were small *"csemege"* similar to the "Mom and Pop" stores or "convenience" stores in the United States. Some of these sold fresh bread and milk and opened at 6 o'clock in the morning. It was very nice to be able to buy fresh bread for breakfast in the morning and many people did. Prices were the same as those at the ABC. It took a while to get used to the fact that it did not matter where you bought an article—the price was the same everywhere. Of course that changed when capitalism began to take hold.

Business space was at a premium and owners of unrelated small private businesses sometimes shared space, resulting in some odd pairings of merchandise, and more enigmatical window displays. One of my students told me his mother had a children's clothing shop in Budapest near the Main Post Office where I often went. He suggested that I stop in sometime and meet his mother. The next time I was in the area, I looked but could not find the place. Later I questioned him about it. "You said it was a children's clothing store; does it have children's clothes in the window?" "Oh, no," he replied. "She shares the shop with a coin dealer. So there are coins in the window."

The dreary ABCs with their dependable stock of meat, bread, canned and packaged foods, and staples – flour, sugar, salt, rice, pasta – at controlled, affordable prices were indispensable for Hungarians and a great convenience for foreigners. They were self-service, and many items, meats, cheeses, bread, pastry were open to view. If you cannot read the labels, packaged and canned commodities usually have identifying pictures; and you can see through clear glass jars. Above all, the prices were clearly marked either on the shelf or on the article itself. So everyone shopped at the ABC out of necessity. But for a glorious adventure in food shopping, there were and still are in Hungary the open air or partially-covered markets. From early Spring, all summer, and through the

Autumn, colorful displays of fruits, vegetables and flowers spill out of large and small kiosks on the streets in cities, towns and villages. The large markets are in more remote areas, often on the edge of the city. They are called by several names which loosely define their type: *"Piac"* and *"vásár"* are open-air, or partially covered; located mainly in rural or semi-rural areas, some resemble country fairs; others are like a combined Farmers' and Flea Market. *"Vásárcsarnok"* may be translated as "market hall," and implies a large, covered market inside the city.

There was an outdoor market (*vásár*) on the outskirts of the city where I spent my first three months in Hungary and lived with the Kovács family. It was open on Saturday and Sunday and János went almost every Sunday morning, as regularly as most people go to religious services. In Hungary, the family marketing is usually done by the women, but Sunday in the summer is father's day at the market when men may go alone or with their wives and children for a family outing.

After I had been there for several weeks, János invited me to go with him one Sunday morning. Anna made it clear by her expression that she did not think much of the idea; she herself never went, and although she said nothing, her manner indicated that it probably wasn't a place for a "lady." I was eager to go and ignored her signals.

That *vásár* covered a very large area, as large as a circus grounds. In two hours we did not see it all. Everything from horses to lipsticks was being offered for sale: men's, women's and children's clothes; pots and pans; fruit; vegetables; handcrafts; goats; used furniture, some antiques; kittens, pastry, candies, dishwashing powder and liquids, jewelry, brooms. Most vendors were Hungarian, but some were from Yugoslavia, 70 kilometers away; others were from as far away as Romania, 200-300 kilometers distance. Eager as I was to see everything, it was not easy because János seemed to know everybody there. Many of them stopped to chat, and he introduced me to them. I understood why these Sunday morning excursions were so compelling. People exchanged information about their families, caught up on what their friends were doing. It was apparent that these Sunday morning excursions were indeed similar to attendance at a religious service where meeting and greeting friends is as important as the primary incentive for the trip.

I bought a cotton head scarf for 150 forints, about $2 at the exchange rate then in effect; János bought a watermelon weighing nearly 10 kilos, about 22 pounds, for the same price, quite expensive at that place and time. He also bought some homemade potato candy, which he liked very much, as did I. It was said to be "good for you" implying some medicinal value. Hungarians love watermelon more than any people I have met since I crossed over the Mason-Dixon Line. The stereotype is the watermelon-loving Southern Black, but the truth is that all Southerners are inordinately fond of it. Years ago, in my youth, a favorite lark of adolescent boys in the South in mid- and late-summer was robbing watermelon patches. Perhaps it still is. Farmers tended to be tolerant about it, as long as they didn't mess up the patch too much. After all, how many of those heavy things can a few boys carry away? The Kovacs family was delighted to have watermelon dessert at dinner that day and consumed all of it.

When I moved to Budapest after my Peace Corps service ended, my first residence was near Moscow Square (*Moszkva tér*), one of the most important traffic hubs of the inner city. Near the Square was a large outdoor and partially-covered market on Fény Street where I shopped regularly. It is now undergoing construction and will eventually be a large market hall, but that summer it had the appearance of a lush garden in full bloom. One side was occupied by flower stalls, the stalls themselves were completely hidden by flowers in a profusion of colors and varieties. Through the uncovered floral area, paths led to the vegetable and fruit stands, covered by tin roofs and tarpaulins, where the produce was displayed in patterns whose shapes and colors rivaled those of the flowers. When I first went there, customers selected the produce they wanted, handed it to the attendant, who weighed the items and computed the cost. That began to change early in 1995. Now, the fruits and vegetables are still beautifully and artistically displayed, but if a customer attempts to pluck one from the arrangement, she is stopped by a loud shout from the attendant, "Don't touch!" If the customer does not look Hungarian, they know the phrase in English and shout it in both languages. It then became the practice for the vendor to select the items, after the customer requested something, as in "One kilo of apples," for example. The clerk then reached under the counter and weighed out apples from an unseen source, thereby not disturbing the decorative arrangement. It took only a couple of such transactions to learn that the produce underneath the counter was not the same quality as that on display. So I began to request that they take my produce from the display, and sometimes they would, but not always. They are very independent. They are also very clever. Often when they acceded to my request and I watched them take fruit from the display box, at home I would find that one piece had a large rotten spot. How did they do that? Fat thumbs?

Some vendors brazenly displayed produce that was old alongside that which was obviously fresh, with only one price posted, and refused to sell the fresh until they sold out the older. Once at the Fény Street market I found some beautiful fresh mushrooms, and beside them a box of brown, tired-looking ones, with only one price posted. I pointed to the fresh ones and asked for half a kilo, but the vendor insisted she could not sell those until the older ones were gone. When I went to another stall, I had exactly the same experience, so I tried another, four in all, with the same result. They were learning some capitalistic techniques, if not the most admirable ones, such as price fixing and cartels, or at least gentlemen's agreements between retailers. My first reaction was indignation, and the second was to wonder how Hungarian women reacted to this. During several weeks, months even, of observation at a number of markets, I never heard anyone complain, and I have never seen a Hungarian customer refuse to buy produce when offered something that was clearly not fresh. It was noticeably startling to other customers when I watched produce being placed on the scales, and if I saw a piece that wasn't good, I removed it and handed it back to the clerk, smiling as I did so. No one refused to take it back. Once when I saw that all the items being weighed were inferior, I insisted that I wanted to buy the fresher ones, but the clerk refused to exchange them. So I smiled and said, "Viszontlátásra!" (Goodbye!) It would be very impolite to leave without saying goodbye. Since my back was to the other customers as I walked away, I could not see their reaction, but I hoped it demonstrated that in a free market society a customer has the right to refuse products of an unacceptable quality. It is interesting to note that nowadays some vendors have refined their marketing technique to the extent that although they still display both fresh and not-so-fresh produce their prices are appropriately different.

Vendors may be either men or women, and generally speaking the women are friendlier and more helpful. Perhaps it is deference to my age, my foreignness, or it may be only an understanding respect for the cook who prefers to buy food of the best quality. It is not unusual to find male vendors who show no respect for female customers and arrogantly tell them what to buy, or at least try to. Their attitude towards me, an obvious foreigner, varies from tolerant, as if they are dealing with a half-wit or a child, to contempt for someone who doesn't speak perfect Hungarian. There are occasional exceptions when they show extra consideration seemingly in recognition of my foreignness and therefore unavoidable ignorance. But even in my earliest shopping ventures when my knowledge of Hungarian was minimal, no store clerk or stall attendant shortchanged me. Some of them may give you rotten fruit or vegetables, but they seem to be scrupulously honest in returning change and also in weighing produce. At times, I have questioned the accuracy of the scales, not because I think they are shortweighting me, just the reverse. It seems to me that half a kilo is much larger than I expect one pound plus one ounce to be, especially lightweight items like spinach and mushrooms; I usually buy only one-fourth kilo of those.

Another large partly-outdoor, partly-underground market stands on Fehérvári Street, near Móricsz Zsigmond Square in front of a large department store (*aruhaz*) named Skála. These state-owned stores sold clothing, large household equipment, books, and almost everything a department store would be expected to stock, at controlled prices, quality and variety. In the early 1990s, they had the same monotonous, dreary, uninviting appearance and the same practical, uninteresting merchandise as the food outlets, the ABCs. The Skála stores have now been sold to private owners and their appearance as well as the quality and variety of their merchandise has been considerably upgraded. Their prices, too. In the early days, the colorful market on Fehérvári Street just outside of Skála benefited greatly from the contrast, and still does, as prices are lower there and the outdoor atmosphere and personal contact with vendors enlivens the shopping experience. There, as in other outdoor markets, flowers, fruits and vegetables spill out in colorful cornucopias of the beautiful and the edible. All spring and summer and through the autumn harvest season, attendants stand proudly in their stalls and beam when complimented on their produce, its freshness or the artistry of the arrangements. Then the Christmas season begins, bringing evergreens, holly, pine cones, decorations and lights for Christmas trees – Christmas trees, too – toys and poinsettias, called the "*Mikulás* Flower." December 6 is "*Mikulás*" in Hungary, the day children receive presents, as in other parts of Europe, and the Holiday Season really begins then. The underground market remains open all year, but during January and February the outdoor portion is a relatively bleak scene until it springs to life again in late March.

During the communist era, state-owned cooperatives offered produce at the Neo-Gothic Central Market Hall (*Központi Vásárcsarnok*) which stands on the Pest side of the Danube at the end of the *Szabadság* (Liberty) Bridge. Restoration of the neglected, nearly-crumbling building was begun in the early 90s and completed in time to celebrate its 100th anniversary in 1996. It is a showplace, rivaling in architectural beauty its neo-Renaissance next-door neighbor, the

University of Economic Science, formerly named Karl Marx University. Visitors are amazed when told that this impressive structure is a market; it might well be a museum or an important government administration building. Doubts about its function vanish as soon as one enters.

A broad center aisle and two narrower side aisles run the full 490-foot length of the building, and are joined by criss-crossing intersecting aisles. They are all lined with food stalls festooned with strings of red pepper, garlic, sausages; their bins are full of dried beans, large white ones, tiny black ones, speckled and plaid ones; cheeses, spices, nuts, breads and pastries, wine, dairy products, fresh and cured meats, poultry, and seasonal fruits and vegetables arranged in colorful artistic patterns. Apples, pears, oranges, bananas, grapes, avocados, kiwi, plums, cherries, strawberries, carrots, broccoli, potatoes, cauliflower, lettuce, celery, spinach, mushrooms fill the stall compartments, some piled so high it looks as if they might tumble into the aisle at any moment. It is a feast for the eyes promising a later one for the palate. There is one stall run by two nice-looking middle-aged women with whom I have established a friendly relationship. They have superb fruits and vegetables, a bit higher priced than others and much of it imported, citrus fruits from Israel, for example, and recently firm heads of iceberg lettuce, country of origin unknown. In the United States, I used to disdain iceberg lettuce but that which comes from their stall is very tasty, or perhaps it is only that five years of iceberg-lettuce-deprivation had made me appreciate it. They recently started displaying very large stalks of celery, country of origin also unknown, but it is a firm and white, and good – and expensive! Occasionally, I treat myself to the celery; the large stalks last a long time. Such extravagances (iceberg lettuce and celery!) have no doubt contributed to our very pleasant customer-vendor relationship. I have no idea what their names are and they do not know mine, but they know what I like. And very often when they see me looking, they whisper that something fresh has just come in and bring me whatever it is from the storeroom. It is always fresh and superior and even though I may not have planned to buy whatever they suggest, I always do and I have never been sorry. A modern supermarket is one escalator flight down.

The supermarket is an amalgam of the former ABC and a Western European or American supermarket, but with a difference. There is no fresh produce to compete with that in the main hall. The shelves are filled with canned, frozen, and packaged foods from Hungary and also from Germany, Austria, Thailand, China, Spain, Italy, the United States, Costa Rica, Denmark, Turkey, Greece, and Russia.

There are some meats and cheeses but scarcely enough to offer any real competition to the upstairs stalls. Of course, there is a sizeable bread section. Hungarian bread is sold in every food market, large or small. Despite the obvious abundance here and on the main floor, a few things have not yet found their way to Hungary – cranberry juice, for example – but compared with only a couple of years ago, the opulence is dizzying.

Along the hallway, adjacent to the supermarket are small specialty shops; one features Asian food and almost makes me feel that I am back in New York's Chinatown. They have not only food items, spices, and such but also cooking equipment from China, Japan, Singapore, Taiwan, and other Far Eastern locales. There are fish shops where you can select live fish out of a tank and take them home, or buy Russian caviar, smoked salmon from Scotland, frozen lobster and crabmeat from various places along the North Atlantic coast. In the small hallway, collapsible stalls are set up to sell books, cosmetics, kitchen utensils, clothing, knives, souvenirs. The basement floor is like a market within the large market.

On what is called the first floor, one flight up from the Main Floor, souvenir vendors offer embroidered linens and clothing colorful Gypsy skirts and vests, and wares from various places – brass from India, leather from Romania, enamel ware and icons from Russia. Food and drink stalls serve the Hungarian equivalent of "fast food," bread with various fillings, grilled meats, and wine, beer, coffee and soft drinks to wash it down.

The Central Market Hall is always crowded. As large as it is, 110,000 square feet, it is sometimes necessary to line up to get in, then the aisles are so crowded that it is difficult to view the produce. Waiting in line to make a purchase is usual. Other markets are often just as crowded. It would seem that with these outlets the Budapest public would be adequately served. Apparently not so. There are now five shopping malls around the city, mainly on the outskirts but within easy reach by public transportation or by car. Once inside such a mall, one might as well be shopping in Richmond, Virginia or Cleveland, Ohio, except that you use different currency. The prices are the same. That is what makes the patronage of the malls so surprising. People still deplore the increase in cost of energy supplies, telephone, transportation, and food, and lament the failure of wages to keep pace, but they shop as frantically as Americans did in the 1950s following the deprivations during World War II. Their hunger for goods and possessions is much the same as people in the United States displayed then. Hungarians are buying new cars, building new houses, including those for week-end and holiday use; household appliances that were unthinkable only a couple of years ago can now be found in many Hungarian homes.

Nothing symbolizes the transformation in Budapest's market place better than the media advertisements during the Christmas shopping season in 1997. The first week in December, Budapest's Mayor, Gábor Demszky, officially turned on Budapest's Christmas lighting in the center of the city and toured the boutique-lined, newly-renovated section of Váci Street which runs South from the Elizabeth Bridge. Among the advertised gift suggestions in that week's newspapers were: hand-made to order shoes for men, antique furniture, video tapes, CDs, and "a wide selection of accessories of the highest quality designer names, many carried exclusively in Hungary." One boutique boasted, "Whether it is the latest design of Bruno Magli or Fratelli Rossetti shoes, Montana bags and accessories, the stunning designs of Lagerfeld, or the shoes that every stylish young man seems to be looking for, Cesare Paciotti, they are all nearby!" Under the heading "Gifts for Him" another boutique listed the names Givenchy, Ungaro, Valentino, Yves Saint Laurent, Pringle, and others; Ungaro and Pringle also appeared under the "For Her" heading with the addition of Cerruti 1881 and Tristano Onofri.

My mind whirled back to my first Christmas in Hungary: no lighted trees in public places, no tree lights or ornaments for sale, no gift-wrapping paper or ribbon in Christmas colors, no gift boxes. And pitifully few gift selections. The drab, familiar stock in the stores – clothing made of synthetic fabrics, plastic toys – the commonplace souvenir-ish goods in the vendors' stalls along the streets, in the squares and almost any open space, were not likely to bring delight to the eyes of children or any recipient. Yet that melancholy memory was tinged with nostalgia. Scarcity throws up a challenge; perseverance, ingenuity, imagination are called upon. Looking for gifts in those dismal days was a treasure hunt. One poked through wares in the stalls hoping to uncover something unique and imaginative. And what a thrill such a rare find could bring! One lucky day, I happened upon the small, obscure stall of a Lithuanian vendor with charming wooden handcraft items. When I got home with the few I bought and saw again their unusual quality, I returned to buy more but they were all gone. The vendor was then displaying the same things shown in other stalls and sadly informed me that there would be no more of the crafts from Lithuania; they were rare, indeed. Friends who received the ones I bought loved them, one of the greatest pleasures of giving.

Five years later, stores, shops, markets and malls were chock-full of gift wrappings, ribbon, boxes, and the same bewildering abundance of gift selections to be found in any Christian country at that time of the year. No adventure awaits the shopper faced with a surfeit of merchandise, only the tedious task of deciding among several appealing choices. And some of the joy of the season is lost.

But Christmas always brings some joy whatever the situation, and that year the economic forecasts were optimistic. Inflation which was then almost 20% was predicted to fall to 14% for the coming year. And people were responding with renewed spirit. From the first week in December, store windows were decorated and brightly lit; strings of lights attached to building tops hung across shopping streets; lighted trees sprang up in every shopping district. Whatever the statistics, current or forecast, the atmosphere reeked of optimism, brisk business, prosperity – one might almost have said "cheer" among the dour Hungarians! What a change from five years earlier.

NOTES FROM THE JOURNAL – ROMANIAN DRAMA

Waking up suddenly to find myself on a red-velvet-upholstered Queen Anne sofa in the office of the famous actor and director of the Romanian National Theatre in Cluj-Napoca, Dorel Vişan, was certainly the most surreal happening on my trip to Romania, but not the only one. It all began with a surprise invitation to give a talk on Shakespeare in America at a theatre conference held in Sepsiszentgyörgy, in the former (pre-Trianon Treaty) Hungarian province of Transylvania, which still has a strong, vocal Hungarian minority population. The Romanian name is Sf. Gheorghe, but throughout the conference I heard only the Hungarian name, Sepsiszentgyörgy. Their interest in Shakespeare surprised me until I met Attila Nagy, president of "The Shakespeare Kingdom House," located in nearby Covasna, and heard that his family had donated land on which to build "Shakespeare's Globe in Romania." My invitation to the conference came through Irén Mátyás, director of the outdoor Zsámbék Theatre, just outside Budapest, who is a consultant and adviser to the Sepsiszentgyörgy Culture House, the sponsor of the conference. She and I traveled to Transylvania together with our mutual friend, Anikó Szabó, a Hungarian-English-Russian language interpreter, who introduced me to Irén. After a 19-hour bus ride (with three rest stops, and of course no toilet on the bus) we arrived at the Culture House at noon to find the director, Gyula Musát, in his office with his entire staff huddled in front of a television set. He greeted us hurriedly, put a glass of something alcoholic into our hands and wedged us into the group. We had arrived on the day and at the hour when the newly-elected president, Emil Constantinescu, was being inaugurated in Bucharest. In good theatre tradition, our timing had been perfect, and along with all of Transylvania, apparently, we saw the entire ceremony. Since the 1989 revolt against Nicolae Ceauşescu, Romania had been ruled by a group of former Ceauşescu cohorts, and most of the country, especially the Hungarian minority, were thrilled at the election of the democrat Constantinescu.

The audience for my talk – which included some excerpts from Shakespearean roles I have played (with Hungarian interpretation by Anikó Szabó and Attila Nagy) – was surprised to learn of Shakespeare's popularity in the United States on the stage, in films, and in television, a measure of the extent to which they were isolated from Western culture for almost 50 years. On the program was an interesting play I had not seen before, *Water Hen* (*Vizityúk*), by the Polish playwright Stanislaw Ignacy Witkiewicz.

After the three-day meeting in Sepsiszentgyörgy, Anikó and I accompanied Irén to Cluj-Napoca where she was invited as a guest adviser to an eight-day drama festival. We were given passes to all festival performances, not only those in the National Theatre of Cluj-Napoca, the organizer of the "Gala", but also for plays in the Hungarian National Theatre. There were performances at one of those theatres every evening at 7 p.m. and at 11 p.m. and most mornings at 11 a.m. It was impossible to see all the plays – I passed up most of the 11 p.m. ones – but I saw Polish, Romanian, Czech and English plays, all performed in the language in which they were written, except that the English language ones were done in Hungarian. Fortunately, I was familiar with the English ones; the program included Anouilh's *Becket*; John Osborne's *Look Back in Anger*; and Shakespeare's *Falstaff* and I now understand enough Hungarian that I was able to understand and enjoy those. The role of Falstaff was played by the theatre's director, Dorel Vişan, one of Romania's most popular actors. We were told by several people that he had just missed being named Best Actor at the previous year's Cannes Film Festival. Of all the plays I saw, the most memorable was *Săptămâna Luminată*, a story written by Mihail Săulescu and adapted for the stage by Mihai Măniuţiu, with music, dance, mime and very little dialog – perfect for those of us who did not understand Romanian. The story was based on a pagan belief that there is one week in the year when all who die are admitted to Heaven regardless of their sins on earth. A mother prays for her very ill, very evil son to die in that week. Her friends and neighbors join her, adding their prayers to hers, and in addition various witches, medicine men and other mumbo-jumbo characters dance, sing, and perform symbolic gestures of entreaty. But the wicked son clings to life until the very last minute when he finally, to the relief of the mother and other characters in the play, and the audience, expires. It was extravagantly costumed, staged, and performed by a remarkably imaginatively versatile cast.

Another outstanding piece was "17 Acte cu Piet Mondrian," staged by Horaţiu Mihaiu with subtext by Ovidiu Pecican. It was mostly mime and stage pictures, based on the works of Piet Mondrian, scheduled to be performed at 11 p.m. I did not consider it worth staying up for. But due to some scheduling difficulty, it was actually done at 11 o'clock the next morning and I saw it unexpectedly, and fortunately as it turned out, because it was much more interesting dramatically than I had thought it would be.

On our last day in Cluj-Napoca, and the last day of the festival, the manager of the National Theatre suggested that we bring our baggage to the theatre in the morning and leave it there, as she had arranged for the theatre's technical coordinator, Estera Bíró, to take us on a day-long tour of the city. In the evening we would attend the festival's last performance, then go to the farewell dinner with the company. The stage crew would transport us and our bags to the midnight train. She did not make it clear that our tour would be on foot, and I was not wearing walking shoes.

We visited the house where, to everyone's surprise, Hungary's great King Matthias I Corvinus Hunyadi was born in 1440. His mother, in the last stages of her pregnancy, was traveling in Transylvania and the baby arrived early. Now the Romanians claim that good and highly revered king as a native of Romania, much to the annoyance of the Hungarians; his birthplace is a main tourist attraction. Estera was a fast walker and we covered a lot of the city, including the linden-tree-lined Mihail Kogălniceanu Street, near the theatre, where we visited the Orthodox Church with the most ornately decorated interior I have ever seen, except that there are no stained-glass windows. All the windows were shattered in World War II and clear glass panes with a very simple geometric design were temporarily installed. Just as in Hungary, religious buildings were largely neglected during the communist regime, so more than fifty years after the damage was done, the clear glass panes are still there.

When we returned to the theatre late in the afternoon I was exhausted (and my feet hurt) and asked where I might rest a few minutes before going to the evening performance. Estera immediately escorted me into the office of the theatre director and told me to make myself comfortable there. "Oh, I couldn't do that," I protested,. "He will need his office." She assured me that he was very busy preparing for the evening's performance and there was no chance he would come in. My reticence was no doubt due to the awe in the voice of the theatre staff when they spoke of him. And the room itself was very intimidating. Make myself comfortable, indeed! I hesitated to even sit down. More of an "expanse" than a room, it was filled with massive carved wooden sofas and chairs, all upholstered in heavy red velvet fabric; several small tables with chairs around them, a richly carved chest with a large-screen television set mounted on it, and several high-backed, upholstered wing chairs. A very large oriental rug covered the floor. A lot of furniture, but for that capacious room not too much. The director's king-size desk in one corner was piled high with plays, posters, brochures, photographs, letters, manuscripts, postcards. Behind it a dark wooden étagère was crammed full of more of the same things, books, papers, programs, photos. Urging me to lie down, repeating that I should make myself comfortable, Estera left me alone. Fatigue soon overcame my inhibitions; I stretched out on one of the long sofas and was asleep before my eyelids finished closing. The next thing I knew the door opened, the light went on, and in walked Dorel Vişan wearing a dinner jacket and carrying a carton of fruit juice. I sat up quickly, apologizing, but he interrupted me with his apology, saying he would only be a minute, that he had merely come in to get something from his desk. He poured some fruit juice for himself and for me, and after we drank it, he left. So I repaired my make-up in the adjoining bathroom, combed my hair and went downstairs to the theatre. After the performance, backstage congratulations and expressions of thanks to the cast and theatre staff, we all went to the hotel where the farewell dinner took place.

Train travel between Hungary and Romania in those days was considered to be a very hazardous undertaking. Travelers expected at least to be robbed, and felt lucky if they arrived home alive. Just mention that you planned to go to Romania by train and you would be offered copious advice and warnings. Above everything, one must never go to sleep – your sleeping compartment might be sprayed with a drug that would render you unconscious — and other dire predictions. The bus trip to Romania had been so uncomfortable that I was somewhat relieved to find that our return transportation was to be by train, but still braced myself for the worst. Exact information was impossible to obtain. We learned that our train would leave Cluj-Napoca at 12:30 at night, that we could buy tickets only one-half hour before departure time, and for only as far as the Romanian-Hungarian border. Nobody knew whether we would change trains at the border, if our luggage would be searched, or where we would get tickets for the Hungarian portion of the trip. We did find out that sleeping-car tickets for the all-night trip had to be bought on the train. The theatre crew drove us and our bags to the station, negotiated in the Romanian language for our tickets (as far as the border) and waved us off.

We looked for the conductor immediately to ask about sleeping car tickets and I was vastly relieved to see that he was Hungarian; that suddenly made me feel that everything would be all right. And it was. He sold us the tickets for the remainder of our journey and for the sleeping car. He told us not to worry about the border crossing, that he would take care of everything. He soon settled us into a sleeping car, said good night, told us to sleep well. I felt that I had already come home, to Hungary, that is. I went to sleep with my passport and Hungarian re-entry permission under my pillow. Sometime in the middle of the night, the border guards – customs and passport–control officers – came through and gently awoke us speaking very softly. I roused up enough to pull out my documents which they stamped and returned. Then they waved a very weak flashlight in the direction of our baggage, and left, whispering, "Now, go back to sleep," which I promptly did.

Later I recalled the miserable border-crossing experience on a bus trip from Budapest to Krakow when we had to pass through Slovakia. We were held at the border for over an hour while they checked our passports before they permitted us to enter; then, a very short time later, we were delayed for the same amount of time in order to exit Slovakia and enter Poland. It was just as bad when we entered Romania by bus – worse, even, because it was dark and raining when we reached the Romanian border. All luggage was removed from the baggage compartment and every piece examined. Eventually the inspectors made one passenger leave a very old, second- or perhaps even third-hand 19" television set – we guessed the border guard needed a television set.

I didn't kneel down and kiss the ground at Keleti Station when we arrived in Budapest the next morning, but the thought occurred to me.

XI

HUNGARIAN WOMEN – AND MEN

"Money is best when counted; women are best when beaten," goes an old Hungarian saying that can still be heard in the villages, and occasionally even in Budapest.

Gyula Krúdy, often called Hungary's finest novelist, recalling his impressions of Budapest when he arrived here in 1896 at the age of 17, wrote: "Women smelled like oranges in Japan." And his lyrical descriptions of the Inner City, today's Belváros, are filled with such images as "...those heart-rending days in spring when the new frocks bedeck the pavements like flowers in the meadows."

These contradictory images of women are eloquently depicted in a painting by Vladimir Ovchinnikov, an artist working in St. Petersburg (Leningrad) in the 1970s. Women are shown repairing railroad tracks, angel wings sprouting from their shoulders. Today's woman in Hungary is the product of almost three generations of Soviet education and acculturation, and the women in Ovhcinnikov's painting could well be Hungarian.

When they are young, Hungary's women are surely among the most beautiful in the world, but their youth doesn't last long. One gets the impression that their lot has not improved greatly since the early 19th century, as described by Kálmán Mikszáth in *A Strange Marriage*, published in 1900: "Men took the view that there were only two classes of women, those who were pretty and fast, and the others who were ugly and faithful. Even this limited classification applied only to women under thirty. Above that age, all women were alike; they were old." As for marriage, Mikszáth wrote, "It was a sad fate, like that of flowers which bloom and scent the air only until they are picked, or perhaps for one further day."

When I first saw Budapest in the Summer of 1992, somewhere in my subconscious, planted there no doubt by novelists of the late nineteenth and early twentieth centuries, lurked an image of Hungarian womanhood which I half-expected to find: thin-waisted as the beautiful Elizabeth, their beloved "Sisi," Empress of Austria, Queen of Hungary, tripping daintily in and out of luxury boutiques, stationers, and confectioners on Váci Street, be-ribboned packages suspended from dainty fingers; or those described by one writer, as "poor office girls who stepped out with the air of duchesses." These images were only slightly blurred by the more contemporary one of Mama Jolie Gabor and her three lovely daughters, Zsa Zsa, Magda, and Eva whose beauty and Hungarian savvy brought a special kind of glamour to Hollywood and brought them fame and fortune. Budapest inspires fantasy; it is one of the world's most glamorous cities with a tradition of culture and refinement equalling that of Paris and Vienna in the nineteenth century. More recently Cold War literature depicted it as a place where secret agents performed daring deeds on behalf of their countries or cravenly betrayed those countries depending upon the writer's imagination.

There was very little to connect those fantasies with the women I first saw in Hungary. In the cities, including Budapest, and villages I visited, women were more likely to be broad-hipped and full waisted, with sturdy feet encased in insubstantial shoes – in the city, sling-back pumps with narrow worn heels were most common – upon which they were always hurrying, sometimes running to catch a bus, tram or train, balanced by overstuffed shopping bags, one in each hand. My own back ached at the sight of those weights straining their hands, arms, and shoulders. "Do Hungarian women have a lot of back trouble?" I asked a physician, and the reply was a shrug and "Yes, of course."

One statistic published at that time indicated that Hungarian women went to the market an average of 1-1/2 times a day and my impression was that they would almost as likely go out naked as without a shopping bag. Those bags were not an accessory, as some "tote bags" are; they were made of strong material like canvas, many of them large enough to hold the contents of an American shopping cart. Consumer goods was then very scarce and one had to be prepared for the lucky opportunity to buy a couple of kilos of something on the spot. Produce was never bagged in the markets and without a large, sturdy bag, the most fortunate finds would have to be passed up. Even now, in places where plastic shopping bags have become available, they are not free; so women use them over and over, and thus still do not go out without a bag.

At first, it seemed that only women cleaned the streets and underground Metro stations; and it was also women who cleaned and attended the public toilets, collecting the "admission fee" and handing each person two sheets of toilet paper. Women workers on construction projects performed such unskilled tasks as sweeping up debris or scraping the exterior of buildings undergoing renovation; they drove buses, trams, and subway trains. The winter of 1995-96 was particularly snowy. Beginning in November it snowed regularly until April. There were only one or two heavy snows, but even fine snow eventually piles up if it falls day after day. There were no snow plows; the streets were cleared by older women, at least they *looked* older, with ordinary straw brooms. As the snow fell, they swept it from the sidewalks towards the road, and when they reached the end of the block, the sidewalk behind them was again covered, so they turned and retraced their steps in the opposite direction, sweeping as they went. Recently, I have noticed that it is more likely to be men who do street-cleaning, and it has been a while since I saw women working on construction jobs, but women still stand guard at the public toilets. Wages for streetcleaning have been upgraded. On warm Spring, Summer or Autumn days, it is most unusual, one might say rare, to see mature Hungarian women sitting together at sidewalk cafés. Those tables are filled with men drinking beer, coffee, or wine, and playing chess or just talking. But middle-aged or older Hungarian women idling away an afternoon in a café? Hardly ever.

Yet on the way home from work men often stop by the flower stalls and pick up a flower or even a bouquet. Márika, a woman I know who works very hard, tells me that her husband brings her a cup of coffee each morning before she gets out of bed. János, the head of the household I lived in for my first three months in Hungary, never bought flowers for his wife, but he would sometimes pick a rose on his way past the garden and present it to her as he came in the door. He often reached across the table and kissed her during a meal, thanking her for something especially tasty, or just because he felt like it. They were both in their late sixties, and she blushed and simpered like a young girl when he made these overtures.

A few older men still kiss women's hands when meeting and leaving them, and all men as well as young people and children greet older woman with the expression "*Kezét csókolom!*" The literal translation is "I kiss your hand," but it has become a perfunctory greeting when meeting or departing from women. The absurdity of that greeting in some situations, as for example to a woman as she scoops construction debris into a truck, attests to its automatic conventional usage; the literal meaning has been forgotten.

At the end of the day's classes in the school where I taught, the banging of desk drawers, and doors of the coat closets and supply cabinets in the teachers' room resounded through the building which was evacuated with nearly as much dispatch as if a fire alarm had rung. Women teachers were already fixed on a destination – market and home in that order – school and classes well behind them. At first, I tried to engage my team-teaching partners in conversation about the next day's lesson plans but found it was impossible. They had switched from the "school mode" into the "domestic mode" and looked at me as if they had never seen me before.

These colleagues often complained about the school administration, scheduling of classes, their teaching load, the curriculum, boring meetings at the end of the teaching day, and the stupidity of their male department heads, but it never seemed to occur to them that they had any power to bring about change. When I suggested that one of them might vie for the position as department head, they looked shocked, not merely by the suggestion, but at my stupidity in not knowing that it would be an impossible undertaking. "But we have children!" they said in chorus, as if that automatically disqualified them.

During my two years there, however much the faculty complained, I never heard any female teacher express dissatisfaction with the system that routinely favored men in the top administrative posts, or say she would like to have more responsibility. The most frequently voiced wish was that they had more time with their husbands and children, more time at home. It recalled the early days of the feminist movement in the United States when an effort was made to bring blue-collar women into the movement. What most of them wanted, it was soon discovered, was the opportunity to stay at home and be fulltime parents and homemakers. The "glass ceiling" was not their problem. Many of the women with whom I worked in Hungary, including university graduates, expressed the same wish.

An International Gallup Poll survey conducted in 22 countries in 1996, found that Hungary had the largest percentage of respondents who favored the traditional family structure; two-thirds of Hungarians polled considered the ideal family to consist of a breadwinner father and a homemaker mother. In the United States less than half of those replying favored the traditional pattern, but still a larger number than in Germany, India, Lithuania, Spain, Taiwan and Thailand, where only about one-fourth of those polled considered that pattern to be ideal. About 1000 adults, described as a "representative national sample," were interviewed in each of the

22 countries. Presumably the sample was based upon the population distribution, and a commensurate number of each sex was interviewed. Africa and Middle Eastern countries were not included in the survey.

In answer to the survey question whether the position of women compared with that of men had improved over the past five years, the reply was positive in all but four countries, Estonia, Latvia, Lithuania, and Hungary.

On questions about resentment toward the opposite sex, Americans were in the middle, with 18 percent of the men and 25 percent of the women reporting that they were often, or very often, resentful of the opposite sex because of behavior that was typical of that sex. Resentment was much higher, among both sexes, in Chile, France and Lithuania, and much *lower*, among both sexes, in Hungary and Taiwan.

This wide difference in resentment of the two sexes toward each other in the United States and in Hungary was evident in one of the few public "scandals" that emanated from the Kaposvár/Taszár installation in Southern Hungary, the staging center for American troops headed for peacekeeping duties in Bosnia. The IFOR base set up there in early 1996 brought an economic boom to the area. Brown & Root, the Houston, Texas-based company contracted by the U.S. Military to procure supplies, equipment and services for the center, estimated at the end of January, 1996, that they had spent $8 million in Kaposvár and $12 million in other cities for goods and services. Many jobs were created for the local community and all of them were well-paying in comparison with Hungarian salaries for similar work. Among those services provided by the contractor was feeding both the approximately 3000 personnel based at the center, and the transient troops who passed through on the way to and from Bosnia. Within the first few months allegations appeared in the press that American employees had sexually harassed some of the local female employees. An investigation was launched immediately but the findings were ambiguous; no Hungarian woman was quoted as having filed charges of sexual harassment or of having used that term in complaining of specific offenses. One of the most serious of the charges was that an American male cook had pat-searched a female Hungarian assistant on three consecutive days, allegedly suspecting she was stealing food from the kitchen. No stolen food was found. The investigation of that incident did not result in a case of sexual harassment; the Hungarian woman was quoted in the newspaper account as saying she did not accuse the American male of "sexual harassment." The report in an English language paper made a general statement about "allegations by Hungarian women," whereas the Hungarian television news report stated that the allegations were made by an AP correspondent working in Hungary, and averred that no women at Taszár had accused any American of sexual harassment.

Some light was cast upon the matter in a letter to the editor of one English language daily from a Hungarian woman, a co-founder in 1994 of the first hotline for battered woman and children in Hungary. She wrote, "...the overwhelming majority of Hungarian women have NEVER heard the term sexual harassment, would probably not understand what it means and would probably have ambiguous feelings about wanting to have anything to do with it. This despite the fact that in Hungary, as elsewhere, sexual harassment is the hard and harsh fact of a great many working women's lives." She went on to state that it would be very good news if, indeed, the women at Taszár had made a complaint, even though it would be a first for Hungary and would definitely have resulted in no legal redress. There are no laws against sexual harassment in Hungary; an effort by a woman Member of Parliament in 1992 to introduce such legislation failed in the committee stage, and her attempt was extensively ridiculed in the Hungarian media.

There are likewise no laws against domestic violence, and no reliable statistics on domestic violence. Many instances go unreported because of a lack of faith in the criminal justice system and the shame and guilt that abused women feel. Law enforcement people, social workers, court officials, and the medical community are poorly informed and inadequately trained to deal with such cases when they are reported. They are often handled incompetently leading to a feeling on the part of the victims that it is useless and sometimes even dangerous to appeal to public officials.

The present Hungarian constitution, enacted by the first democratically-elected parliament following the downfall of the communist regime in 1989, contains a provision, aimed at righting past wrongs, which asserts the "inviolability of one's home." The intent of this was to prohibit random entry into and searches of private homes, a routine occurrence in the communist days and a bitter memory for Hungarian citizens. This provision is, unfortunately for abused women and children, being interpreted to mean that the government cannot interfere with the domestic lives of its citizens, thus denying families protection against domestic abuse. There are to my knowledge cases where friends and neighbors know that a wife is being abused, but they are helpless to do anything about it. They say the police would not reply to a call from anyone outside the home, as they cannot legally enter the house without the express consent of the head of the household. A man's home really is his castle, protected by a legal provision as secure as a moat. General laws against assault make domestic battery illegal but charges are hard to prosecute. Willing witnesses are seldom available. Doctors do not document bruises; if a case is reported to the police, they ask if there is any blood. If there is none, they say it is a "private affair."

In preparation for membership in the Europe Union, Hungary is required to enact legislation to criminalize violent acts in the home along guidelines established by the UN and the Council of Europe. But many members of the current parliament are dragging their feet on this issue. They give as their reason a fear of the return to government intrusion into the home as it existed under communism, and caution that extreme care must be taken in drafting such legislation. It is impossible to say whether it is only a revulsion for the past that motivates reluctance to deal with the matter expeditiously. In the meantime, the ambiguous provisions for citizen protection against the state continue to be interpreted so that cases of spousal and child abuse are almost impossible to prosecute.

The organization NaNe (Women for Women against Violence) set up a hot line for battered women in 1994 to give out information on shelters where women and children can stay but in 1998 there is still only one shelter specifically for battered women. It is run by the Salvation Army, and cannot begin to meet the need. It is staffed by about 30 Hungarian women and one English woman, all volunteers. One legal advance has been revision of the law against rape that formerly excluded marital partners--rape was a crime only when unmarried couples were involved. The exclusion has been omitted.

Wives who leave their homes have no right to reclaim them. And the attitude of the public regarding spousal and child abuse is not unanimous in denunciation. In the English language weekly, *Budapest Week*, in 1996, seven years into Hungary's democratic government, a Hungarian-American columnist, opposed to the idea of shelters for battered women, wrote:

"It reinforces and justifies the woman's injury, strengthens grievances without providing the opportunity to examine her role in creating a violent atmosphere... .... the unfortunate consequence of importing such interventions wholesale from the West is that as men are debunked for their chauvinism . . . their traditional roles as fathers also become diluted."

This excerpt contains the gist of a common attitude towards wife abuse; it is probably the woman's fault; and the male position as head of the family, the authoritarian role, must be maintained at all cost.

Even if the Constitution is brought into compliance with the guidelines of the UN, there is no guarantee that such revisions will result in really effective legislation, or that they will bring about a change in the behavior of men and women toward each other. There are some indications, however, that public opinion is influencing the behavior of men, and I have learned of specific cases in which there has been a real turn-around – the men in question have stopped the abuse.

When the communist regime ended in 1989, a number of state-owned enterprises closed down, and many people were thrown out of work. The unemployed were mostly factory workers and others with no marketable skills. At the same time, foreign business people were flocking to Hungary to explore investment opportunities, and tourists were coming to have an unhampered look at a former Iron Curtain country, creating new job opportunities of various kinds for local people. A large demand arose for tour guides, interpreters, taxi- and bus-drivers, and people with other skills requiring special education and/or training. There also arose, particularly in Budapest, a demand for certain kinds of service providers, such as paid escorts, masseuses, and prostitutes, requiring minimal skills, especially for beautiful young women of which Hungary has a plenitude. In a surprisingly short time, the number of massage parlors, escort services, "singles" bars for both sexes (or, as one commenter phrased it, "all three sexes"), and streetwalkers multiplied. Many attractive young women found that these jobs offered better money per working hour than they had ever earned before. Prostitution has always existed in Hungary, and Budapest has a long, and what many consider respectable, history of that profession, specifically in District 8. The current district mayor, who grew up there says, "Everyone knew whose mother and whose sister was a prostitute; the old timers can tell you which buildings were built specially as brothels."

In 1950, the communists outlawed brothels on the principle that prostitution was exploitative; they arrested prostitutes and forced them to work in (presumably non-exploitative) clothing factories. But as throughout the world, throughout history, streetwalking continued, although somewhat limited and somewhat clandestinely. Society seems unable to explain why this "world's oldest profession" flourishes in spite of almost universal religious, legal and social disapproval, but the Hungarian novelist Kálmán Mikszáth, threw some light on the matter. One of the characters in his 1900 novel, *A Strange Marriage*, the old Antal Szirmay, described as "our beloved and honourable deputy at the diet," says: "Marriage is like food: he who takes his meals at an inn, yearns for plain cooking; whereas he who eats at home is continually tantalized by the thought of the innkeeper's food."

After 1956, during the Kádár years, as the Hungarian government grew more liberal, some restrictions were eased on escort services, massage parlors and other managed sexual activities. The democratic parliament, elected in 1991, decriminalized streetwalking in 1994, but prostitutes were still subject to fines. Officials of District 8 would like to establish legal brothels that would be regulated, taxed, and periodically inspected to insure that health standards are maintained. Concern about the spread of AIDS, not yet a large problem in Hungary, but threatening to become one, has led the National Institute of Public Health to support the idea, which is strongly opposed by the prestigious public schools in the area. The schools may win; brothels have not yet been legalized, and approval for them does not seem likely in the near future. In 1998, legislation was introduced prohibiting prostitutes from working in towns with a population of less than 20,000 and on main city roads, turnpikes, and highways bearing one or two digit numbers. Prostitution is to be completely outlawed in the vicinity of courts, city halls, schools (including kindergartens), railway stations and religious institutions. Local municipalities would have authority to restrict prostitution in other areas within their own jurisdictions. The draft bill provides that media advertising of sexual services, now a reliable source of income to newspapers, magazines, and TV stations and to the agencies that provide them with copy, is punishable by fines up to 1,000,000 forints ($5000). It also makes it illegal for prostitutes to accept clients under the age of 18.

It is an unsurprising corollary that a city where prostitution flourishes, has come to be known also as the "Porno Capital" of Europe. Many beautiful young women without other marketable skills have found that with an uninhibited attitude toward sex and a small amount of acting talent they can have a career in films that is preferable in several ways to streetwalking. Pornographic films are made in a few days, or a couple of weeks at most, and an actress can move from one to another once she becomes established. Hungarian sex films have become popular in other Eastern European countries also, and some neighboring countries are beginning to make their own. Hungarian actresses, known for their beauty and reputed to have a more liberal attitude about sex, are often hired for films that are made in other countries.

It is not only porno films that are made in Hungary. International television and movie producers have discovered that Budapest provides the European grandeur required for some film scenery at budget prices, and its eclectic architecture makes it adaptable to almost any European locality with a minimum of effort. One producer who chose Budapest as a "stand-in" location for a Parisian love story, shrugged off the substitution saying, "O.K. It's not Paris, but you've got 70 percent of it at one-third the price."

The Hungarian film industry at one time had the highest technical standards in Europe, and produced generations of high-quality technicians. That industry, state-owned and state-controlled under the communist government, collapsed in 1989 when Mafilm studio laid off between 2000 and 3000 employees. Less than a year later, however, American and West European filmmakers discovered Budapest's adaptable architecture and lower production costs – stage hands who earn more than $2000 weekly in the United States are paid about $450 in Hungary – and soon most of Mafilm's former employees were working again. Since 1990, in Hollywood films and television commercials, Budapest has doubled as Berlin, Paris, Vienna, Geneva, Casablanca, Warsaw, Moscow, Toronto, and in a torrent of publicity, Buenos Aires, when Madonna came here to film "Evita."

Film industry workers in Hungary have nothing like the union protection they have in the United States and other places, so there is rampant exploitation in all fields and skills and at all levels, involving both men and women. However, even in the absence of any statistical evidence, it is safe to say that young women, especially those engaged in films of the pornographic genre, are the most exploited. At the same time, it is also safe to say that they can still earn more from such work than they would earn doing other jobs that might be available to them.

Until 1996, the retirement age for women in Hungary was 55 and 60 for men. In that year the retirement age for men was set at 62. The pension plan is still being revised and a retirement age of 62 for both men and women is being phased in gradually. It is expected to be fully established by 2009. The government pension plan, referred to as Social Security, was never generous but after 1989 when the forint was steadily devalued, pensions bought even less and many retirees who could find part-time jobs supplemented their pensions with earned income.

When I inquired about the availability of household help in 1992, my Hungarian friends and colleagues were scandalized. It didn't exist, they told me. No Hungarian woman would ever pay someone to do her housework, and certainly no Hungarian woman would do another woman's housework, except in the case of a sick friend. But after a few discreet inquiries, I found that a neighbor, who had recently become a pensioner, would be glad to earn the extra money. She was a widow living with an unmarried grown daughter whose salary was insufficient to cover the household expenses. Every cleaning woman I have had in Hungary was past retirement age and on a pension. A question I was frequently asked was, "Doesn't your family miss you?" That question made sense to me only after I found out that most retired women, including those with part-time jobs, routinely make weekly visits to the homes of their children, where they clean, cook, do the laundry, and sometimes prepare food for the next few days. One woman approaching 40 years of age, married, with two children, said, "If I didn't see my mother at least once a week, I couldn't get along." I understood her remark better when I learned that her mother visited one day a week and did the household chores that are usually paid for in the United States. When I ask young women whose mothers help them so much if they plan to do the same for their sons and daughters after retirement, no one answers; they only smile.

In the villages and on the farms, women share in all the drudgery not consigned to the domestic animals, in addition to the cooking, housework, and child care. Observing the life of such women even for a few hours, one easily comprehends that they might be considered "old" after the age of 30.

Today's Hungarian women whose physical endowments easily justify Hungary's reputation as the home of great beauties often wear dolorous or angry expressions, thus obscuring their loveliness. One very beautiful colleague at my school had seemingly never learned to smile. When, in the context of certain situations, a smile was called for, her expressions ranged from bitter-grim, almost a sneer, to resigned, as if to say, "What can I do?" She never smiled broadly in my presence, much less laughed aloud with open enjoyment.

In truth, women have less reason to smile than men do. All babies are pampered, spoiled, their every whim noted and if possible satisfied, but boys are doted on, especially by their mothers. It is easy to make a connection, albeit superficial, between this mother-child relationship and the Hungarian male attitude that values women according to their willingness and proficiency in fulfilling male needs. When it comes to fulfilling needs, nobody in the world does that as well as a good mother, and mothers are revered in Hungary, even as their unceasing labor is taken for granted. The husband who brings home flowers at the end of the day is not far removed from the six-year old who picks field flowers for his mother on an afternoon walk.

My friend Sally in New York has Hungarian roots: a grandmother born in Hungary married a Hungarian in the United States. Her mother, born in the United States, married a man of Russian heritage. She told me this before I came to Hungary and said that her earliest memories included her grandmother's Hungarian cooking, and her mother's repeated admonition, "Whatever you do, never marry a Hungarian man!" When Sally pressed for an explanation, her mother only said, "They make terrible husbands."

The unspoken assumption of male superiority is instilled and reinforced in boy children from birth. While that often makes them arrogant and overbearing, it also imposes upon many a burden that may be too heavy. Not all Hungarian men are equipped to take the leadership role, to make decisions and be responsible for the actions of wives and children, and above all for carrying on the myth of male charisma and strength. Not all Hungarian men are physically and emotionally strong enough, or even have the desire, to become domineering family rulers. But such a model is held up to them as the ideal. That would be challenging in any society. But in the last half of the 20th century Hungarians lived under a system in which the individual was denigrated and every element of life was controlled by the state. Home was the only place where most males were the dominant figure, and where they could give vent to their frustrations.

It should not shock us to learn of a recent study showing that approximately 49% of Hungarian adult males are "heavy drinkers," a term that is defined as one stop below "alcoholic." Between 40,000 and 50,000 deaths were due to alcoholism in Hungary in 1995 out of a population of just over 10 million; cirrhosis has become the No. 2 killer in the country. Most alcohol-related deaths occur among males, but not all; alcoholism among women is on the rise.

In 1996, an English language newspaper reported results of a recent survey that indicated approximately 75 percent of Hungarian men have sexual problems. This seemed so extreme that I asked my Hungarian women friends whom I knew well enough if they thought this was true. (It was a small group, of course. Who, besides sex researchers could ask a lot of people about that subject?) Their replies were unanimous and emphatic. "Of course," said one, "Everybody knows that. That is why they are so macho and boastful in public." Numerous Hungarian women and some from foreign countries have made similar remarks to me. Most of them said they thought alcohol was largely responsible.

Hungarian men are not all swaggering braggards, but most simply take it for granted, without even thinking about it, that as males they will be accorded precedence. This is nowhere more evident than in the behavior of male pedestrians in certain situations. Budapest streets today are clogged with more automobiles than anyone ever dreamed of during the communist regime (sometimes referred to now as the "good old, bad old days,") and there is no parking space for them. So automobiles are regularly parked on the sidewalks, sometimes on both sides of the street. They may be laterally parked, completely covering the sidewalk, in which case pedestrians are forced to walk in the road. Most often, they are parked diagonally, the front wheels resting half-way across the sidewalk. This leaves very little space and when two people walking in opposite directions meet, it is like driving on a single-lane road, one must get off to allow the other to pass. When I am about to meet a man on such a street, he usually appears not to see me, and I am the one who steps aside between two cars, whereupon he goes by without a word or any slight recognition of my presence. Occasionally, I pretend not to see him, and if I hold out long enough that a collision seems imminent, he will step aside, but never acknowledges my presence or replies to my cheerful, smiling, "Thank you," or usually, "Thank you very much!"

The sidewalks are narrow even without automobiles and frequently three or four men will block pedestrian traffic by standing together in lively conversation oblivious to any other activity on the street. When approaching such a group, no amount of throat-clearing, paper-rustling, or clicking of heels on the concrete alerts them. It is as if they are deaf and have no peripheral vision. Some passersby simply walk out into the road around them, but I refuse to do this, I walk right up to the group and stop. Do they turn, in surprise, and look at me? Never. Do they hastily separate with perhaps a muttered apology? No. They sway outward in slow motion, leaving barely room for one person to squeeze by, with no sign of recognition and no response to a "Thank you." This studied indifference to other people seems to be a national characteristic, much more pronounced in men. Even when forced, by direct request, to adjust their stance to give someone space to pass, they do not acknowledge the presence of that person.

This is mysterious to the point of being a little eerie, and in my opinion it is insulting. It says, "You do not exist." At first, I speculated that this was a form or protective behavior, developed in police states where nobody wants to become a "witness." It is a way of saying, "I am not here, and if you think I am, I do not see you. Thus, I can never be a witness to anything that happens here." But Hungary is now eight years into democracy and it begins to seem more like an ingrained national characteristic.

Men never hesitate to give advice to a woman even if none has been requested. She has only to say, "I must go to such-and-such a place," and a man is certain to speak up and say something like, "You should take the Number 3 Metro, and …" If she interrupts, saying, "Thank you. I know the way; I have been there," he may continue. When I spoke about this to a Hungarian woman friend, she said that was a world-wide male characteristic; not just Hungarian, and cited John Gray's *Men are from Mars, Women are from Venus*. But I find it hard to believe that a conversation with a man I encountered in the lobby of my building one day could have occurred anywhere except in Hungary.

A young man appeared and opened his mailbox as I was also collecting my mail. We greeted each other with the perfunctory "Good Day," as everyone does in the lobby, on the elevator, or in hallways in my building, and this conversation followed:

He: Do you live in this building?

I: Yes, I do.

He: Well, the lock on the front door isn't working well. You should have it fixed.

I: The Housemaster (building caretaker) is in Apartment Number 1. (I pointed to it.)

He: (Ignoring my remark, and with some impatience.) Well, can you have it fixed?

I: Do you live in this building?

He: Yes.

I: (Laughing) You can have it fixed better than I can, maybe even do it yourself.

His expression showed no embarrassment or even indignation. He only looked puzzled, as if my behavior was strange.

Up to now, I have seen very little to indicate that Hungarian women resent such behavior. In private, they may complain, but in the presence of men they are models of compliance and docility. The pressure to marry is so strong that women learn at a very young age to make themselves agreeable to men. When I ask women if they feel or felt pressured to marry, everyone denies it. "Oh, no," they say, "not from my family." Close friends who have married admit that they did feel pressure from society in general, but usually maintain that the family had exerted none. Their assertion of this may only mean that they were unaware of it. Inculcation of the importance of marriage begins at such a young age that both women and men may feel it never occurred.

Once I took an American guest to visit a very attractive Hungarian family. The parents are both university educated, and their two children, a boy and a girl in their early teens are both intelligent and very attractive. It is always a pleasure to visit them; they are gracious hosts, interested in and informed about many things. The family had recently moved into a large new house, a happy event for them, and at first much of our conversation centered on the house, the garden, the neighborhood. In the course of the conversation, both parents at different times referred to the amount of living space they had and stated that when their daughter married there would be enough room for her and her husband – not once, but several times. Thinking that I might be overly-sensitive to such remarks, I asked my friend when we left if she noticed those references, and she exclaimed, "Of course! I was shocked!" No mention has ever been made in my presence of what that exceptionally promising young girl might do with her intelligence and talents in addition to being married.

Every Hungarian woman I know well, regardless of her professional accomplishments, feels that a male companion, husband or not, is essential. Those who escape from miserably unhappy marriages often plunge into another marriage or live-in relationship very soon, even when it is no more promising than the previous one. In this they may not differ from many American women, but there is an element in the Hungarian psychology that is distinctive, the idea that women are defenseless and need protection. It has nothing to do with strength or even competency; the man may be manifestly less capable than the woman, but because he is male, she reveres him and considers him necessary to a successful life.

A long-divorced Hungarian woman friend, very competent and well-educated, whose son was a student in the high school where I taught, appeared in the school one day, accompanied by her live-in male companion. I was surprised to see them and concerned when they went into the principal's office. Her son was a good student and not likely to be in trouble. Later I asked her if anything was wrong. She laughed and said, "Oh, no. We are going on a trip and I wanted to get permission for my son to be out of school for two weeks. I asked Peter to go with me because I know such a request is more likely to be granted if I am accompanied by a man."

Another woman, a well-known and much admired professional, divorced, and living with her 12-year-old son, was having some repair work done in her home. She and the workman agreed that he would come on the following Saturday to do a job, and she asked him what time he would be there. He said he wasn't sure. "At least give me some idea, morning or afternoon," she replied. "I don't want to be waiting here all day," and he said, "Why not? What else have you got to do?" When she told me this story, she was angrier than I had ever seen her, but her decision about how to handle the situation was to me the most shocking part of the incident. She said, "I am going to ask my former husband to be here when he comes, because with that attitude, I am sure I won't get a decent job done unless I have a man to deal with him."

After hearing many stories along this line, it did not surprise me when I asked fourth-year high school students how they would like to see themselves ten years hence, hoping to get some insight into their ambitions and dreams, and every girl with one single exception said she wanted to be married and have children. Two or three mentioned that they would also like to have some kind of job outside of the home, but none spoke of a profession. The school was a gymnasium, a secondary school from which graduation is a prerequisite to a university education. When asked what age they thought was best for a woman to marry, the consensus was the age of nineteen. Three years later, when I was no longer teaching, Peter and Imre two former students, then in higher education institutions, were visiting me and the subject of marriage came up. I reminded them of the time we had the class discussion and the girls said 19 would be the best age for women to marry, and Imre interrupted me. "That has changed," he said. "The girls in my college now talk about 30 as the best age!" Marriage and the family still get strong official support. Maternity leave time for working mothers is still very generous although the pay has been reduced.

The status of women in Hungary, especially educated women, has improved since the democratic government was installed, but without a comprehensive survey it would be impossible to say how much. They are paid less than men doing the same jobs, as is still true in the U.S., but the gap is greater in Hungary. They are being given more responsibility in the work place, or at least better-sounding titles. My estimation is that they are about where American women were in the early 1970s when a young woman in New York said to me, "I am now a vice president in my firm, but I'm still the one who gets the coffee."

Early marriages often end in divorce, and the divorce rate is rapidly approaching that of the United States. Divorce was relatively easy during the communist regime since education, medical care and housing were provided by the government. Personal property was not a factor as the state owned everything, and there was no "alimony." Children usually stayed with the mother and a set percentage of the father's income was allocated to their support. The main problem was housing since one spouse had to leave the home and needed official assignment of another domicile. There were often delays in approval of the additional housing and some couples continued to live in the same residence after divorce, even after one of the partners married again and brought a new spouse to live in the same residence.

Now, divorce is an option only for those women who earn enough to support themselves and provide a major part of the children's support. Others are literally at the mercy of their husbands who may mistreat them, and can divorce or abandon them at will. They live very precarious lives, fearful of losing their only means of support, and many feel they have no choice but to endure abusive treatment from their husbands both to themselves and to their children.

When one says that Hungarian women or men do this or that, it is of course a broad generalization that does not include every individual. There are beautiful, slender, well-dressed women; there are women members of parliament – not many – and female entrepreneurs, who have probably been the most successful in achieving financial independence. There are also some men who help with the housework and care of the children, most of them younger people who live in the cities. In general, however, men prefer not to own up to helping in the home; it isn't something they brag about to their male friends. One Saturday morning, I stopped by a neighbor's apartment and surprised her husband in the midst of scouring the bathroom. He looked a little sheepish as if he had been caught in a compromising situation, although he knew I would only applaud such action. Another friend and neighbor told me one day in an apparent slip of the tongue that her teen-age son helped her by vacuuming the apartment floors. Then she realized what she had said and immediately asked me not to mention it to anyone. "He would be very embarrassed if any of his friends found out!" she whispered. There are very few Hungarian women who would tell a mother-in-law that her husband helps with the housework, must less with the cooking! In the cities, quite a few young couples are beginning to share the household duties and child care, but just as in America, women who work outside the home still carry the heavier load.

NOTES FROM THE JOURNAL – JUDIT'S WEDDING

The Kovács's granddaughter, Judit, graduated from college in June and in September married András, a college classmate. As an adopted member of the family I was invited to the wedding and plans were made for me to join Budapest relatives who would be making the 130-kilometer trip by car and returning late in the evening after the wedding supper. It was my first Hungarian wedding, and I was delighted to be invited and to have the transportation arranged so conveniently. It never occurred to me to ask about the car or the driver so it was a very pleasant surprise to be called for by a cousin of the bride with her two children in a brand new red Opel which her husband was driving. The road we traveled was mostly two-lane, despite which our driver, apparently unmindful of the possibility of any oncoming traffic, took off at a pace that rendered me breathless and clench-fisted. My worries were groundless; he was probably the best driver I have ever ridden with. We made the trip in two hours with no mishap of any kind. On a two-lane highway, on a Saturday afternoon! There were so few cars in Hungary then that highway traffic was very light. And that was only on the trip going there; on the return trip – but I'll get to that later.

The wedding party and guests assembled at the modest-sized *lakótelep* apartment of the bride's parents, where the bride, her maid of honor, her parents and brother, and the groom's best man were getting dressed. The approximately 100 guests, therefore, gathered in the parking lot. For the trip to the place where the ceremony was held, we were assigned to cars which traveled in a caravan. The bride and her family were in the first car; the groom and his family in the second; and I was in the third with the next closest relatives. The bride and groom were both members of the city's police force, so we had a police escort all the way. Two motorcycle policemen led the procession and stopped traffic at every intersection until we passed. At large intersections, other motorcycle policemen were already holding back the traffic when the procession approached.

The building where the ceremony took place was a former synagogue that had been converted by the communist government into an art museum and a venue for weddings. Officially, it was designated as *"házasságköto terem"* (Registry Office), where civil marriage ceremonies were performed. Some couples chose to have both kinds of ceremony: first, the civil service, at the *házasságköto terem*, dressed in their wedding finery, followed by a religious ceremony in a church.

Either because our travel was unimpeded by other traffic or because there was an unusual number of marriages that day – Saturday was a popular day for weddings – we had quite a long wait outside the building for the previous wedding party to depart. It was a beautiful early fall day; people milled around in the sunshine greeting relatives and friends and nobody seemed to mind the wait. When the other wedding ended, we watched the departing ritual which our group would repeat later. All the guests came out and lined up on each side of the walkway leading from the building. When they were in place, the newlyweds came out preceded by two pretty little flower girls, looking like flowers themselves, carrying baskets of rose petals which they scattered in the pathway of the bride and groom. The guests followed the couple as they departed in the opposite direction from where we stood, and we realigned ourselves to enter the building in proper order.

The bride went first, escorted by her brother; it is the Hungarian custom for a young male member of the family to escort the bride; their parents followed. The groom with his parents was next, and then the other members of the wedding party and the guests.

The building had not been altered from the original traditional synagogue design: a main auditorium with a balcony for female worshippers. The balcony had been turned into an art exhibition space and the works of some contemporary Hungarian artists were then on display. The municipality not only provided the space for wedding ceremonies, but also furnished the decoration. There were some flowers in the area where a church altar would have been, flowers that looked fresh although they had served several weddings already and would serve still more that same day. It was a pleasant auditorium with simple lines and unadorned wooden seats. A slightly raised platform was at one end where there would be an altar in a house of worship. To anyone accustomed to church or cathedral weddings, the setting seemed rather stark. No imposing neo-baroque doorway decorated with bronze reliefs, no Carrara marble font; no high altar with scenes depicting the life of Christ; no steep-roofed Gothic nave; no statues of saints, no arches or high dome to reverberate the sonorous tones of an imposing pipe organ, no stained-glass windows. Still, there was an air of solemnity arising from the occasion itself: friends and relatives had gathered to witness the pledge of two young people to spend the rest of their lives together, to hear them vow to remain faithful and loyal through the inevitable vicissitudes that were to come. Marriage ceremonies, like christenings, are expressions of humanity's best hopes for the future, inspiring for the moment whatever comes afterward. Later, I asked János why the building had not been returned to its original function as a synagogue after 1989. He thought for a moment, then said quietly, "I don't think there are more than three Jewish families left in this city."

The bride and groom, third-generation communists, had both grown up with no religious education or experience, but they wanted to have a ceremony that was beautiful, moving and memorable. So they designed a ceremony that satisfied the legalities of the prescribed socialist-communist civil rite combined with some elements of the Christian marriage ceremony, and incorporated a few traditional Sárköz wedding customs into the *lakodalmi ebéd* (wedding feast). The bride wore an elegant white satin gown that would have been appropriate for any church on New York's Fifth Avenue. She carried a beautiful bouquet of Arum lilies and roses. Her brother, who escorted her, and the groom were both in black tie.

There was an organ in the building that may have been added at the time of the conversion to a wedding hall, but I am not sure, and a brief program of light classical music was played at the beginning. Then the local government official who performed the ceremony took her place on the platform. When I asked what title she had, they said, "She came from the office of the Mayor." She was a nice looking woman, probably in her early-forties, wearing a two-piece navy and white dress with her badge of office ostentatiously draped diagonally across her ample bosom. It was a striped riband in the colors of the Hungarian flag, red, white and green, one end attached at her right shoulder, the other at her waist on the left side. The bride and her attendant, the groom and his best man stood facing her on the platform. She performed the brief ceremony with perfunctory dignity just as a clerk in the New York City Registry Office might do. Then the bride and groom read to each other their personal vows which they themselves had written. The official ended the ceremony with a somewhat warmer but obviously obligatory lecture on the responsibilities of marriage. The couple signed the register and together with their attendants turned to stand at the edge of the platform facing the congregation to accept individual congratulations. The guests went up one by one and there were good wishes, tears, hugs and kisses enough to make up for any perceived lack of sentimentality. Then, as the guests at the previous wedding had done, we took our places along each side of the walkway leading from the building and murmured more good wishes as the tiny, doll-like flower girls bestrewed rose petals in the path of the newlyweds. Then all departed for the restaurant where the wedding feast was held. The police department again provided escort service.

The restaurant was quite spacious, with a second floor designed for large banquets and receptions. In the main room on the second floor tables were arranged in a U-shape, and places were set for the approximately 100 guests. Separated from that room only by arches were two smaller rooms, one at each end. An orchestra was in one of the smaller rooms and played throughout the night. The other room was arranged for dancing. And what a wedding feast it was! Even by Hungarian standards, the meal was overabundant. Course after course of soup, beef, chicken, pork, potatoes – boiled, fried, and in salad – rice, noodles, cabbage salad, pickles, bread, wine, vodka, beer, mineral water and coca-cola. And after all that, the desserts: not just a wedding cake, but huge layer cakes, chocolate, walnut, coconut, lemon, strawberry, distributed to each ten-place table. The food was not prepared by the restaurant but by the bride's family and friends. Anna told me she had been cooking for weeks, baking her famous pastry (*sütmény*) and other things that could be frozen. Every family in attendance brought something, at least a homemade layer cake, very large layer cakes, and those I sampled were delicious. Restaurant personnel served the foods very professionally and efficiently. Platters of pastry, fruit, and candy stood on tables at the end of the dining room. The wedding cake, when it came late in the evening, was a spun-sugar sculpture in the shape of interlocking wedding rings, large enough for each guest to be served a piece of it.

The social grace of the bridal pair was most impressive. The groom was confidently in charge, offering toasts to the bride and her family, to his family, and during the meal, visiting every table and speaking personally to every guest. If I had not known that he grew up in a small village where piped-in running water and electricity were rarities, I would have assumed that he was the product of a privileged family and had acquired his social grace as a matter of course.

At midnight, the bride and groom disappeared, took off their wedding costumes and reappeared wearing clothing symbolizing their new status. She was dressed in a red, full-skirted peasant-type dress with an apron, ready for the kitchen, obviously. He wore slacks and a casual shirt. Ready to lounge? The mother and grandmother of the bride also went out and changed clothes, the symbolism of which I never learned. When they returned, everyone was ushered into the room set up for dancing. The orchestra in the third room continued playing.

In one end of the "ballroom" there was a table with a silver tray on it. The mother of the bride was seated at the table, behind the tray. Guests took turns placing an envelope containing money in the tray after which each contributor was rewarded by a dance with the bride, the groom or both.

When I had inquired about the proper way to present wedding gifts, I was told that they were brought to the wedding. Thus I brought with me a package wrapped in white paper tied with white satin ribbon containing a silver picture frame and a gift of money. When I arrived at the bride's parents' apartment before the wedding, I tried to give the package to the bride's mother, but she said, "Not now." So, I was forced to hold onto it all afternoon, through the ceremony and finally carried it with me to the restaurant. By the time the giving ceremony began, I was more than eager to make my presentation and be rid of it. But to my dismay, no one else carried a package, and I felt conspicuously cloddish to be holding one when, as far as I could tell, no one else arrived bearing a gift except the money they placed upon the silver tray, the appropriate gift, obviously. But my money gift was buried deep inside the securely gift-wrapped package which, with apologies, I handed to the bride's mother, and whispered that there was money inside. She accepted it most graciously, not at all disconcerted. I was suitably rewarded by a dance with the groom; after a few minutes the bride joined us and we three danced together. The dancing was very free and informal and everyone joined in, children as well, so there were groups of three or more as well as couples on the floor.

After the guests had all kicked in with their contributions and everyone had danced with the newlyweds, a shower of coins was thrown onto the dance floor, almost covering it. The bride and groom knelt down and attempted to pick up the coins as the guests made it difficult for them by kicking the coins away as they reached for them. It was an exhausting exercise for the newlyweds, and its significance was lost on me. The only function I could see that it served was to tire them out, which seems to have been the idea of the overlong party and the rituals performed in that part of the celebration. After the couple's efforts to retrieve the coins had gone on for quite a while and there were still many coins on the floor, the bride's mother brought in a broom and dust pan and swept up the remaining ones, thus ending that ritual in order to move on to the next.

The next one was an old Sárköz wedding custom probably unique to that region. No one in Budapest whom I asked knew anything about it. The bride and groom stood in the center of the room in clear view of the guests who sat or stood around the walls. The reason for the groom's change of costume into lounging slacks then became clear. The bride inserted an uncooked egg into the bottom of one leg of his slacks and, manipulating the egg through the cloth, moved it up his leg across his pelvis and down the other leg until it reappeared at the bottom of the pants leg opposite the one into which the egg had been inserted. The bride's movements provoked titters and giggles especially as the egg approached the pelvic area, and its reappearance as it emerged unbroken was greeted with applause and much merriment. The merriment it provided was such that even weeks later, when the bride's grandparents visited me in Budapest, they recalled that particular part of the wedding festivities and laughed until tears came into their eyes. I tried to indicate pleasure at the memory but it was difficult.

It was past midnight when this part of the evening ended and I was already thinking about the return trip to Budapest assuming it to be the end of the celebration. But we were ushered back into the dining room where the tables had been cleared and reset with fresh china, glassware, and eating utensils. Puzzled, I pointed to the table and said to the woman sitting next to me, "What is this for?" She replied, "Oh, now we will have some roast!" And sure enough, to my unbelieving eyes, we were served another meal of chicken, pork, potato salad, and what they call "Francia" salad – which I believe to be a name they have given to Russian salad – containing green peas, carrots, onions, potatoes and other vegetables in a thick mayonnaise dressing. More wine, of course, and more sweets on the table.

It was a great relief when the driver of the car in which I had traveled to the wedding told me with profuse apologies that he had to open his benzene (gasoline) station at six o'clock the next morning, and we would have to leave before the party was over. Considering the speed we traveled early in the day on our way to the wedding, I assumed we would get back to Budapest in about two hours. What I had not taken into account was the difference in the time we were traveling. There wasn't much traffic at two o'clock in the afternoon, but at two o'clock in the morning there was none. It was like driving on a race track, and the return trip took one hour and fifteen minutes! I was sitting beside the driver and once I courageously glanced at the speedometer. It read "140"! That was kilometers, of course, but still on a two-lane highway! As I said he was the best driver I have ever ridden with. It would have been nice to fall into bed immediately, but as we departed from the restaurant, Anna had pressed upon me a large package containing samples of the party food, various sweets, of course, and also chicken, pork, and even salad. So I had to store the food in the freezer before the long day finally ended.

Judit's great-grandfather, the family patriarch, who lived through most of the twentieth century, died before her wedding, reducing the current family to three generations, and I wondered if she and András would hasten to restore it to four. But they had other plans. Soon after the wedding, they both entered law school at a university within commuting distance and arranged their working schedules so they could continue to work and attend school. Before the century ends, they will both have law degrees, and thus enter the twenty-first century as a young married couple the like of which their great grandparents or even grandparents could scarcely have imagined.

NOTES FROM THE JOURNAL – INSIDE SERBIA, A GLIMPSE

Once, traveling from Vienna to Budapest, I took a Yugoslavian train and swore never to make that mistake again. But in 1997 when my former Peace Corps colleague Jeff invited me to visit him in Belgrade where he was working with the Organization for Security and Cooperation in Europe (OSCE), there was no other reasonable way to go. Jeff also invited our mutual friend James who was teaching at a Budapest University, and although I would have hesitated to go alone, the promise of a traveling companion made the invitation irresistible. We bought First Class tickets and were so pleased at the very low cost that we failed to consider its significance. A hint of apprehension set in when we boarded the train marked "Thessaloniki" and found no car marked "1" indicating First Class. Our seats were in a car marked "2," but we both had window seats – we sat facing each other – and there were only two other passengers in the six-place compartment, so we were reassured. It was early in the day and a snack cart come through the car as soon as we left Budapest. We bought coffee and mineral water from the vendor, a young Hungarian man. He seemed to want to talk with us, so we chatted a bit, and when he came back later we bought more drinks and some snacks. As we approached the Yugoslavian border, he returned and said if we wanted anything more we should buy it because he was leaving the train at the next station, and we said our goodbyes. And that was the last time we saw of any train vendor during the entire journey.

At Subotica, our first stop inside Yugoslavia, the two other people in our compartment got off. The platform was crowded, and as soon as the border officials had finished checking the papers of all seated passengers, people swarmed onto the train frantically grabbing any available seat or standing room. A number of people tried to crowd into our compartment to claim the four vacant seats, and in the end seven remained. Any semblance of "First Class" had disappeared at the border. Unreasonably, perhaps, I felt that we had been invaded, and tried to make myself as small as possible, wishing I could become invisible. But when I relaxed and looked at our compartment mates, I saw that the seven young men were all neat and clean and well-behaved. They took turns sitting and standing – those whose turn it was to stand went into the corridor and smoked cigarettes. They all smoked! The only language they could speak was French. I used to think I spoke French but after more than five years of concentration on the Hungarian language and no use for any other language except Russian on rare occasions, I have lost whatever facility I had. Besides, they were speaking with an accent I had never heard in Paris or in Grenoble where I once spent a summer at the university. It turned out that they were from Tunisia! We managed to exchange a bit of information, but our communication was limited. Finally, as people all over the world seem to do at times, we began singing French songs, to show we were people of good will, I think. By the time we said goodbye at Belgrade we parted like old friends.

The OSCE was organizing the participation of former Bosnian residents in the upcoming Bosnian municipal elections. The Dayton accord provided that all displaced Bosnians were eligible to vote for local officials in the Bosnian municipality where they had formerly lived. Jeff was responsible for the "out-of-state" voting program in Serbia and Montenegro, "Rump Yugoslavia." This required getting out information to former Bosnian residents about the election and their eligibility to vote, registering them, training poll workers and finally, setting up polling stations on election day. It was about six weeks before the election and the most difficult work had been done – getting the information to people about establishing their eligibility, and informing them where and how to register. The registration phase had also been completed, and the staff was in the process of training a very large number of poll workers to handle the actual voting on election day.

Jeff invited us to stay in his spacious apartment, but I preferred to stay at the local hotel used by the OSCE. In my experience, bachelor apartments seldom offer much privacy or quiet, and being aware of Jeff's openhanded hospitality, I knew better than to expect either if I stayed there. It was a wise decision because when we arrived we found two other unexpected houseguests. One was an OSCE staff member from Warsaw and another was a young woman from Ireland who needed a place to stay temporarily while she looked for a job. The man was an Englishman with a Polish wife and family and had been living in Poland for some years. His expertise was in training poll workers and he had been sent by OSCE to several countries since the demise of communism in Eastern Europe to assist in elections, which is what he came to Belgrade to do. The pretty young woman had been living with a young Chinese man, a refugee following the Tiananmen Square demonstration, who had wound up working with the OSCE in Belgrade. Well educated and intelligent, she had learned to speak Serbo-Croatian, but her job ended at about the same time she and her Chinese friend parted company. So Jeff with his characteristic hospitality invited her to live in one of his guest rooms until she found another job. She had long, dark hair worn loosely, with one strand hanging down the middle of her face, a la Michael Jackson. Both of the unexpected guests were interesting, well-informed and congenial, so we had good company for the week-end. But I was very glad to be able to repair to the hotel at the end of our evenings together.

The hotel, moreover, was something I was glad not to miss. It was a huge, ugly, rectangular building, only eight stories high but very, very long. My guess is that it had about 1000 rooms. The dimensions of the lobby were approximately those of a football field, and when we entered in the late afternoon, it was quite empty. One clerk attended the registration desk. They accepted credit cards, but preferred payment in American dollars, and cut the cost by about 75 percent to make that an attractive option. My room was large, well furnished, with all modern appurtenances, including television, and had a balcony overlooking the Danube River. The cost was $32 a night and included a sumptuous breakfast and one other meal, a choice of lunch or dinner. The only drawback was the eerie feeling that I was all alone in that mammoth establishment. When I went down to breakfast the next morning, the lobby was as vacant as it had been the night before but there were three desk clerks on duty who greeted me with bright smiles. The dining room was set up with enough tables-for-four to seat about 100 people. A headwaiter welcomed me; several uniformed waitresses were busily laying tables, filling salt and pepper containers. They all greeted me cheerily. At first, I was the only guest, but later two more people came in, and as I was leaving, one other person entered. It was the kind of buffet breakfast I came to expect in Eastern Europe: a long table containing several varieties of cold cereals, a couple of hot cereals, fruit, three or four juices, milk, yogurt, croissants, bread rolls, sweet rolls and toast; plates of cold meats, cheeses, fresh tomatoes and cucumbers; zucchini or eggplant fried in batter, jam, butter, honey. Warming ovens contained hot dishes, eggs – creamed, scrambled, boiled – bacon, sausages, ham and creamed meat dishes. Coffee, tea, hot chocolate or soft drinks could be ordered at the table and served by the waitresses. As I left the room after breakfast, I glanced at the buffet table, and the beautifully arranged, lavish spread looked as if it had been scarcely touched. I began to feel like a character in a mystery novel with a title like, "The Deserted Inn." It was puzzling. When I asked Jeff if they were expecting a large tour group, he thought not. Then I wondered what they did with all that food; he laughed and said they had a very large staff! He said he had the same eerie feeling when he lived there while searching for an apartment, and when he also expressed curiosity about the sparse occupancy, someone suggested to him that accommodating guests was not the hotel's main purpose. That was all he would say which left me with only an out-of-control imagination. Later I asked some other people I met about the hotel, and got vague replies in which expressions like organized crime, money laundering and associated activities were used but not in complete sentences. It seemed useless to pursue the subject.

James and I spent the next morning at the OSCE office where Jeff introduced us to Stjepan (not his real name), the young Serbian who was his chief assistant and indispensable aide, interpreter, translator, authority on local geography, public opinion, customs and courtesies. Stjepan told us about the out-of-state voting program they were conducting, and talked about the Bosnian-War – from the Serbian point of view. His bias was so pronounced that it began to seem like an indoctrination session. At one point, James mildly interposed, "We have the impression that it was the Bosnian Serbs who first attacked the Muslims." Stjepan did not change expression or raise his voice, but with an air of quiet patience, as if he had been through this before, set about "explaining" the situation. "You see," he said at one point, "when people are close neighbors, living side by side, and they quarrel, they have the right to attack, don't they?" When I got my breath, I said, with more vehemence that I intended. "No!" He looked as if I had hit him, so in a calmer voice, I added, "You have a right to talk, to discuss, hopefully to reach agreement even, if necessary, to compromise, but not to attack." He backed down immediately, and admitted that "attack" was perhaps a poor choice of words, that it was not exactly what he meant. He was being a tactful host. He was intelligent, university educated, not yet 30 years old, a representative of the country's voters and upcoming leaders. Later, when we told Jeff about this exchange he said the point of view expressed by Stjepan was typical among the Serbians he had encountered.

That afternoon we went to see the castle which sits on a great ridge of rock overlooking the Danube and Sava Rivers. The highest point in the city, it is an ideal location for a fortress which was its original purpose. We strolled along the outer perimeter until we came to the exact point where the Sava Tributary flows into the Danube River. There are varying opinions about that confluence. One person had told me that the difference in the colors of the water was quite obvious, that the Sava on the left, at the point where we stood, was grey-brown and the Danube on the right was almost blue! They looked exactly the same to me – water flowing along all the same color, brown with a greenish tinge, despite the change in name at that point. Whatever the color of the water may be, the view is sublime. A small, heavily timbered island, seemingly uninhabited and unused, sits in the middle of the water; a wide expanse of sky and water extends in both directions; and we were favored with a delicately-tinted, not fiery, sunset.

In the evening, a Serbian friend of Jeff took us to the district of Zemun where we first visited two small, exquisite churches. They were like over-sized jewel boxes, in which one is surrounded by walls and an overhead canopy of treasures arranged in mosaic-like closeness so it is impossible to focus on individual pieces.

Our host then led us to a waterside restaurant where he was obviously a favorite patron and we could understand why. He took great care in ordering the meal, especially the wine and the fish. The waiter brought several fish for his inspection and selection, all very large. The one he chose was more than sufficient for the six of us, and it was probably the best fish I have ever eaten, white, flaky, cooked just right. We sat outdoors under trees and it got very chilly as the evening wore on. Our companion from Warsaw insisted on giving me his jacket, a gallantry for which I was very grateful.

The next day Stjepan drove us to the village of Oplanac, situated on a hill about 75 kilometers south of Belgrade, to see the Mausoleum of the Karageorgevitch family, the Church of St. George. On the way out of the city, we drove through the elite residential section of Dedinje where Slobodan Milosevic then lived. His house was hidden behind a tall, very thick hedge and I craned my neck trying to see it. Stjepan apologized for not stopping, saying that if he even slowed down, the police car sitting across the street would immediately approach us and inquire about our business. I had not even noticed the inconspicuous, unmarked car on the other side of the street.

The Karageorgevitch family Mausoleum, built by King Peter I at Oplanac in 1912, was destroyed during World War I, and rebuilt in 1922 by King Peter's son, Alexander, who inherited the throne when his father died in 1921. Alexander also brought to the mausoleum for burial the bones of the founder of the Karageorgevitch (*Karadjordjević*) dynasty, George (*Djordje*) Petrović, born in 1752 known as "Black George", the "First and Supreme Hereditary Leader of the

Serbians." He was buried in his home village of Topola in 1817, where his bones lay until 1922 except for a few years when they were removed for superstitions that arose during the rule of the Obrenovitch dynasty. Black George dominates the mausoleum and apparently the village – pictures of him seemed to be everywhere. He was very handsome, though his face was deeply scarred, six feet six inches tall, with wild coal-black hair, and burning eyes. He was a brilliant warrior who frequently outfought and/or outwitted the Turks, who controlled and oppressed the Serbians for more than 400 years. He and his grandson who became Peter I, King of the Serbs, Croats, and Slovenes, are the only two Alexander honored by placing them in the church itself, both under headstones of plain black marble. Others are buried in the crypt below. Alexander, who became the first King of Yugoslavia, was assassinated in Marseille, France in 1934. He is buried (as his will directed) in the crypt beside his mother, Princess Zorka of Montenegro, who died when he was a baby. A slab of onyx marks his grave. It was the plan of King Peter I that the only decoration in the church would be the battle-torn regimental banners from the Balkan wars and World War I, but when Alexander rebuilt it he added colorful mosaics, copied from Byzantine frescoes. Some art critics have deplored this contribution to the decor on the basis that the mosaic medium is not appropriate for copying painted frescoes. But to the untrained or uncritical artistic eye, they are very appealing, and for those who take the time to observe them, I understand that they are excellent renditions of medieval Serbian art, and accurate depictions of historical events.

Our guide could tell us nothing about the last King of Yugoslavia, King Peter II, known as "the young King", who was 11 years old when his father was assassinated in 1934, and who later, during World War II, established an exile Yugoslavian government in London. At this point, I realized with sneaky pleasure, that this was one of those rare times when being the oldest member of the party was an advantage and I enjoyed telling them that I could remember when Peter, then 18 years old, fled to England (by way of Athens and Jerusalem) after the Luftwaffe razed Belgrade on April 6, 1941, and the Yugoslavian army surrendered to the Germans on April 12. In exile, King Peter appointed Colonel Draža Mihajlović, leader of the Četnik Partisans, as war minister. Although Mihajlović eventually lost out to his Partisan rival, Tito, he was much admired in the United States and England for sheltering and helping to evacuate British and American airmen shot down or forced to bail out over Četnik territory. After the war, Yugoslavia, under Tito's leadership, became a communist republic. King

Peter was never allowed to return to his home country. In 1944, at the age of 21, he married Princess Alexandra of Greece, whose cousin Princess Marina was the widowed Duchess of Kent. The Duke died in the war in 1942, and Marina was much admired not only for her beauty but for her war work in England. Peter and Alexandra, called Sandra, had one child, named Alexander. They were later divorced and Peter moved to Libertyville, Illinois, in the United States. He died in a Los Angeles hospital in November 1970, and is buried at the Serbian Church Monastery in Libertyville. All our guide could tell us about young King Peter is that the American actress and model Catherine Oxenberg is related to him but he was not sure of the exact relationship.

When Peter inherited the Yugoslavian throne at age 11, his regent was Prince Paul, first cousin to his father, who had been raised by Peter's grandfather, Peter I, and so was like a brother to King Alexander, young Peter's father. Thus he was like an uncle to young King Peter, rather than a cousin first removed, which he was. Paul, who died in 1976, was Catherine Oxenberg's grandfather.

In Oplanac, we also saw the home of the man who is referred to locally simply as "The Prince." He is young King Peter's brother, Tomislav, born in 1928, five years younger than Peter. His home, not at all ostentatious, is a large wooden structure that from the outside seems well-designed. We did not see the inside, so I do not know about the furnishings. Only one feature is suggestive of a "royal" residence; it is surrounded by a park and thick forest, very private and serene. He was not at home; Stjepan guessed he was away for the summer, but when he is there, Stjepan said he lives like any country gentleman, rides horses, takes long walks, is friendly with people in the village and well-liked locally.

Our train back to Budapest was scheduled to leave at 9 o'clock in the morning. There was no chance of missing it as Jeff, James, and Stjepan called for me at 7 a.m. We had coffee at the station which was quite crowded even at that early hour. A little before 9 o'clock our train had not appeared but Jeff and Stjepan had to go to work, so we said goodbye, and James and I went out to wait on the platform from which our train was scheduled to depart. A Russian train was sitting on the tracks there, marked Thessaloniki to Moscow, all sleeping cars, all shades drawn. We sat down on a backless bench to await our train, assuming it would arrive as soon as the Russian one pulled out. Ten o'clock came and nothing happened. No train arrived; none left. A young man came along the platform and asked us in slightly accented English if that was the train to Budapest and we told him that we also were going to Budapest and that we expected our train to come in when the Russian one departed. He walked on toward the front of the train and disappeared. Soon we saw other people walking in the same direction and heard someone say it was the train to Budapest. We didn't understand it but followed the crowd to the end of the train where they had hitched a coach to the Russian sleeper and were taking on Budapest passengers. We followed the crowd pushing through the car looking for seats. In the second compartment, the young man who had spoken to us on the platform signalled us to join him. He was in a six-seat compartment and there were three other young men, all students, two French and one American who was studying in France. Our young benefactor, who seemed to have saved seats for us, was a student at Montenegro University. At age 18 he had been in the army, in the fighting at Sarajevo, and was also at Mostar when the Croatians bombed the famous bridge there. He felt very lucky to have come through it all unhurt, and when he got out of the army, he went immediately to the university where he is studying mathematics. When he took out a package of cigarettes and asked if I minded if he smoked, I said, "I won't ask you not to smoke, but we've been in smoke-filled rooms and cars in Belgrade for three days, and my eyes…" He didn't let me finish, but immediately put his cigarettes away and said he could smoke in the corridor. "I was once a smoker myself," I added, "and I feel guilty about objecting-" but he interrupted again and said very pleasantly that it was no problem, then went out into the corridor without a trace of rancor or resentment. The others in the compartment observed this and also went into the corridor to smoke.

The young Serb, whose name I never learned, said his family had formerly lived in Bosnia and now lived in Novi Sad where he was going to visit them. I told him we had visited a friend in Belgrade who was with the OSCE and asked if he knew about the Out-of-State voting program for former residents of Bosnia. He did know about it, and I asked if he and his family were going to vote in the upcoming election for the officials in their former municipality. He said they were going to vote, but not in the municipality where they formerly lived. "It would be no use," he said, "everyone who lives there now is Muslim." I was sorry when he left the train at Novi Sad, but glad to be detached from the Russian train that went on its way to Istanbul, Bucharest, Kiev and thence to Moscow. Our car was then attached to a Yugoslavian train headed for Budapest.

We looked forward to reaching the border of Hungary, assuming that conditions would improve. Our car was less crowded as many people got off at Novi Sad, but nothing else improved. Especially the toilets – no paper and no water, except on the floor. Neither James nor I had thought to bring bottled water or food with us. We must have foolishly assumed that the young vendor we left at the Yugoslavian border on the way down would rejoin us as soon as we returned to Hungarian soil, but it was not to be. After coffee at the Belgrade train station about 7:30 a.m. we had no food or drink until we arrived in Budapest at about 7 p.m. My vow never to ride on a Yugoslavian train was speedily reinstated, but in the right circumstances it will probably be broken as easily as it was the first time.

XII

HUNGARY – THEN AND NOW

In 1995 a Hungarian film *Sweet Emma, Dear Böbe*, directed by István Szabó, was awarded a Silver Bear at the Berlin Film Festival. It was the story of two young Hungarian teachers struggling to cope with the effects of their country's transition from a collectivist to a free-market economy. Their salaries, already low, fell steadily as the currency was devalued and prices soared. They shared a room in a hostel and tried to keep cheerful, but in the end one of them, Böbe, jumps to her death out of the window of the high-rise building in which they lived. Böbe gave up too soon. If she had hung on only a while longer she would have seen considerable improvement.

By the end of 1995, approximately 60 percent of the economy was in the hands of the private sector, up from 3.5 percent in 1989; industrial production grew by 6 percent during that year, and Hungary was receiving more foreign investment than any other Central European country, approximately 50 percent of the total in the entire region. However, the inflation rate was still high, 28 percent, so the government applied strict belt-tightening despite the risk that it could hurt them at the polls. They closed down unprofitable state-owned businesses and cut jobs. There was deep pessimism among the populace and widespread criticism of the new government. But the reforms paid off and by 1997 Hungary was being hailed as Post-Communist Europe's economic success story. In that year, for the first time in the life of the new democracy, wage increases exceeded inflation. Gross wages grew by 21-22 percent while inflation was just over 18 percent. That was very good news after years of inflation rates ranging from 20 to 30 percent, and the concomitant decline in real income.

One did not have to know the details of the improved economic situation in 1997 to see that the general population was feeling more optimistic. People seemed to smile more and those whose work brought them into contact with the public had lost some of their surliness and began to be pleasant, almost friendly. This impression was confirmed by surveys made that year which indicated that people had become more optimistic. According to some analysts, optimists outnumbered pessimists and people's expectations for the future were rising. It is notable that in 1997 Hungary lost its world-leading position in number of suicides. Looking back to when I arrived five years earlier it was hard to believe it was the same country.

Hungary began to experience a major retail boom in 1997. In Budapest, huge shopping malls and "hypermarkets" mushroomed. Mall prices were high by Hungarian standards, but it was estimated that about 50 percent of the population earning moderate incomes patronized hyper- or supermarkets, attracted by lower prices and the selection and quantity of goods available in one place. Food freezers and large refrigerators were becoming common, which made buying in quantity feasible, thus reducing the frequency of trips to the market, a real boon to working women.

The shopping malls look very much like those in the United States and Western Europe with many stores and boutiques offering goods at a wide range of prices, most of them on the high side. They are, nevertheless, often crowded with shoppers or at least with people wandering through and looking, and new malls are being built and still more planned, so somebody must be buying there. Some of them have fast food restaurants and multi-plex theaters, which will always attract young people.

The amount and variety of consumer goods that has become available since 1989 is dazzling. In addition to the shopping malls, retail outlets of various sizes, designer boutiques, indoor and outdoor markets, offer luxury commodities from all over the world – clothing, household appliances, electronics equipment, furniture, silver, china, linens, jewelry. In Budapest, internationally-known designer boutiques dispense men's and women's clothing and accessories, and perfume boutique shelves are filled with every scent known to the fashion world. Casinos are flourishing, seemingly as ubiquitous and as easy to patronize as Woolworth's used to be in the United States.

Amid such prosperity it is hard to recall Hungary as I first saw it, when store shelves were almost empty and the whole country looked poor and sad. In the small city I first lived in, soap, shampoo, toothpaste, laundry and dishwashing soap or detergent were exceedingly scarce, and when a diligent search turned up any of those things, the quality was so poor that it hardly seemed worth the effort. Toilet paper was the coarse, brown paper seen throughout Europe during and after World War II; attendants at the public toilets counted out two sheets to each customer as they paid the entrance fee. Any other household paper goods was nonexistent.

Women's clothing was scarce and what was on display was drab, made of flimsy fabrics with poor workmanship. Most of the footwear worn by women in the streets was made of synthetic material and was sometimes inappropriate to the season. Once I saw a middle-aged women wearing light colored sandals on a cold day. I told a friend about this. She said many people could afford only one pair of shoes and the color and style depended upon what the state-owned stores were selling at the time they were bought. If a women's shoes wore out in mid-summer and the only ones on the market were white, she might still be wearing them in December; they would be worn as long as they lasted.

After I had been here for more than a year, my shoe heels were all quite worn. Even in Budapest, no one could tell me where to find a shoe repair shop. It was not a lack of shoe-making expertise, but lack of the necessary materials and equipment. As soon as a shoe repairman set up shop in one of the residential buildings near me, I rushed right over with several pairs of shoes. The tall, soft-voiced man, about 40 years old, who greeted me, held my shoes in his hands and inspected them with the same care he might give to emeralds. Acting on my experience in the United States where several grades of repair material are offered at different prices, I said, "Please use the best materials." He smiled sweetly, shook his head and said quietly, "I don't have the best." Charming exchanges such as that keep those days alive in my memory. It would be easy to suppress them amid today's abundance.

That abundance has not come without a price. Not all of the changes have been desirable; the winds of change inevitably blow in both the good and the bad, and Hungary still has some serious problems. The inordinate power of the police during the communist era has been reduced, a good thing with an unfortunate result – crime has increased, an unwelcome side effect of Hungary's prosperity.

Strategically located in the heart of Europe, it was inevitable that modern-day, liberated Hungary would become a pathway for contraband of all kinds, as well as illegal movement of human beings. Many transient smugglers, observing Hungary's new affluence, decided to end their journey here, and soon commodities such as drugs, alcohol and cigarettes from foreign places became available in the underground market. Also, people from neighboring countries where life is considerably harsher than in Hungary flooded into the country, legally if possible, but many came illegally, seeking a better life. They were willing to work for lower wages and endure a lower standard of living than Hungarians, and added to the problems of housing, public health, and unemployment. Resentment of the newcomers has focused mainly on Gypsies, a minority group that historically has been discriminated against throughout Europe.

Now, in 1998, Váci Street has changed, not only from what it was in 1896 but what it was in 1989. It is still a pedestrian street where shoppers may stroll leisurely – it must be leisurely in order to dodge the throngs of tourists and the vendors' stands that line both sides of the street, especially in summer and on holidays. Books, souvenirs, ice cream, newspapers, magazines, flowers, postcards, sunglasses are sold from the temporary collapsible kiosks. There are shops, some almost elegant, selling perfumes and cosmetics from Paris, London and the United States, and store windows display fashionable clothing, including luxurious furs. But there are not many. At some of the choicest locations where in bygone days imported merchandise may have been sold, signs indicate that imported products of another kind are offered there, garish neon signs that say McDonalds, Burger King, Dunkin' Donuts, Pizza Hut. At the end of the street nearest to Hungary's highly esteemed, scholarly university, Eötvös Loránd, a scintillescent neon sign blinks out "Flash Dance Bar."

One of the saddest changes in my opinion is the transformation of the coffee house, bearing the name of the owner who bought it in 1884, Émile Gerbeaud. He made it a traditional European coffee house famous for its delicious pastry and its charming, unhurried atmosphere where one could sit for hours over an excellent cup of coffee and read, write, or talk with a companion. There used to be a little side room reserved as a meeting place for the *Gerbeaud Ladies* where old ladies who once had a better life met their friends and talked about the past over coffee with whipped cream, but it has disappeared. When I first went there, Gerbeaud was a place to have pastry and coffee, and occasionally excellent caviar sandwiches were on the menu. Now the building is owned by the German-based firm Immo-Müller and Gerbeaud has become a place that serves sandwiches, salads, and in addition to coffee and pastry, they now offer alcoholic drinks. It is far from the traditional Europeans coffee house that Gerbeaud created. *Sic transit gloria*!

A welcome change reminiscent of the Budapest of the late 19th century is that banks now issue not only brand-new bills, but bills in brand-new denominations. New 200-, 2,000-, 10,000-forint bills have been issued; new 3,000-forint ones are promised for next year. The old 100-forint bill has been retired, replaced by a shiny new vending-machine compatible 100-forint coin, heavy enough to strain pocket linings and coin purses.

Hungary's economic success, so admired by the rest of the world, especially in Eastern Europe, has not benefitted all sections of the country equally. Western Hungary, including Budapest (where a fifth of the population lives and where the headquarters of most business and industry are located), enjoys the major impact of the growth and a marked rise in living standards. But the eastern and northern sections of the country have remained stagnant or undergone a decline. Hungary's overall unemployment rate at the end of 1997 was between 10 and 11 percent; yet in the northeastern city of Miskolc, for example, it was 15 percent. That section of the country has not attracted foreign investment, the major source of prosperity in the western area, because of its underdevelopment in facilities and resources vital to business and industry. In recognition of this inequity the government has pledged to improve the transportation infrastructure and educational facilities in the northeast and both the national and local governments are offering potential investors attractive tax incentives. Significant improvements have already been made in the telephone service. Now, some foreign investors are considering the comparative underdevelopment in eastern Hungary to be an advantage because of the tax incentives, and because labor costs are 50 percent cheaper than in the western part. GE, which in 1994 bought out the Hungarian bulb manufacturer, Tungsram, and has six plants in western Hungary, has decided to put all new investment into the east; and companies from Asia, Europe, and others from North America are planning new factories and the expansion of existing ones in that region.

Unemployment throughout the country is still too high. The number of people without work for over a year rose in 1997 to approximately 203,000. The only bright spot was among school-leavers – unemployment in that group decreased. This seems to indicate an increase in entry-level positions, not surprising during a period of rapid privatization and aggressive foreign investment.

Böbe, had she lived, would have found herself in a more prosperous country, but her own situation might not have improved commensurately. Teachers' salaries in Hungary remain among the lowest in Europe and although I would like to add "while their competence ranks among the highest," I am not sure about that. When the communists, in the late 1940s, announced their plan to turn Hungary into a "country of iron and steel", despite the lack of iron ore and coking coal, and other raw materials, they revised the education system to reflect this objective. The "new socialist man" produced by the new curriculum would be able to overcome such technical obstacles! Much of the classical education that had prepared graduates of Hungarian gymnasiums for entry into the best universities in Europe disappeared or was distorted by the revisions ordered in 1949. Hungarian history texts were replaced with versions written from the communist point of view; social sciences were eliminated or de-emphasized; priority was given technological subjects. Later revisions restored some social sciences to the curriculum, but the emphasis on technological subjects remained; and Marxist economic and social theory, as well as mandatory study of Russian language were a large part of teachers' education. My colleagues and friends who were acquainted with world literature and social thinking, and also had an accurate knowledge of Hungarian and world history, grew up in homes where the family contributed extensively to their education. So a teachers' competence and skill depended to some extent on what they learned at home. Yet there was a dark period between 1949 and 1962 when the communist government forcibly moved the Hungarian upper and middle class (the so-called "elites") out of Budapest, confiscated much of their property, and did not permit their children to register at the universities. Those were the families most likely to be educated and to have books at home to augment their children's education. Thus for a time higher education was available almost exclusively to children of the working classes and of Communist Party officials, whose education was unlikely to be supplemented at home by undistorted information.

Reform of the education system was one of the first undertakings of the new democracy. Beginning in 1989, an army of people at the Ministry of Culture and Education undertook to overhaul the national school curriculum and provide a comprehensive road map and script for Hungarian teachers in primary and secondary schools, scheduled to begin in the fall of 1999. The package, called the National Base Curriculum (NAT), replaces a curriculum that was in effect for about twenty years which included such things as 33 hours of primary-school instruction on workers' movements worldwide. Part of the new plan requires that teachers be re-certified every seven years, but nobody is sure how this will work, and the teachers are understandably very apprehensive. Some retraining will be necessary for those who must teach such things as computer science and economics, and some gymnasium teachers are already being required to take computer courses in which they must pass an examination at the end. They must also be prepared to include in their lesson plans information on the European Union and the International Monetary Fund, as well as on basic issues concerning the rights and responsibilities of Hungarian citizenship. Teachers' salaries have been increased but not as much as those of other professions, and still lag behind Western European countries. Unless this is adjusted, the teaching profession risks losing some of its best people who will be the ones most likely to find higher-paying positions in other fields as the country's economy continues to expand.

Pensioners, like teachers, are also less likely to be found among the optimists. Living on fixed incomes, they were the biggest losers in the years of government "belt-tightening," but even for them the government had some good news at the very end of 1997. Beginning in January 1998, citizens over 65 became entitled to free travel on all public transportation including lines of the Hungarian State Railways (MAV). They were also promised preferential rates on the Hungarian Airline Malév. The majority of Hungarian pensioners have never in their lives boarded an airplane; it will be interesting to see how many take advantage of this senior citizen "perk." Commenting on this concession to the older sector of the population, one person said, "It is a last-minute trick of the out-going government; most of them still cannot afford it." He was right in describing the then-current government as "out-going." In May 1998, the Socialists were defeated by a moderate right-wing party, Fidesz, headed by 36-year old Viktor Orbán who became the Prime Minister.

Income from tourism reached a record high in 1997 when nearly five million tourists spent more than 15 million nights in the country; tourism among Hungarians also increased significantly. They embraced the new freedom to travel with great enthusiasm. It is no longer surprising to hear someone say, "We're going to the Canary Islands in January," or "We were in Crete (or Tunisia, Morocco, Egypt, France, Germany) in September." Although not many can afford luxury travel, there seems to be no discomfort they will not endure in order to visit a new place. My colleagues at the gymnasium organized a bus trip to Venice in 1993 and invited me to join them. The cost was unbelievably little which made it very tempting, but after inquiring into the arrangements, I had to decline. They traveled on a chartered bus and everyone carried food. For the five-day, four-night trip, they slept and ate on the bus, which did not have a rest room. It is all the more remarkable when one considers that Hungarian teachers have high standards of personal hygiene and, like Americans, consider the daily bath a necessity. All who went gave glowing reports of a wonderful trip! This was not unusual; such excursions are common and I never heard a complaint about inconvenience or discomfort.

The difficulties that accompany the improved economy have inevitably given rise to some negative voices. Criticism is still heard from writers and commentators in the media, from opposition political figures, and from those whose boats the tide has not lifted. And not all manifestations of democracy are pleasing to everybody. Protests against Gypsy families moving into a neighborhood occasionally erupt into violence. The government has enacted legislation aimed at improving the lot of minorities, some specifically relating to Gypsies, but it is a slow process, so slow that it may seem more like a gesture than a real will to bring about change. They are tackling the problem with emphasis on education, a laudable concept but inherently long-range. Plans were made in 1997 for colleges to offer places to talented Gypsy students – in that year, there were only 300 Gypsies among the nearly 200,000 university and college students. There are also proposals to provide assistance in training and promotion to the Gypsy minority councils and the Romany social organizations promising somewhat shorter-range results.

In speaking with Hungarians about Gypsies one hears statements very similar to those made in the United States about Blacks. It is often assumed, before the culprit has been apprehended, that any offense was committed by a Gypsy. One friend who had her wallet stolen on the metro told me about it, and her opening sentence was, "The Gypsies got me." Often, that is true. Everyone seems to have a personal Gypsy outrage experience. And the statistics, like those in the United States regarding Blacks, indicate that Gypsies are responsible for a disproportionate number of crimes, particularly petty thievery and other misdemeanors; they also make up a large portion of the prison population. One person said to me that the Hungarians hate Gypsies more for personal reasons than as an abstract stereotype. But that does not seem to be supported by recent surveys of Hungarian attitudes toward minority groups.

According to a Gallup survey taken late in 1997, one in two Hungarians dislikes Gypsies, one in three thinks it would be better to limit the number of colored people in the country. Another study indicated that Gypsies were hated more than drug dealers and neo-Nazis; only the militant "Skin-heads" were hated more than Gypsies. That study concluded, interestingly, that the population was "neutral" regarding Jews and another "minority" in the survey, Feminists. In comparison with some other European countries, the Hungarian "Skin-heads" (political and social heirs of the Nazis and the Hungarian fascists, the Arrow Cross) are small in number, but they are an ominous reminder of the past. However, they may be their own worst enemy. Their very presence may contribute to the low level of anti-Semitism reflected in recent attitude polls.

During the communist years, overt anti-Semitism was forbidden, and famous Hungarians, past or contemporary, were never identified as Jews because it would be considered discriminatory to do so. The effect was that even today middle-aged and young Hungarians are often surprised to learn how many of their most famous musicians, scientists, composers, writers, and other artists were Jews. And it has been my observation that there is still a reluctance to identify someone as a Jew. During the 1994 election campaign, I asked a teaching colleague about the membership make-up of the political party she favored. She replied, "The intellectuals," then paused. We were in the teachers' room. She looked over her right shoulder, then over her left shoulder, leaned closer to me and lowered her voice, "and Jews." It seemed to be an automatic cautionary gesture.

One conversational exchange that I wrote an American friend about and described as an overt expression of anti-Semitism was challenged; the remarks, he said, were crude, but could not be characterized as "anti-Semitic." This was my story: A Hungarian native who grew up in the United States was visiting his home country in 1994 and staying with relatives who invited me to join them for an evening at the opera. We met at the Opera House and went directly to our seats. Waiting for the heartbreakingly beautiful Puccini music that opens "La Bohème," I was disinclined to make small talk but felt it was my social duty to do so, and so I spoke:

"I understand you were born here. When did you leave?"
"In 1945. That was the bad time, the really bad time. When the Russians came."
"Some people I have spoken with refer to 1956 as the 'really bad time.' I have heard that in 1945 many welcomed the Russians, seeing them as liberators from the Germans at the end of World War II."
(His anger was immediate)
"Bull shit! Liberators! Bull shit! That's bull shit Communist propaganda!"

"Weren't the Hungarian people happy to be rid of the Germany army, and their own fascist Arrow Cross?"

"The Germans never did anything to us!"

"You call shipping hundreds of thousands of people off to death camps nothing?"

"They didn't do anything to us! We're not Jews!"

The lights went down. The music began.

My friend's opinion that this was not an expression of anti-Semitism puzzled me. At the time it occurred, I took it to be arrant anti-Semitism. But after a while, I realized what made the difference. It was one of those "You had to be there" stories. One had to hear the inflections and see the facial expression; the words alone were not enough. The simple statement that one was not killed because he was not Jewish would not necessarily be anti-Semitic. But the tone of voice and the expression said, "Why would you think the German atrocities would affect me? Surely you don't think that I am a Jew!"

If any evidence was needed that my opera companion did not reflect today's Hungarian viewpoint, it was supplied conclusively by the public response to the re-opening in September, 1996, of the 137-year old Budapest Synagogue, the largest in Europe, and the second largest in the world after Temple Emanu–el in New York. After being blasted by bombs during World War II, the resplendent synagogue with its twin golden Moorish-style domes and the gold-leaf Ark of the Covenant, suffered years of neglect and disrepair. The restoration cost about 9 million dollars, 80 percent of which was paid for by Hungarian taxpayers, and the remainder by the international Jewish community. When I have commented on this remarkable (to me) fact that during Hungary's worse economic times, they financed the restoration of the synagogue, Hungarians are surprise to hear it. They rarely know the details about how public money is spent. Their democracy has not yet reached the stage where individual citizens or citizen groups are told or can ask about their national budget including how it is being administered. But at the re-opening ceremony, it was made very clear that the Hungarian government strongly supported the synagogue restoration.

That event, described by one speaker as the restoration of Jewish life in Hungary, attracted more than 7,000 people, including Hungary's President, Arpád Göncz, cabinet members, the speaker of Parliament and opposition politicians. Israel's former Prime Minister, Yitzhak Shamir, speaking at the ceremony, said the attendance by the country's highest ranking officials "symbolized a new relationship between Jews and non-Jews in this country..." Before World War II, Hungary's Jewish population was estimated to be between 800,000 and one million, of which, despite the heroic efforts of Raoul Wallenberg and others, approximately 600,000 perished in the Holocaust. The population today is just over 80,000, the largest in any Central European country.

Hungarian attitude and policies toward Jews have been ambivalent, even capricious for centuries. Before Joseph II came to the Habsburg throne in 1780, the Catholic church regulated the spiritual life of Hungary. In 1781 Joseph's Patent of Toleration edict extended the "free practice" of religions to all confessions, and gave all non-Catholics full rights as citizens, excepting Jews. (Some restrictions remained: non-Catholics could not ring church bells or erect steeples; the entrance to their churches could not open on main streets.) Two years later, Joseph went further and gave Jews the right to practice their religion freely, but they still did not receive full citizenship rights.

The initial momentum toward a liberal Hungary began in the second quarter of the nineteenth century. The Parliament (the "Diet") of 1832-36 was divided on the Jewish question but there were some liberal groups that, although under constant police surveillance, openly called for emancipation of the Jews. In the latter half of that century the legal equality of all citizens was proclaimed, finally giving Jews full citizenship rights. There was still active opposition to the liberal governments of that time (in 1883 the short-lived National Anti-Semitic Party was established), but assimilation of Jews into Hungarian society was astonishingly successful. Many attained positions of importance, and a recognized Jewish "financial aristocracy" emerged. By 1900 there were sixteen Jewish members of Parliament and two dozen Jewish professors in the universities. Some of the better social clubs in Budapest admitted Jews to membership. About 120 Jewish families were given noble titles by Emperor Franz József, most of them in 1905 and after. In 1910, Hungary had a Jewish Minister of War; in 1912, the Minister of Finance was a former Jew (conversions were rather common at that time). For a short time in 1913, Budapest had a Jewish mayor.

Béla Kun's Bolshevik Hungarian Soviet Republic took over the country for a short time after World War I. Kun was Jewish as were 32 of the 45 commissars of the Communist Republic, and even though most Hungarian Jews did not join Kun, many people associated his regime with Jews. In the chaotic period known as the "white terror" that followed Kun's defeat, democrats, socialists and Jews were beaten and hanged. The communists and the Jews ("Judeo-Communists") were blamed for the military defeat and the country's devastation. The *numerus clausus* law enacted in 1920, when Count Pál Teleki, the scion of an old Transylvania family, was Prime Minister under the regency of Miklós Horthy, restricted the number of Jewish students admitted to the universities, making anti-Semitism constitutional for the first time in the history of modern Hungary. The law was modified in 1928, under the leadership of Count István Bethlen, who became Prime Minister in 1921. Bethlen, also a Transylvanian, had inherited a liberal-leaning conservative outlook, but after events following the war, such as the Béla Kun revolution, he believed that liberalism had to be controlled. However, he brought about some noteworthy reforms, including land reform, extension of health insurance to some new social classes, and educational reforms.

The *numerus clausus* law did not fit into his political and economic concepts and created difficulties for him abroad. So, in 1927 a new proposal was introduced which continued to limit the number of students admitted to institutions of higher learning to prevent the growth of an intellectual proletariat, but changed the qualifications for admission. Racial and nationality considerations were eliminated as criteria and more weight was given to social origin. This did not mean an end to discrimination or anti-Semitism, but the hope was that political and economic order and the general improvement in the standard of living might revive the peaceful coexistence that had begun late in the 19th century. This hope was unfortunately not realized. The Hungarian fascist movement began to take shape during the 1930s, and discrimination did not end. Instead, several anti-Jewish laws were enacted, one which declared that the criterion for being considered Jewish was no longer religion but racial background (so religious conversion did not render one "non-Jewish"), and restricted Jewish participation in the professions and civil service to five percent. Liberal elements in the government protested these laws but the trend was clear. After Hungary joined the Germans in their attack on Yugoslavia in 1941, thereby breaching their treaty of friendship with Yugoslavia in exchange for the return of some of Hungary's lost territory, the die was cast. They were in the German camp. That year, the Hungarian parliament ratified a new law that prohibited intermarriage between Jews and Christians and decreed severe punishment for extramarital sexual relations between Jews and non-Jews. It is no wonder that the few Jews who survived the holocaust at first welcomed the arrival of the Russians and the communist government that, whatever else it did, outlawed anti-Semitism.

Today's Hungarian constitution guarantees religious freedom and has no restrictions on rights for any citizens. But centuries of discrimination, abuse, and attempted genocide have left their mark. Memory is long and people are cautious; there are metal detectors at the entrance to the now-restored, magnificent Budapest synagogue, although there may be reasons for that other than fear of anti-Semitic expressions. The world has changed and terrorists of other kinds threaten all institutions, including places of worship.

Hungary was the first socialist country to move directly from a collectivist to a free market economy and from a one-party dictatorship to a multi-party democracy, and so it had no model to follow. It has had three national elections, one in 1990 in which the electorate favored moderate right-wing candidates who had never held office in the communist governments during the previous forty years. While this position was understandable, it insured that the elected leaders had little or no past government experience to prepare them for their enormous task. In 1994, the electorate did an about face, and gave a landslide victory to the socialist party, led by and comprised largely of former communists, bringing fear on the part of some people (and hope on the part of others) that the clock would be turned back and the democratic progress annulled. But the second government followed the lead of the first and after a slow start even accelerated privatization. In May 1998, the socialist government was defeated by Fidesz, a formerly radical liberal party that redefined itself and added "Hungarian Civic Party" to its name. It is now considered to be a moderate right-wing party resembling the Hungarian Democratic Forum that governed from 1991 to 1995. The present government is a coalition—Fidesz is the senior partner; the junior partner is the FKGP, Independent Smallholders, described as a populist right-wing party. Hungary continues to look to the West for guidance and support, and welcomes the prospect of formal alliance with NATO and the European Community.

In July 1997, Hungary along with Poland and the Czech Republic, was invited to become a member of the North Atlantic Treaty Organization (NATO), and in December of that year the three countries signed an accession memorandum, expecting to become formal members on April 4, 1999, NATO's 50th anniversary. Hungary was the only one of the three countries that chose to hold a referendum on the issue. Although there is some opposition to the idea in Hungary, in the November 1997 referendum, 85 percent of those who voted, more than 50 percent of eligible voters, favored the idea. President Clinton's proposal to expand NATO beginning with the three Eastern European countries was ratified by the U.S. Senate in May 1998 against negligible opposition.

Few Hungarians have a clear idea of what membership in NATO really means. If NATO itself has a clear understanding of what it will mean, it has not fully conveyed it to either the existing member nations or to Hungary. Nobody seems to know exactly what the costs of the expansion will amount to for new members or for existing members. Neither has NATO fully set forth to the public the extent of the military commitment NATO membership implies on the part of Hungary or on the part of NATO vis-á-vis Hungary. Nevertheless the invitation to join NATO is welcomed by Hungary as a token of acceptance into the community of Western nations.

On the day of the Hungarian referendum, I was invited by a friend to accompany her, her mother and her son to the polling station. It was not only a historic occasion for Hungary, it was also a rite of passage for my friend's son: it was his first time to cast a vote, since he had only recently reached the eligible age of 18. I took photographs of the three generations at the polling station where they all voted "Yes," reflecting the nearly unanimous vote of the nation. It was highly gratifying to be present when a young Hungarian graduate of the school where I taught for two years cast the first vote of his life, and especially since it was a vote in favor of Hungary's placing herself politically among the democracies of the West.

Hungary is also among those countries that have been invited to participate in accession talks leading to membership in the European Union (EU). Hungary took the first step toward EU membership in 1996, by becoming a member nation of the Organization for Security and Cooperation in Europe. Membership in EU will require further legislative, legal and other requirements which Hungary is preparing to meet by the year 2000, expecting to become a member of EU early in the next century. It is easy for Hungarians to see the benefits of EU membership as it will open up markets that have hitherto been restricted or closed to them; at the same time, some EU members are not enthusiastic about meeting competition from some Hungarian products. The French are not looking forward to the increased exportation of Hungary's excellent wines and paté, for example. The future of this tiny country with a history both glorious and tragic looks more promising than it has for many years.

* * * * *

The expression "over the hill" connotes an ending, and at the time I was writing the notes that became this book, I thought of my sojourn in Hungary as an ending, my last big adventure. But now I am not so sure. The title does not seem to fir with my present view of the Hungarian "happening," nor my feelings about the future. Instead of an ending, it now feels more like a beginning as I peer into the future trying to see where the next hill may be looming.